THE POLITICS OF THE HEADSCARF IN THE UNITED STATES

THE POLITICS OF THE HEADSCARF IN THE UNITED STATES

BOZENA C. WELBORNE,
AUBREY L. WESTFALL,
ÖZGE ÇELİK RUSSELL,
AND SARAH A. TOBIN

CORNELL UNIVERSITY PRESS
Ithaca and London

First published 2018 by Cornell University Press

Printed in the United States of America

Library of Congress Cataloging-in-Publication Data

Names: Welborne, Bozena C., author. | Westfall, Aubrey L., author. | Russell, Özge Çelik, author. | Tobin, Sarah A., 1977– author.
Title: The politics of the headscarf in the United States / Bozena C. Welborne, Aubrey L. Westfall, Özge Çelik Russell, and Sarah A. Tobin.
Description: Ithaca : Cornell University Press, 2018. | Includes bibliographical references and index.
Identifiers: LCCN 2017046634 (print) | LCCN 2017047979 (ebook) | ISBN 9781501715389 (epub/mobi) | ISBN 9781501715396 (pdf) | ISBN 9781501715365 | ISBN 9781501715365 (cloth ; alk. paper) | ISBN 9781501715372 (pbk. ; alk. paper)
Subjects: LCSH: Hijab (Islamic clothing)—Political aspects—United States. | Hijab (Islamic clothing)—Social aspects—United States. | Muslim women—Clothing—United States. | Muslim women—United States—Attitudes. | Clothing and dress—Religious aspects—Islam. | Islam—United States—Public opinion. | Public opinion—United States.
Classification: LCC BP190.5.H44 (ebook) | LCC BP190.5.H44 W45 2018 (print) | DDC 297.5/76—dc23
LC record available at https://lccn.loc.gov/2017046634

🍃 Contents

❧ FIGURES AND TABLES

Figures

Tables

✒ ACKNOWLEDGMENTS

This book would not have been possible without the help of many people. We owe the deepest debt of gratitude to the Muslim women who participated in our survey and focus groups. Because we refer to them by pseudonyms in order to keep their identities confidential, we are unable to name them. They should know, however, that their thoughtful insights are the heart of the book. We were outsiders in their communities, yet we found ourselves welcomed with kindness and generosity. We are so grateful that they were willing to share their thoughts and experiences. They enriched the book and our lives.

The seed of the idea of this book was planted when most of us were finishing graduate school. As this work progressed, a number of friends and colleagues at many different institutions offered various forms of intellectual and emotional support and encouragement. We are grateful to the many members of our academic departments and writing groups who provided encouragement and insight along the way. Special thanks to Jonathan Brumburg-Kraus, Bill Eubank, Peony Fhagan, Bojana Fort-Welborne, Susanne Martin, Simon McPherson, Kathy Morgan, Robert Ostergard, Tristy Vick-Majors, and Cindy Westfall, all of whom read and provided feedback on parts of the manuscript and this project. We are especially thankful for Susan Clarke's mentorship. Susan's was the first opinion we sought with questions on the substance of our work, on advice pertaining to manuscript negotiations, and on insights into the difficulties of collaboration. She always urged us not to undervalue our work and to be ambitious in our expectations.

The faculty and staff at various institutions provided us with the time, space, and finances to complete this project. Smith College; the University of Nevada, Reno; Virginia Wesleyan College; and Wheaton College all provided grants to cover the costs associated with distributing the survey, conducting focus groups, transcription, and editing the manuscript. We also relied on the help of Georgetown University, Loyola University in Chicago, the University of Houston, and the University of California at Berkeley for help in setting up and hosting the focus group interviews. In particular, we thank Aminah

McCloud and Farid Senzai for connecting us to relevant Islamic organizations and research participants, as well as helping us brainstorm and formulate some of the ideas presented in this book. Finally, we offer a special thanks to Hannah Harder, who painstakingly transcribed our interviews, and to Rudy Leon for her work copyediting the manuscript.

We owe a great deal to the reviewers of our book chapters and of the related articles that appear in the journals *Politics and Religion* and *Social Science Quarterly*. They offered us useful feedback, which helped shape the content of the book and the interpretation of the findings. The insights of Paul Djupe were particularly valuable. We are also thankful to the participants and discussants in panels at the Midwest Political Science Association and the American Political Science Association conferences, who offered feedback on our preliminary results as well as encouragement to continue with the project.

We were privileged to work with Jim Lance, our editor at Cornell. Jim was our cheerleader as we were writing the manuscript, and he bolstered our confidence in every interaction. Throughout the process, he would send us thoughts and articles that connected to our work, constantly affirming the importance and timeliness of the research. He cheerfully and graciously provided feedback whenever we asked and was patient with our questions. It was a joy to have such an encouraging, enthusiastic collaborator in our corner.

We can't imagine completing anything worthwhile, let alone this multiyear project, without our families. We are grateful for the love and support of our parents and siblings, who took an interest in the research process and project. We appreciate the tolerance of our partners, who held down the fort during weeks of fieldwork and presentations, many late nights, and over one hundred hours of collaborative phone calls in the early mornings and weekends.

Finally, we are grateful to each other. This work was a collaborative effort every step of the way, and we constantly learned from and alongside each other. High-stakes cooperation challenges the strongest relationships, and we are so pleased to have emerged from this project as better scholars and friends.

❧ A Note on Author Contributions

Bozena Welborne and Aubrey Westfall contributed to the majority of this book and in equal amounts, followed by Özge Çelik Russell and Sarah Tobin.

ॐ THE POLITICS OF THE
HEADSCARF IN THE
UNITED STATES

Introduction

On a cool December evening in 2015, then-presidential candidate Donald Trump stepped on to a stage in Mount Pleasant, South Carolina, and positioned himself in front of a large banner bearing his campaign slogan "Make America Great Again." Above the cheers from the crowd, he read a statement prepared in response to the December second shooting in San Bernardino, California, in which the male shooter was a Muslim American, and the female shooter was a legal immigrant from Pakistan. Trump spoke of Muslims' "great hatred" of America, and he repeated false claims that Muslims around the world affirm violence against the United States and believe legal forms of *Shari'a* law should be implemented in America (Taylor 2015). His rhetoric extended to policy promises as he indicated that he would introduce a registry or database of all Muslims living in the United States, that he would ban Muslims from entering the country, and that he was open to surveillance of Muslim communities and warrantless searches of mosques.[1]

---

1. The concept of such a registry is not entirely new. For example, the National Security Entry-Exit Registration System is the Bush era attempt at a registry of noncitizens, initiated in 2012 as part of the War on Terror. The Obama administration dismantled the registry before leaving office (Goodman and Nixon 2016).

While Trump's statements were met with immediate criticism and condemnation, they resonated with a segment of the American electorate—one
poll of North Carolina voters estimated that among self-identified Trump
voters, 67 percent support the creation of a national database of Muslims,
51 percent want to close mosques, and 44 percent believe that Islam should
be illegal in the United States (Public Policy Polling 2015). Such opinions are
not limited to hard-core Trump supporters. A later YouGov poll found that
a majority of Americans support the idea of a registry and also found strong
support for enhanced surveillance of Muslim neighborhoods (Hussain 2016).
These high levels of public support suggest that the American public would
countenance Trump's policy proposals.

It was therefore unsurprising when, following the election of Donald
Trump nearly a year later, Muslim women took to Twitter to report they
feared wearing the headscarf in public (Markovinovic 2016). The Muslim-
American human rights advocate Alaa Basatneh observed that "it's no
longer safe to walk on the streets with a headscarf" (Richmond 2016).
Her fear and the fear of other Muslim women was well founded: hate
crimes against Muslims spiked in late November 2016, emboldened by the
perception of support for anti-Muslim vigilantism. Covered women are
the most identifiable Muslims, placing them in the crosshairs of Trump's
ethnonationalistic ideology and making them inadvertent and unwilling
political symbols.[2]

This book explores the politics of the headscarf in the United States and
argues that the politicization of the practice occurs almost exclusively in the
social rather than the institutional sphere. For the women who participated
in our research, the act of head covering is not explicitly politically motivated,
nor is it regulated through American governmental institutions. However,
wearing the headscarf accentuates Muslim identity, which carries significant
social and political costs for Muslim-American women and for the communities to which they belong. The headscarf functions as a symbolic boundary
marker in that it identifies a religious individual, differentiates between Muslim communities, and serves as a point around which women create personal

---

2. Anti-Muslim discrimination experiences are not limited to Muslim women, despite their visibility. Federal Bureau of Investigation (2016) data reveal that hate crimes against Muslims of both
sexes have increased in the years since September eleventh. Specifically, in 2001 the percentage of anti-
Islamic hate crimes increased thirteen times from that of the previous year, surging from 2.1 percent
of all hate crimes motivated by single religious bias up to 27.3 percent. Between 2002 and 2014 the
percentage of anti-Islamic hate crimes ranged between 7.5 (2008) and 16.3 (2014), making Muslims
the second most targeted group after Jews.

and collective understandings about what it means to be "Muslim" and "American."[3] Such boundaries can create opportunities for engagement and social enrichment, but they can also form the basis of discriminatory practices, depending on who is engaged in the work of boundary construction. In other words, the head covering is not always a boundary itself, but it is a marker around which others (including covered women) create boundaries—some people will use the headscarf as a symbol around which to create a community, and others will see it as something that signals difference and conflict.

Muslim women create and maintain multiple meanings and values through the practice of head covering, which shapes particular group identities and interactions while simultaneously conveying religious value orientations that prioritize piety and modesty. By wearing the head covering, Muslim-American women often become subjects of exclusionist social behaviors and experience political and social marginalization. Ultimately, women's experiences with symbolic boundary construction through their head-covering practices carry important political consequences that may well shed light on the future of the United States as a model of democratic pluralism.

Head Covering in North America and Europe

The United States is experiencing a critical moment regarding whether and how symbolic boundaries associated with Islam and the headscarf are translated into social boundaries. Thus far, the debate over Islamic practices has been restricted to the sociopolitical sphere. The formal legal institutions of the United States' government unequivocally protect Muslim women's right to wear the headscarf in all manner of commercial and public space, helping the headscarf to maintain its status as a symbolic boundary rather than a social boundary.[4] The headscarf has historically been protected at the local

---

3. Symbolic boundaries are conceptual constructs that allow social actors to create categorical and meaningful differences between objects, people, practices, space, and time (Epstein 1992, 232; Lamont and Molnár 2002, 168–69). Our social lives are influenced by the way these symbolic boundaries shape notions of membership, identity, similarity, and difference as well as inclusion and exclusion. They also emerge as mediums within which people can overcome stereotypes and gain social status. When symbolic boundaries are widely agreed upon and when the systems of social differences they represent become entrenched and institutionalized and systematically inform behavior, they create social boundaries, which ultimately transform and institutionalize difference in the polity.

4. It is not surprising that the United States would set a precedent for protecting religious practice, as its foundational institutions and national narrative billed religious freedom and practice in the private and public sphere as sacrosanct. The Establishment and Free Exercise clauses of the US Constitution have thus been held as a beacon of religious tolerance enforced through legal institutions, marking the country as a haven for refugees fleeing religious persecution the world over.

and state level. However, in 2015 a civil case, *Samantha Elauf v. Abercrombie and Fitch Stores, Inc.*, made its way to the Supreme Court and raised the possibility of a shift in this protection.

Samantha Elauf was an American teenager who in 2008 applied for a job at Abercrombie and Fitch in her local mall—the quintessential store for fashionable teenagers—wearing a black headscarf to the interview. Samantha was known to fuse her fashion sense with her religious sensibility, commenting that she "tends to make anything . . . in [her] wardrobe *hijabified*" (Liptak 2015). Abercrombie and Fitch did not hire her, claiming the scarf clashed with the company's "look policy." In the aftermath of this experience, Samantha felt she had been discriminated against because of her religious beliefs. The offense was further compounded by her disillusionment: "I was born in the United States, and I thought I was the same as everyone else" (ibid.). When the Equal Opportunity Commission sued on Samantha's behalf, ultimately taking the case to the Supreme Court, Abercrombie and Fitch responded that it was not aware that Samantha was wearing the headscarf for religious reasons. In May of 2015 the Supreme Court ruled that Title VII of the Civil Rights Act of 1964 protected Samantha's right to wear the headscarf at work, and even conservative Justice Antonin Scalia opined that the decision was "really easy."[5]

The system of legal precedent in the United States creates an environment in which the practice of head covering is legally protected. Such protection is unusual worldwide. In many European countries, the interpretation of secularism often requires that religious individuals refrain from showing any type of religious fervor in public space. This interpretation has translated into a zeal for legislating against Islamic head covering at the national or local level across the European continent. France prohibited students from wearing the headscarf in public secondary schools in 2004, and followed it up with a 2011 ban on face-concealing garments such as the *burqa* and the *niqab* in public places. Belgium also banned the niqab in 2011, and the European Court of Human Rights upheld bans on the burqa and the niqab in 2014.

---

5. A spate of lawsuits for workplace discrimination against covered women aimed at high-profile companies such as the Walt Disney Corporation and the Sodexho-Marriott Services, among others, have been successfully litigated in favor of the plaintiff (Business & Human Rights Resource Centre 2010). Many prominent civil society organizations such as the American Civil Liberties Union (ACLU) and the Council on American Islamic Relations have gone to court in Oklahoma and in Michigan (2008), California (2005), and Florida (2002) in support of a women's right to wear the head covering in a variety of public settings from work to photographs taken for the Division of Motor Vehicles (DMV). Lawsuits over religious attire in the workplace have overwhelmingly been settled in favor of the plaintiff. In fact, in a 2004 Oklahoma case the federal government actually supported a motion against the Muskogee School District, which had ordered eleven-year-old Nashala Hearn to remove her headscarf when attending school (Frieden 2004).

Controversies arose in 2016 when the banning of the *burqini*—a full-body swimsuit—in Nice, France, reignited the debate surrounding Islamic attire in Europe. The burqini ban was later overturned by France's highest administrative court on the premise that it violated individual liberties and because officials had failed to demonstrate that the swimwear posed a threat to public order. However, twenty-two cities along the French Riviera persisted with the ban (Breeden and Blaise 2016).

In the wake of the burqini ban, Germany's conservative interior ministers called for a partial ban on the niqab in their "Berlin Declaration" stating, "We unanimously reject the burqa. . . . It does not fit in our open country" (Deutsche Welle 2016a). Along these lines, Chancellor Angela Merkel said that "a fully covered woman has little chance of integrating in Germany." Merkel later supported a formal ban of the burqa, and many Germans appear to agree with her: 51 percent of individuals polled by Infratest Dimap stated that they would be in favor of such a ban despite the fact that Germany's constitutional guarantees of religious freedom would legally prohibit this course of action (Deutsche Welle 2016b). Other European countries, including Spain, Switzerland, and Germany, have left banning the niqab, burqa, or headscarf to the discretion of their municipalities.

In May 2016, the European Court of Justice, the European Union's highest court, issued an advisory opinion stating that companies could bar Muslim female employees from wearing the headscarf at work as long as they banned other forms of religious attire as well (Chan 2016). This ruling strongly contrasts with the United States Supreme Court's ruling in the *Equal Employment Opportunity Commission v. Abercrombie & Fitch Co.* case. In North America, Canada overturned a niqab ban for citizenship ceremonies in 2015, but a contemporaneous poll conducted by the Canadian broadcast network suggested that about 72 percent of sampled Canadians agreed with the ban (CBC News 2015). The Canadian scholar Lydia Clarke commented that the government's initial reasoning for the ban was based on false assumptions that wearing the niqab was an involuntary act and that the garment symbolized women's oppression (Clarke 2013).

In comparison with its Western counterparts, the United States is one of the few secular Western countries that do not regulate women's religious attire in any form (Pew Research Center 2016a).[6] Furthermore, the American public does not appear to be interested in banning religious attire: only 28 percent of respondents in a 2011 Pew survey approved of banning face veils (Pew

---

6. According to Pew Research Center data from 2012 to 2013, Ireland, Finland, and Portugal alongside most of the eastern E.U. member states were the only European countries that did not restrict women from wearing religious attire in some fashion (Pew Research Center 2016b).

Research Center 2010b).[7] Yet public resistance to banning head covering and the legal protections of religious expression do not indicate general public support for Islam or the practice of head covering itself. In the United States, Muslims continue to shoulder the weight of "othering" and discrimination in the social sphere.

Because of the head covering's visibility, covered women are easy targets for social marginalization. For example, despite legal protections, a majority of Muslim-American women fear the headscarf reduces their economic opportunities (Ghumman and Jackson 2010). The Workplace Religious Freedom Act of 2012 in the California State Assembly explicitly mentions religious dress as a protected right, and its passage highlights the very real harassment and discrimination faced by covered women in the public realm and the lengths states have gone to protect them. The bill was passed after a marked rise in cases of religious discrimination in 2011 and 2012. Between 2000 and 2006, civil rights complaints filed by Muslims increased by 674 percent, with 6 percent of cases related to the headscarf—most commonly women were prohibited from wearing it (ACLU Women's Rights Project 2008).

Head covering has also had direct and important ramifications for Muslim women even in the political realm. Campaign managers for President Obama during the 2008 election cycle "prevented two Muslim women wearing the *hijab* from sitting in the televised audience behind the candidate on stage citing concerns over their religion" (Barreto and Bozonelos 2009, 7). On the 2016 presidential campaign trail, then-candidate Donald Trump had a covered Muslim woman, Rose Hamid, ejected from a campaign rally for silently protesting his statements linking Syrian refugees with Islamic terrorism (Diamond 2016).

The contrasting attitudes between the American legal and social environment illustrate the daily conflict inherent in the lives of many covered Muslim-American women: the central political ideologies and institutions of the United States permit and protect head covering and facilitate its use as a symbolic boundary marker in public space. However, the social climate makes wearing it a risk and threatens to turn the symbolic boundary into a social boundary with accompanying structural inequalities. As the practice of covering has become more popular over the past few decades—head cover-

---

7. Daniel Gordon explains this phenomenon with cross-religious sympathy, which is a distinctive feature of American culture that is reflected through the legal briefs issued by the American Supreme Court protecting the free exercise of religion in public space (2008, 37). Unlike Europe, the United States does not have an inclination to regulate religious symbols, and this difference is partially due to varying interpretations (and enforcement) of what secularism connotes in different countries in the West.

ing has doubled internationally since the 1960s (Carvalho 2013)—it has also inadvertently created more opportunities for the proverbial cultural clash between Muslim and non-Muslim Americans. Furthermore, as the headscarf is adopted by congregants in Muslim communities and among new converts in non-Muslim states for the first time in larger numbers, it draws increased social scrutiny outside the Muslim world. Certainly the religious, social, and political significance of covering is growing, especially since many women are covering in a socially deliberate and politically engaged way (Mahmood 2012).

America after September Eleventh

Though the legal institutions in the United States are relatively neutral, and therefore theoretically accepting of head covering in the public sphere, the social environment is less accommodating since the terrorist attacks of September 11, 2001, which now appears to be the major inflection point for social conversations surrounding head covering. This was not the United States' first encounter with Islamic terrorism, but it was the first major threat to the domestic population. The widespread fear and insecurity following the attacks changed the way Americans viewed Islam and Muslims, even the Muslim citizens who had been living peaceably in American neighborhoods for decades (Panagopulos 2006).[8] Almost overnight, Muslims changed from being a protected religious minority group to being a minority group associated with a specific threat to American society.

Governmental institutions soon began to reflect public perception. Whether through the rampant profiling unleashed by the USA PATRIOT Act, the 2004 Department of Homeland Security data share,[9] or the openly Islamophobic statements made during the 2016 presidential race, Muslim men and women feel under siege by their own government, and the societal response is even more distressing. Over half (55%) of Muslim Americans report that being a Muslim after September eleventh is more difficult, and large percentages also report being looked at with suspicion (28%) and called offensive names (22%) (Pew Research Center 2011b).

---

8. The FBI reported a 1,700 percent increase in hate crimes against Muslim Americans between 2000 and 2001 (C. Anderson 2002).

9. In 2004, three years after September eleventh and the beginning of the United States' War on Terror, the Census Bureau gave the Department of Homeland Security access to data on Middle East and North African (MENA) populations, including zip codes of where MENA households are located. MENA organizations and national civil rights advocacy groups like the ACLU compared this to the unethical use of census data in locating Japanese Americans for forced placement in internment camps during World War II.

A spate of attacks against covered women—two women were physically assaulted while pushing their baby strollers in Brooklyn and a sixty-year-old Muslim woman was stabbed in Florida—all in the space of a month in the fall of 2016, speaks to what Muslim activist Linda Sarsour calls the unparalleled courage needed by covered women just to leave the house (Sarsour 2016). She notes how Muslim communities now face a civic and political environment more poisonous than anything encountered since the weeks right after September eleventh, when mosques were defaced and Muslim Americans attacked. In the quote below, Sarsour calls for both formal and informal political engagement by both Muslims and non-Muslims to change the atmosphere of fear that is pervading American politics.

> Bigotry against Muslims has become the norm and often has no consequences. It is time for all Americans to speak out. When we allow one faith community to be targets then we open the doors for others to be targeted. I believe the worst is yet to come unless more people actively intervene with their voices, their votes and in public acts of solidarity with their Muslim neighbors. In a time of growing tensions we must uphold our fundamental freedom to worship in the land of religious freedom and it's why I choose to be unapologetically Muslim every day. As a Muslim woman, not only is wearing my religious headscarf in public an act of faith, but it has become an act of courage. (Ibid.)

Ironically, these attacks and the rampant Islamophobia in the American public sphere foster precisely what so many proponents of liberating Muslim women from presumed subjugation hope to root out—the relegation of Muslim women to the home and their disengagement from public space for reasons of safety. The new security measures enacted in response to the September eleventh terrorist attacks and the subsequent profiling of Muslims inadvertently served to isolate them from the mainstream population and provided suitable social environments for the creation of symbolic boundaries. In many cases this amounted to discrimination, othering, and the marginalization of covered Muslim-American women based on negative stereotyping. Many women stopped wearing the head covering because of the discrimination and aggression they faced in their everyday interactions with non-Muslims.

But for other women, the context has prompted them to wear the headscarf and defy the societal stigma lobbed against Muslim Americans. Thus a religious symbol is increasingly becoming a self-styled tool of civil resistance and a means to reclaim "Americanness." These women embody a contradiction: they experience a sense of precarious membership in American social and political identity while simultaneously enjoying full legal protection for their religious practice. The current situation for Muslim-American women, and more specifically the role of head covering in boundary construction, is the ultimate example of the potential disconnect between forms of inclusion fostered through formal institutions and alienating informal sociopolitical processes. Therefore, the experiences of covered Muslim-American women and the politics underlying their choice to cover constitute an important test case for understanding the limits of American pluralism.

The Boundaries of American Pluralism

Contemporary understandings of the place and significance of religion and diverse cultural practices in the public space are informed by America's history of providing refuge for those seeking freedom of worship and equal treatment—in short, democratic pluralism (Gvosdev 2010, 226; McGraw 2003). Since its foundation, American society has been characterized by ever-increasing religious and cultural diversity, primarily due to immigration. This new religious and cultural plurality corresponded with shifts in attitudes and policies about assimilation, Americanization, and the idea of a cultural melting pot. In line with the shift toward a more pluralist approach to immigrant integration, new groups often used their religious faith as a primary resource for integrating into an American way of life (MacHacek 2003). In this respect, most of the new groups added to the religious and cultural landscape were not significantly different from previous waves of immigrants who used Protestantism as a mechanism for integration. Yet the divergence of more recent immigrants from a cultural and religious consensus grounded in the Judeo-Christian tradition, and their active renegotiation of American social and cultural identity, pushed against the predefined symbolic boundaries of American pluralism (ibid.).

In the last few decades, Muslims in America, and particularly women who cover, have become part of public and academic debates on whether religiously and culturally diverse groups can be brought together under the sociopolitical umbrella of American identity (McGraw 2003). With the growing emphasis on multiculturalism in the late twentieth century came the encouragement of greater acceptance of religious and cultural pluralism, but this process often culminated in a "benign neglect" of the groups that constituted this new pluralism.

In many ways, American political institutions operate from a liberal universalist frame, in which issues related to religious and cultural pluralism are left to society. The political and legal system is formally open to all members of the polity through individual rights and liberties, and legal institutions continue to protect individual religious expression under the First Amendment. However, the increasing cultural and religious diversity of society and the mainstream American perceptions of that diversity produce dynamics that manifest in de facto exclusion of many cultural and religious minorities within the mainstream American polity. One of those communities is represented by Muslim-American women who choose to cover as a way to express their religious and personal identity but have been alienated from the public sphere for this choice. Our book uses their lived experiences as pious and patriotic American citizens to reflect on the health and sustainability of democratic pluralism in America.

Covering in America: Our Survey Methodology

The central argument of this book is developed through a quantitative analysis of survey data from nearly two thousand Muslim-American women in forty-nine states, supplemented by additional focus group interviews. Ours is the largest academic online survey of Muslim-American women on the issue of head covering (see appendix A for descriptions of the questions asked and summary statistics for each variable). We distributed the online survey in 2012 and used a snowball sampling mechanism to find research subjects by referral from one subject to the next (Atkinson and Flint 2001). We adopted snowball sampling as our recruitment mechanism because of the strong social and cultural linkages that occur within and across the American Muslim population but also because of the difficulties of tapping into a population that is variously estimated as comprising at most 2 percent of the US population.[10] Snowball sampling allowed us to quickly grow our sample beyond the initial contacts reached via e-mail or online exchanges with more than 1,300 mosques, Islamic centers, Islamic organizations, Muslim student associations, and vendors of Islamic dress and head coverings across the fifty states.

Though our survey is not intended to be representative of the female Muslim population in the United States, our survey demographics compare favorably

---

10. The American census has no clear estimate of how many Muslims currently live in the United States since it does not collect religious data. Statistics on the size of the American Muslim population are usually garnered from privately and publicly administered surveys by organizations such as the General Social Survey (GSS); the Religious Landscape Survey by the Pew Research Group; the Gallup, Institute for Social Policy and Understanding, and Mori polling agencies; and many others, with estimates ranging from 2 to 7 million Muslims. In 2011, the GSS ventured that there were approximately 1.2 million Muslims, while the Pew Research Group calculated some 2.75 million in the United States. CAIR put the number closer to 7 million. See, for example, A. Khan 2011.

with other large-scale surveys of Muslim Americans, such as the Pew Surveys of Muslim Americans conducted in 2007 and 2011 (Pew Research Center 2007, 2011b; see appendix B for a comparison of our findings with these Pew surveys). Generally, the participants in our survey are slightly younger, more educated, more likely to be employed in part-time labor, and more likely to be United States citizens than the female participants of the previous studies conducted by Pew. While the demographics of our interviews roughly lined up with the expected breakdown of the estimated ethnic composition of Muslim Americans, our survey undersampled African Americans. This is surprising since 52 percent of our survey respondents were born in the United States, and the plurality of American-born Muslims identify as African American, according to the latest survey research (Ahmed 2014). Conversely, the size of the white and Asian populations in our sample is overrepresented by comparison with the Pew samples. Gallup maintains that the largest ethnic group among Muslim Americans is African Americans (35%) (Hodges 2009), while according to Pew the plurality (over 30%) of their respondents identified themselves as "white" both in 2009 and in 2011 (Pew Research Center 2011b). Ultimately, there is no clear consensus on the exact size of the specific ethnic groups underlying the Muslim-American population even across Pew and Gallup (Keeter and Smith 2009). However, we suspect our sampling outcome is partially due to the nature of the organizations that distributed the survey. These include, among others, the Council on American-Islamic Relations (CAIR), the Islamic Society of North America (ISNA), and Muslim student associations (MSAs), which traditionally tend to skew toward Arab and South Asian Muslims (Ahmed 2014), though we also contacted local mosques and other Islamic organizations across the fifty states.

The differences in the demographic profile can also be explained by other factors. The most important is the online survey method, which may not be equally accessible across all socioeconomic and generational strata in the Muslim-American survey population. Online survey distribution requires potential participants to have access to a computer or smartphone and the Internet. According to the 2010 US Census, populations under the age of forty-four have wide access to the Internet, and Internet usage rises with age and school enrollments as well as household incomes (US Census Bureau 2012). This makes our relatively young survey respondents likely to have accessed our survey through their educational networks and/or their socioeconomic positioning. For example, MSAs provided frequent assistance in distributing our survey, leading to the overrepresentation of college-age survey participants.

The survey research is supported and enhanced with rich qualitative data from seventeen focus group interviews during the summer of 2013 with seventy-two women in seven American cities with large Muslim populations: Boston, Chicago, Detroit, Houston, New York, Norfolk, and Washington, DC. We recruited participants using many of the same contacts from our survey distribution network. We contacted local academic centers that focus on religion with a request to host our focus groups, which provided an education-centered space and granted institutional legitimacy to our requests for interviewees. For example, several of our interviews in Washington, DC, were held at Georgetown University, and a few of the interviewees indicated that they had come to the interview—at least in part—to check out the campus and see the space.[11]

Focus group interviews are a useful tool for our project because they are more sensitive to cultural variables than survey methods and are well suited for exploring the ideas and views of marginalized groups who might feel threatened or intimidated by more conventional interview or survey methods (Kitzinger 1995). Given the culturally complex nature of our research topic and the incidence of discrimination against Muslim women, these concerns are very relevant. Furthermore, interviewing in groups made the conversations flow more naturally between our respondents, and it allowed us to behave more like bystanders than moderators or interviewers. However, we did use six key questions to stimulate discussion, and there is a slight likelihood that our interview subjects were susceptible to the Hawthorne effect.[12] (Our interview questions can be found in appendix C.)

Observing the interplay between respondents and listening to their comparative experiences helped us better understand the diverse perspectives on the topic within the Muslim-American community and how they interacted with and informed one another. Our participants were cheerfully generous with their time and seemed to enjoy the opportunity to share their stories and to hear from other women. Many said that it was a religious obligation for them to participate in events that allow them to share their faith (referring to it as *da'wa*),[13] while others emphasized a feeling of responsibility to share as a representative of a vilified and misunderstood community. Because of this vulnerability, throughout the text we have changed the names of our respondents and have provided a footnoted description of their demographic

---

11. We also relied on the help of the University of Houston, Loyola University in Chicago, Virginia Wesleyan College, the University of Nevada at Reno, and the University of California at Berkeley to help us set up focus group interviews.

12. The Hawthorne effect—named after research at the Hawthorne Works in Cicero, Illinois, which suggested that worker productivity improved when the workers knew they were research subjects—warns us that respondents' discourse and responses to these questions might have been geared to appeasing other participants and us as the interviewers and moderators of the focus groups.

13. See Mahmood's 2012 discussion of this concept in Egypt.

profiles at the first mention of each in the text (summary statistics of the demographic profiles of our participants can be found in appendix D).

All interviews were conducted in English, recorded, and transcribed verbatim. Our analysis of the data is based on a close reading of the hundreds of pages of transcripts and coded using a qualitative software program. We used the qualitative data generated by the focus groups to both affirm the results from our survey and supplement the survey data, helping us to understand complex concepts and to highlight important experiences that might be overlooked in a survey. Our focus groups provided us with evocative content, and we directly engage with quoted material from over two-thirds of our seventy-two focus group participants throughout this book.

The vast majority of our participants cover (85.5%); therefore, we cannot use this sample to analyze hypothesized differences between covered and uncovered women in the general population. Rather, we generate insights through these focus groups to illuminate possible mechanisms linking Islamic practice and political opinions and participation.[14]

Different Terms for Muslim Head-Covering Practices

Up to this point, we have referred to the Muslim head covering as the hijab, the burqa, and the headscarf. There are numerous other ways to denote forms of Muslim head covering, and this diversity reflects the variety of styles used by Muslim women in covering their bodies to varying degrees, often reflecting diverse understandings of female modesty across Muslim communities (Shaheed 2008, 290).

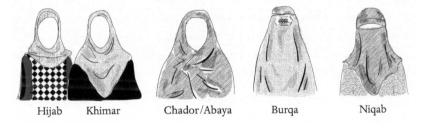

Hijab   Khimar   Chador/Abaya   Burqa   Niqab

FIGURE I.1.   Types of Islamic head covering. Right to left: hijab, khimar, chador/abaya, burqa, niqab.

---

14. Throughout the analysis of our qualitative data, it is important to recall the selection effect produced by the way we solicited participation for both our online survey and focus group participants. In both instances, the individuals were likely interested in discussing the headscarf, and the willingness of our focus group participants to voluntarily surrender their time reflects a level of social engagement that may not be representative of the population of Muslim women in America.

As Islam spread, historically, through conquest, trade, migration, and conversion, head covering increased in frequency, and new forms and names for covering emerged, resulting in "new geographies of vocabulary" related to the practice (Moors and Tarlo 2007, 136). Each new community of believers embraced the Arabic or local descriptors of the practice on their own terms, in many cases redefining the original meaning of Arabic linguistic imports. In the modern era, Muslims in North America and Europe have largely adopted the Arabic term *hijab* for the generic headscarf commonly used in the Middle East and usually describing a shawl specifically wrapped around the head and neck.[15] It is still an open question whether the Qur'an suggests standardizing the practice of female covering, since only the word *khimar* (head cover) and *jilbab* (cloak) appear as styles of women's dress in the holy text itself. In fact, the word *hijab* specifically references the Arabic verb for the act of "covering" rather than an explicit clothing item (Lewis 2007, 248).[16]

Geographical variations in the use of Arabic terms describing the head covering and other forms of Islamic attire (i.e., concealing more of the body) often make it difficult to discern the exact style of covering when one of these terms is used. For example, in Indonesia the Arabic term *jilbab* describes the headscarf itself, whereas much of the Middle East uses *jilbab* to refer to a full-length coat or cloak. However, this style of attire is specifically called a *balto* in Yemen, indicating there is linguistic variation across Arab countries as well (Moors and Tarlo, 2007). The term *burqa* has a particularly confusing etymology, with South Asian Muslims using it to refer to a complete face-body garment akin to the *abaya* in the Persian Gulf, while traditional Pashtuns in Afghanistan and Pakistan use burqa to refer to a covering style that leaves a small mesh or grille opening for women to see through. Yemenis and some other Arab communities use burqa to describe the modern face veil, or niqab, which leaves a slit opening for the eyes. The notorious burqa ban in France also invokes some of this linguistic confusion, because, in fact, what is being banned is the niqab (veil), not the hijab (headscarf).[17] The South Asian *dupatta*, a loose scarf covering the head, is the closest equivalent to the hijab

---

15. Sometimes the hijab will be referred to by how the wearer ties it: the *al-amira* (two-part head covering composed of a skullcap and a tightly wound headscarf) or shayla style (loosely tied headscarf).

16. *Surah An-Nur* (24:30–31) and *Surah* (33:59). These are the two passages in the Qur'an that most explicitly mention women's attire—though some scholars invoke a third, which warns against adopting the "finery" characteristic of women during the pagan, pre-Islamic period (32:33). More detail available at http://veil.unc.edu/religions/islam/quran.

17. The replacement of niqab with burqa in the burqa ban is particularly confusing since the communities most likely to wear the niqab in France are Arab, while the burqa is an Afghani garment.

when styled in the *shayla* fashion common in the Persian Gulf. In Iran and other ethnically Persian communities, the word *chador* describes a combination of head covering and shawl, loosely wrapped around the upper body. Yet it can also refer to a full-length black cloak similar to the abaya, covering the wearer from head to toe. This same cloak is called the *paranja* in Central Asian Muslim communities, while Balkan Muslims refer to it as *feredza*.

To dispel some of this linguistic confusion, in this book we use the terms "head covering" or "headscarf" and *hijab*, which can refer to a specific garment or to the practice of modesty, since we surveyed and interviewed American Muslims. We also refrain from using the term "veil" unless specifically referring to face coverings, as veiling entails a very distinct act and object that many Muslims consider not ordained by Islam but rather specific to cultural and tribal traditions.[18] The majority of our research participants formally reported wearing the hijab (77%), and only a small number of them reported wearing the niqab (3%) and the abaya or jilbab (6%).[19]

Chapter Descriptions

We argue that in the United States the politicization of the headscarf has occurred primarily in the social, rather than in the institutional, sphere. In the following chapters, we develop the ways in which the headscarf serves as a symbolic boundary marker, highlighting the United States as an intriguing case for exploring the politicization of the headscarf within society. We investigate the effects of head covering on Muslim women's social, religious, and political lives. While head covering in the United States is understood primarily as an act of religious piety (as is discussed in chapter 1), the practice also reflects a complex set of crosscutting processes within modern democratic society: it influences the structure of personal social networks, feelings of belonging, and group and personalized identity, as well as political attitudes and actions.

This introduction contextualizes the case of the United States and illuminates our conceptual framework. Chapter 1 lays the groundwork for later analysis by reviewing the historical and theoretical basis for modern head-

---

18. The former sheikh of Al-Azhar, Dr. Sayyid Muhammad Tantawi, as well as many other senior clerics and Islamic scholars, have disputed that the niqab is ordained by doctrine.

19. In our survey, the head covering was referred to most frequently as hijab, with 642 mentions, followed by the headscarf with 601 mentions and the veil with 187 mentions. Other descriptors were used less frequently. Khimar was referenced 37 times, abaya 34 times, and niqab 25 times, and burqa and dupatta were each mentioned 3 times.

covering behaviors. It also sets up a crucial part of our argument by demonstrating that the individual decision-making process around head covering is not politicized but is primarily a feature of religious piety and secondarily an expression of personal identity. Most important, we show that head covering is very much a choice in the American context and is therefore emblematic of the religious agency of our research participants.

While wearing the headscarf is conceived by our respondents as an individual choice, it also has collective implications for Muslim communities. Chapter 2 analyzes the role of Muslim head covering as a symbolic boundary marker mediating community belonging and social interaction within and across Muslim communities in the United States. The head covering visibly identifies Muslim women as part of a religious community, making it a crucial facilitator of identity politics as it identifies Muslims to each other and aids in constructing a unified Muslim community. However, the head covering can also highlight difference, particularly in suggesting different levels of piety between women who do and do not cover. This carries important ramifications for group-based politics and the emergence of a coherent and stable group identity among Muslim Americans.

While the head covering is a powerful marker of religious group identity facilitating social interactions within the Muslim community, it also visibly associates a woman with a religious minority that has been marked as a physical and ideological threat in the post–September eleventh context. Chapter 3 focuses on the experiences of covered Muslim women as the visible "other" within mainstream society in the United States and explores our participants' self-reported experiences along a continuum of othering behaviors, ranging from benevolent to exclusionary actions and attitudes toward Muslim individuals. We also engage with the consequences of social marginalization by paying particular attention to instances of discrimination, which erode Muslim women's sense of belonging in mainstream American society.

As the everyday lived experiences of covered Muslim women influence their political attitudes and patterns of political participation within the American state, Muslim women also define and justify informal political participation with reference to their Islamic worldview. Chapter 4 examines the ways by which they reconcile their lived and often negative experiences as covered Muslim women living in non-Muslim society with Islamic scripture and lifestyle ethics. In this chapter we engage with our respondents' views on the complementarity between Islam and political participation and the ways in which head covering informs these understandings.

It is not always easy for our participants to reconcile their spiritual and political lives, but most of them are active participants in the political system.

Chapter 5 analyzes the relationship between the practice of head covering and formal political participation. This chapter argues that the practice of head covering is indirectly associated with Muslim women's formal political participation through its role as a boundary marker in constructing religiously homogeneous personal social networks. These networks decrease turnout and political party affiliation. However, participation in more formalized social networks through mosques and Islamic organizations increases formal political participation, which demonstrates that the ethnic, racial, and denominational heterogeneity within the mosques has a mobilizing effect on covered Muslim women in the United States. This chapter reveals that the nature of women's social networks facilitates distinct types and levels of political engagement with the American political system.

Despite their formal and informal political engagement in the United States, Muslim-American women express feelings of disaffection from the American political system. They are particularly disappointed with the levels of representation they get in return for their political input. Chapter 6 extends the analysis of their relationship with the political system to explore notions of citizenship. Our participants self-identify as Americans and naturally invoke citizenship rights, connecting their religious expression to the protected freedoms of speech and religion. Their American political socialization is further demonstrated through a strong individualism and expectations of civic benefits in return for their political engagement. This chapter discusses the perceived disjunction between our respondents' sense of belonging and investment in the American political system and their lack of representation and voice within formal political institutions.

Finally, we revisit the role of head covering as a symbolic boundary marker in the United States and how it mediates the sociopolitical realities of Muslim-American women once they've chosen to embrace the practice as an expression of their religious agency and personal identity. In particular, we consider how the increase in Islamophobic sentiment redefines the ability for covered women to enact their identities as religious American citizens and offer policy prescriptions for managing and sustaining democratic pluralism—how to maintain the novel "one" out of the diverse "many" (*e pluribus unum*)—within American institutions and society.

✖ CHAPTER 1

The Islamic Head Covering

[Prophet], tell believing men to lower their glances and guard their private parts: that is purer for them. God is well aware of everything they do. And tell believing women that they should lower their glances, guard their private parts, and not display their charms beyond what [it is acceptable] to reveal; they should draw their veils over their breasts and not reveal their charms except to their husbands, their fathers, their husbands' fathers, their sons, their husbands' sons, their brothers, their brothers' sons, their sisters' sons, their womenfolk, their slaves, such men as attend them who have no sexual desire, or children who are not yet aware of women's nakedness; they should not stamp their feet so as to draw attention to any hidden charms. Believers, all of you, turn to God so that you may prosper.

—Surah 24: 30–31

This chapter explores the practice of head covering in the United States by unpacking generational and fashion trends and the demographics of those who cover and through investigating the reasons for adopting the practice as explained by our survey participants. We situate this analysis within a contemporary historical frame, highlighting women's agency and choice in embracing the practice within the American setting. Since the 1970s, head covering has become increasingly popular among Muslim women across the globe. In consequence, there have been intense academic debates about the reasons for its increasing popularity and whether Muslim women exercise free agency in adopting the headscarf.[1] While it is impossible to do justice to this vast literature in one chapter, we observe that the contested nature of this topic is largely due to the complexity of choices and actions underlying the practice itself—especially in a quasi-secular, democratic country.

---

1. See, for example, Ahmed 2014; Charrad 2011; and Mahmood 2012.

The iconic Surah al-Nur (the Chapter of Light), with which we begin this chapter, is the scriptural genesis of the Islamic head covering and most explicitly describes its function in enacting both symbolic and social boundaries related to piety and gender within Islam. While many other verses in the Qur'an speak to the necessity of "barriers" between men and women, the requirement of demure, conservative, and pious comportment is clearly stated in these verses for both genders. However, there appears to be a greater onus placed on women to facilitate and maintain this boundary through the practice of covering.

Head covering was not invented by Muslims, nor is the practice specific to Islam. Jewish, Christian, and Muslim women have all practiced head covering during the past two millennia (Amer 2014). In fact, it has pre-Islamic roots and was often used to signal status rather than piety and even ethnic background across a variety of religious and ethnic communities who first adopted similar practices in the Middle East and the Mediterranean Basin (Lewis 2007). Covering the head with cloth was used as a symbol of women's status and sexual availability as far back as the thirteenth century BCE in Assyrian society. Later it was both adopted and adapted in ancient Greek, Roman, Sassanid, and Byzantine societies (Amer 2014). The use of head covering as a marker of women's status was partially due to its "contextually interactive" role, in which the covering transcended religion and added a spatial dimension to its function by enforcing gender separation and thereby governing "who can interact with whom . . . and the nature of those interactions" (Lewis 2007, 151).

In the modern era, Muslim head covering has become a particularly powerful symbol of religious identity, women's piety, modesty, and—depending on the audience—their subordination and submissiveness. Because of this powerful symbolic role, Muslim head-covering practices have provoked heated and emotional debates in both Muslim majority and Muslim minority states (Amer 2014). Most clothing styles have the potential to "create boundaries between people and shape collective identities" as a result of their symbolic, religious, and contextually interactive roles. However, Islamic head coverings have become a particularly powerful symbolic boundary marker in the last few decades (Shaheed 2008, 294).

Symbolic boundaries are conceptual constructs that allow social actors to create categorical and meaningful distinctions between objects, people, practices, space, and time (Epstein 1995; Lamont and Molnár 2002). Our social lives are influenced by the way these symbolic boundaries shape notions of membership, identity, similarity, and difference as well as societal inclusion and exclusion. These symbolic boundaries also emerge as mediums within which people can overcome stereotypes and gain social status, depending on an individual's group affiliation and identity. The strategies informing this type of symbolic identity production are often referred to as "boundary work." In the case of Muslim women in the United States these strategies represent opportunities for them to use religious and social resources to "craft distinctive identities that selectively appropriate values from the American cultural mainstream" while still projecting and safeguarding a personal Muslim identity (Bartkowski and Read 2003, 86). The symbolic boundaries associated with head covering are thus often contingent on the interplay between the religious, social, and political meanings attributed to the practice by a variety of social actors. These symbolic boundaries represent crosscutting individual and collective identities demarcating boundaries between non-Muslims and Muslims; differences across race, ethnicity, and generation within Muslim communities themselves; and most explicitly the gender differences between men and women. Ultimately, the iterative and interactive processes underlying the meanings, functions, and motivations associated with the headscarf reflect a complex set of choices and behaviors on the part of those women who choose to adopt it.

In the United States, Muslim women can best be understood as citizens embodying religious norms who enact, claim, and negotiate their religious but also social and even political identities through the practice of head covering. Most important, our research participants perceive head covering as a choice and express their agency by connecting it to their social and political lives. We explore the religious, social, and political motivations informing the practice of head covering through our survey and focus group data. While our research shows piety to be a primary reason for covering among our research participants, we distinguish it from other social and political motives for the practice among our respondents.

Modern Trajectories of Head Covering

In the late twentieth and early twenty-first centuries the significance of Islamic head covering came to the front and center of religious, social, and political discourse as a result of a global increase in the practice and in the global reach of Islam (Mahmood 2004). Several studies suggest that a growing number of Muslim women are covering, in both majority Muslim and Western societies.[2] This is a surprising development considering the Arab historian Albert Hourani's prediction in the 1950s that the hijab would disappear by the end

---

2. See Ahmed 2011; Carvalho 2013; Morin and Horowitz 2006.

of the twentieth century,[3] which he based on personal observations of the trend of "de-veiling" across Egypt, Syria, Lebanon, Jordan, and Iraq.[4] Despite these predictions, head covering has doubled since the 1960s and 1970s (Carvalho 2009, 2013).[5] Wearing the headscarf became an important symbol in the pro-Islamist movements in Egypt, Morocco, and Iran in the late twentieth century, while shedding the headscarf increasingly came to be identified with Westernization and imperialism (Hirschmann 2002). The latter interpretation is most often attributed to the ascendance and rhetoric of political Islam in the 1970s.[6]

It is important to note that head covering signals different political commitments depending on the context. For example, during the Iranian revolution, women donned the hijab as a sign of defiance against the shah's regime (Nashat 1983), while during the headscarf affairs in France (1989–2003) it symbolized a complex act of identification with and defiance against the French secular state (Benhabib 2004), showcasing a determination to be both French *and* Muslim (Wing and Smith 2005). There are also veiling regimes or the "spatially realized sets of hegemonic rules and norms . . . produced by specific constellations of power" related to women's head covering in both Muslim and non-Muslim settings (Secor 2002, 8). In these regimes, women experience varying possibilities for choice within a given space and thereby exercise "a series of cultural and subcultural competencies in their adherences to and destabilizations of veiling regimes, often moving between different regimes in the space of a single day and over the course of their lives" (Lewis 2007, 427–28). Adopting and shedding the headscarf both symbolize the varying political struggles reflected in women's political agency across different national contexts (Golley 2004). Consequently, there are significant differences between adopting the headscarf in a liberal democracy where women are legally autonomous and wearing it in contexts of legal obligation, such as in Iran and Saudi Arabia. Over the past few decades the revival in head-covering practices has become the symbol of a "return to traditional values" (Winter 2008, 28) and "resistance to the perceived loss of cultural purity resulting from Western power and influence" (Hirschmann 2002, 179).

---

3. See Ahmed 2011; also cf. Berger 1990 for a treatment of secularization theory.

4. The notion of de-veiling was launched by the prominent Egyptian feminist Huda Sha'rāwī's dramatic removal of her veil in 1923 after returning from an international conference of feminists (Sha'rāwī 1987). Subsequently, a host of secular Arab feminists organized movements to de-veil and even coordinated collective de-veiling street demonstrations akin to the bra burnings of American feminists.

5. Also cf. Bayat 2007a on Egypt; Rheault 2008 on Turkey; and Smith-Hefner 2007 on Indonesia.

6. See Bayat 2007a; Carvalho 2009, 2013; Franks 2000; Hoodfar 1991; Stillman and Stillman 2003.

The global increase in head covering from the 1970s onward has also affected the Muslim population in the United States. Head covering became much more commonplace after the 1990s, especially among the second- and third-generation immigrant populations (Carvalho 2013). The increase in covering among younger, American-born Muslim women, sometimes against their parents' will, also challenges the view of religious socialization as a linear "transmission [of values] from one generation to the next" (Kühle 2012, 114). Further, the revival of head covering among second-generation immigrant women coincided with the debates on the integration and cultural adaptation of immigrant populations in Western societies. As a result, questions about Muslim women's agency and choice in adopting the head covering have been common in both academic and policy circles.

Agency and Choice in Head Covering

The increase in the popularity of covering has sparked intense debates about women's agency and choice in adopting the practice. In Western academic debates, covered Muslim women have often been portrayed as victims of patriarchal religious norms, and in the 1990s liberal feminists expressed concerns about covered women's access to and enjoyment of their individual rights in both non-Muslim and Muslim countries. These debates mainly centered on questions of whether the head covering symbolizes and maintains patriarchal gender inequalities and relatedly, whether cultural group rights can therefore be antithetical to the individual rights of women (Okin and Cohen 1999). Even Muslim women who actively invoked their personal autonomy and choice in adopting the practice were often perceived as suffering from cognitive dissonance—essentially, while they may have thought their choices were "free," they were seen to be in denial of the paternalism behind head covering. This argument challenged the authenticity and questioned the autonomy of their agency (Sheth 2006). The conception of head covering as a falsely desired choice is driven by narrow understandings of individual agency as limited to active resistance against what are deemed to be oppressive norms. However, such assumptions about the headscarf often invalidate Muslim Americans' sense of their own personal and especially moral autonomy.

Furthermore, in the aftermath of September eleventh and more recent US terrorist attacks perpetrated by Muslims, covered Muslim women are paradoxically portrayed as religiously fundamentalist and potentially dangerous while simultaneously cast as subjugated and oppressed (Aziz 2012). Paradoxically perceived as both victims and threats, Muslim women are turned into an "allegory of undesirable cultural difference" (Bilge 2010, 10). This paradox drives the continuum of "othering" behaviors toward Muslim-American women discussed in chapter 3.

Head covering can symbolize both resistance and subversion—an interpretation that moves beyond the binary of oppression and/or false consciousness but remains squarely within the bounds of liberal notions of agency as being authentic only when arising in response to externally imposed norms, acts, or institutions. Some have argued that head covering may constitute a strategic way to facilitate freedom of movement and employment and enable social interactions outside the private domain. It may also be a resistance to sexual objectification or Western hegemony.[7] The headscarf can be "both a part of the material being and have an independent character from it," effectively containing the seeds of both regulation and subversion within itself, depending on the wearer's opportunities within a given veiling regime (Tanir 2009, 6). This notion of the head covering as a means for subverting hegemonic norms certainly attributes a form of agency to Muslim women. However, the view of head covering as a subversive act has also been criticized for excluding the possibility of an agency situated beyond resistance to externally imposed norms (Mahmood 2004).

More recently, the head covering has been analyzed as an embodied religious practice through which the agency of Muslim women emerges.[8] This scholarship draws on poststructuralist understandings of agency and the role of embodiment in agency formation. Poststructuralist approaches challenge the idea that agency necessarily requires autonomy from external norms and power structures and instead views agency as created within systems of power (Butler 1990). Drawing on Michel Foucault's understanding of power as both repressive and productive, Laborde suggests that agency does not exist *prior* to social forces but is rather developed within and constituted by those same forces (2006, 364). Thus embodiment—the expression of norms and values in physical forms—has become an important analytical tool for exploring how women's agency is constituted within patriarchal systems of power.[9]

From this perspective, Muslim women's embodied submission to religious authority through head covering could be a condition enabling their agency. The act of wearing the head covering enables the development of specific moral dispositions and virtues that are associated with being a "good Muslim." This embodied practice in which the wearer voluntarily submits herself

---

7. See Hirschmann 1998; Hoodfar 2001; Gaspard and Khosrokhavar 1995; Laborde 2006.
8. See Bracke 2008; Mahmood 2005; and Winchester 2008.
9. See Butler 2011; Gatens 1996; Grosz 1994.

to religious norms and her subjectivity (her conscious experience of head covering) is premised on a chosen docility, which reflects her religious agency (Mahmood 2005). Thus, in head covering, agency is driven by neither resistance to nor compliance with external social norms but is rather subjectively marked by a desire to submit to and please God, straddling the line between duty and choice (Bracke 2008; Bracke and Fadil 2012).[10]

Our research demonstrates that among our respondents, head covering is almost universally framed as a free choice. However, that choice reflects the complex religious, social, and political motivations informing the practice in the United States. Head-covering behaviors unfold across ever-dynamic circumstances for Muslim-American women, and consequently these behaviors suggest a kind of agency that is influenced by multiple and often competing sociopolitical factors (Sheth 2006). In the following section, we explore how these women enact their religious agency more broadly through the choice to cover.

Agency in the United States

Muslim women in the United States come from a variety of social backgrounds associated with differences in race, ethnicity, culture, class, and even immigration status, and we further explore this diversity in chapter 2. Their social positions within American society are mediated by the nature of their religious practice and gender, which effectively confine them to minority status within the current social and political system. This is often the case even though they might have privileged status within other socially significant demarcations in American society (based on income, education, race, etc.). The complex interplay of Muslim women's social positions, which are shaped by intersecting power structures, requires accounting for the "specificities of material and symbolic conditions" affecting their agency as religious minorities in an increasingly Islamophobic environment (Bilge 2010, 24). To the extent that Muslim women in the United States are oftentimes simultaneously members of multiple minority groups, their head-covering practice is both a religiously informed and a socially and politically determined decision. The agency of Muslim women is thus shaped and developed both through

---

10. Framing covered women's agency in terms of an embodied act of submitting to the will of God has been criticized for introducing a "certain kind of cultural and ethical absolutism" since religious agency is therefore understood only contextually (Waggoner 2005, 247). This "absolutism" disallows questioning the contemporary religious revival in the Islamic world and prevents an examination of inequalities potentially created within religious social structures (Vasilaki 2016).

their embodiment of religious norms and through the social environment that emerges from symbolic boundaries that create their individual and group identities.

Our research participants overwhelmingly report that they perceive the headscarf as an autonomous, individual, and informed choice in the United States—a context that allows them to exercise their legal right to religious expression and build communities and identities through the headscarf. While they commonly believe they embody their religion, they do not generally envision themselves as championing or embodying gender subjugation, patriarchy, or inequality through the act of head covering. Though our research participants explain their practice primarily in terms of their piety and choice, our data reveal they often have social and even political reasons for adopting it. These other reasons usually reflect the lived experiences of Muslim women as minority citizens in the United States.

Recent scholarship on religious identity and religiosity underscores that religious agency "is not practiced in a vacuum but is enacted within specific social contexts" shaped by symbolic boundaries that manage understandings of individual and group identities (Leming 2007, 74). Therefore, religious agency and the creation of symbolic boundaries both involve a "personal and collective claiming and enacting of dynamic religious identity" in which identity is both "received" and "claimed" by covered Muslim women (ibid.). Rather than being an exclusive matter of ascription or choice, the development of religious identities in contemporary America involves elements of both (Cadge and Davidman 2006). Conventional views assert that "choice" weakens traditional religious commitments, hastening the process of secularization. However, choice has been found to strengthen religious commitments by enabling individuals to personalize and claim ownership of their faith as an act of religious agency (Berger 1969; Warner 1993).[11]

While the explanations for how choice is involved in the enactment of religious agency may differ, it is important to consider what Muslim women themselves make of this discourse on choice when it comes to analyzing the headscarf as a symbolic boundary marker—especially in response to non-Muslims' expectations and perceptions about their agency and vulnerability. The women who participated in our focus groups often aspire to follow in

---

11. Much scholarship on Islamic practice in Europe argues that a personalization of the faith is taking place. This personalization could be a byproduct of myriad factors: the fragmenting of religious authority structures, the democratizing influence of Western values, the effects of immigration, or reformist traditions within Islam itself (Peter 2006).

the footsteps of the Prophet Mohammed and his wives and daughters, citing them as role models and examples of religious agency. In one of our Chicago focus groups, this notion of agency informs a discussion of how exposing one's body and covering it were equivalent choices. Lara, an African American in her late fifties, observes, "Why do non-Muslim American women care if somebody has something on their head or not? As they move to expose increasing amounts of their own flesh, what bothers them about women who choose not to do that, if indeed, women have choice? Because if it is about choice you can't dictate when their choice is not your choice."[12]

In response to Lara's comment, Xara, another African-American participant in her late forties, links the practices of exposing one's body to non-Muslims' perceptions of freedom: "For the average non-Muslim American women, they think taking off more clothes, the fewer pieces of clothing you have on, the more freedom you have."[13] Lara challenges this idea that wearing less represents freedom: "Put it in context. The women's movement started with trying to take women off billboards. Having women not be forced to take clothes off to be attractive and giving them power over their own bodies. Their daughters have come full circle and decided to take off all their clothes. Liberating? Maybe [as] enslaving as anything else."

Comparing their choice to cover with the non-Muslims' choice to wear less, these Muslim women implicitly challenge the mainstream public and even academic perceptions of what constitutes free will. By proposing the counterargument that exposing one's body by wearing less connotes a submission to equally oppressive secular norms about women's sexuality, they comparatively situate the practice of covering within a discourse of freedom and choice. In this discourse, the presence of the non-Muslim "other" serves as a reference point for the emergence of a religious agency that is grounded in the observance of an embodied religious practice.

Muslim-American women enact their religious agency in ways that reflect their engagement with issues of gender equity and feminism within the Muslim-American community. Many Muslim women have been public in their activism; these include the Qur'anic scholar Amina Wadud, the political activist Linda Sarsour, and even the community of women who launched an all-female mosque in Los Angeles in 2015. Both Amina Wadud and Edina Lekovic (from the Muslim Public Affairs Council) have led *jumah* (Friday) prayers for Muslim congregants. Amina led the *khutba* to a mixed-gender mosque, and

---

12. Lara is a fifty-year-old covered black native-born American living in Illinois.
13. Xara is a covered black native-born American woman living in Illinois.

Edina led prayer in a single-gender mosque. Both of them effectively and controversially redefined the role of women in the mosque from being passive recipients of a sermon to being its active creators (Street 2015).

In general, Muslim women are openly redefining Islamic gender roles through their participation in the fashion industry and media, thereby reinventing what it means to be a pious Muslim woman in public space. In some cases, they invoke the language of Islamic feminism. The 2016 New York Fashion Week hosted a historic and critically acclaimed all-hijab runway show, with many pundits highlighting that designer Anniesa Hasibuan represented a trailblazer in the fashion industry (Murray 2016; Roberts 2016). In September 2016 *Playboy* featured an article with covered journalist Noor Tagouri, as its "2016 Renegade" (Blair 2016). Elsewhere, Muslim women's understandings of feminist politics interact in compelling ways with symbolic boundaries. In an interview in the *New Yorker*, Nailah Lymus, the founder of the Underwraps Modeling Agency, commented on the connection between the hijab and the symbolic and social boundaries it creates with notions of feminism:

> Boundaries are a feminist issue. . . . A hijab is a refusal to objectify yourself sexually, a refusal to court desire from strange eyes, it's a boundary between you and the public. When you are uncovered and walking down the street . . . you are sort of a morsel to be devoured visually. Covering is a way of saying "no, I don't consent. I don't consent to be devoured visually, I don't consent to be looked at with lust." It is a question of consensual participation in the public sphere. In that sense, it seems to be in line with many of the sexual guidelines that have been passed in universities about what constitutes appropriate sexual contact, making sure that everyone is in agreement: These are my boundaries, these are my boundaries for being looked at, these are my boundaries for keeping my body private. (Wickenden 2016)

While much of the literature pits Islamic piety and the hijab as antagonistic to feminism,[14] our respondents demonstrate that ideological challenges from feminist politics are resolved through personal understandings of themselves and their practice as connoting a new type of feminism. In particular, Islamic feminism and head covering are connected as a rejection of objectification in order to focus on the content of one's speech and fight oppressive Western gender norms. As one survey respondent from Boston notes, "Being an independent woman and going to a top college in the United States and still

---

14. See, for example, Afshar 2008; Fekete 2006; and Moghadam 2001, among others.

choosing to wear a headscarf shows that I'm not oppressed, and I choose to cover my body because it helps people not to objectify me. When men talk to me they don't see my physical features, they tend to focus on what I'm saying, on my opinions. So, this shows the other side and how a headscarf protects, provides modesty, and it's not oppression." The ways in which Muslim women come to terms with their religious agency within a largely non-Muslim and secular country suggests that head covering is not merely the result of submission to an ascribed religiosity. As their understandings of gender equity and feminism illustrate, some of our covered respondents develop a personal feminism as a solution to the simultaneous demands of contemporary life and religious proscriptions. Ultimately, Muslim-American women's religious agency is the product of a socially and politically embedded choice to embody religious norms and enact religious agency in visible and performative ways.

Changing Trends in Head Covering

Notions about what constitutes proper dress are often a contentious issue, especially among diverse Islamic congregations such as those in the United States. Further, people raised in the United States may have a very different understanding of what constitutes pious attire than do those who spent their childhood in a Muslim country. Generational differences across immigrant and native Muslims can be a significant factor in emergent covering trends, in which young Muslims are developing a new style of dress that is radically different from that of their elders. Modern forms of head covering therefore symbolize what the scholar Bronwyn Winter calls a "new veiling" rather than a mere "re-veiling" trend, since the *hijabi* (a colloquial expression for a woman who wears the hijab) is, in fact, "a thoroughly modern woman" (2008, 43). Particularly within Western societies, women who cover see themselves as fashionable, independent, self-asserting, and educated. They are women who want to take their place in the public sphere as individuals, claiming their personal right to a distinct religious and cultural identity.

Head covering has a natural performative role as it constructs and communicates individual and cultural meaning while expressing individual piety.[15] One of our survey respondents captures this complex sentiment well:

While I do express my ethnic heritage in clothing and symbolism, I feel that women should have the right to wear it and right not wear it,

---

15. Judith Butler wrote in *Gender Trouble* that "identity is performatively constituted by the very 'expressions' that are said to be its results" (1990, 33).

whether the purpose is religious or cultural. The hijab is not an exclusive trait for Muslim women, as women of other faiths do wear similar head coverings, but I feel that Islam is a personal faith and there are several instances in the Qur'an that describe it as a personal creed and not a religion. . . . The element of society is being removed in terms of faith but reinforced when it comes the duty to one's community. My hijab, there or not, is part of a personal creed and is not a duty to my community. It is a choice.

In the introduction to the edited volume *Modest Fashion*, Reina Lewis notes that women who dress modestly are often considered "representatives of essentialized, unchanging collective religious identities rather than as individual youthful style seekers" (2013, 3). Yet head covering seems to be a practice driven by young Muslim Americans and, as previously mentioned, has become much more common since the 1990s, especially among the second- and third-generation immigrant populations (Carvalho 2013). In particular, second-generation American women are more focused on reinterpreting the headscarf as a mechanism for negotiating a unique, nonimmigrant identity than were their immigrant mothers, who primarily saw it through the lens of religious obligation (Hu et al. 2009). Other research reveals that second-generation women explain their choice to cover in terms of a "purer" Islamic piety untainted by "cultural Islam" (Peek 2005; Williams and Vashi 2007). In fact, cultural Islam is often associated with maternal figures as the primary vector for religious practice, yet that transmission is anything but linear with a younger generation who chafes against a parental, "old world" vision of the faith.[16] Consequently, the headscarf and changing trends in hijabi fashion are a potent tool for the creation of a reconfigured and more inclusionary American Muslim community.

With all the meanings associated with the headscarf, it is legitimate to ask whether it dangerously dilutes religious identification by layering other uses onto a piece of clothing. Lewis (2007) finds fashion trends in head covering turn women into religious interpreters and intermediaries straddling the line between religious ideology and consumerism. In particular, the growing popularity of modest fashion online has led to an interesting discussion especially among hijabi women on how consumerism and the consumption of Islamic fashion relate to the production and construction of Islamic identity. Overall, the fashionable hijabi seems to be the cultural carrier of the extraordinary,

---

16. Still, some studies have shown young women wear a *hijab* to accommodate these parental expectations and thereby increase their public mobility and security (Hoodfar 2003).

while those pushing more conventional, mainstream American attire such as blue jeans are cultivating the norms of the ordinary. In some ways, the hijab may become ordinary as ad campaigns featuring hijabis such as those by H&M enter the mainstream (Bridge Initiative Team 2015).

Woodhead argues that fashion is significant to the discussion of religion precisely because it is a sphere in which "women can act autonomously and creatively, outside of male control and as leaders in their own right" (2013, xviii). As covered and uncovered Muslim women increasingly enter the media mainstream through their roles in political campaigns (e.g., Huma Abedin, adviser to Hillary Clinton), activism (Linda Sarsour and Amal Clooney), broadcast journalism (Nour Tagouri), cooking and construction (Amanda Saab on the television show *Master Chef* and Aidah on *Home Free*), and Olympic sports (Ibtihaj Muhammad), we see women embodying the full range of what it means to be Muslim, mobile, and often keenly fashionable and media savvy as well. The renaissance of hijabi fashionistas on Instagram promoting modest fashion and often DIY or even commercial fashion speaks to how "their presence on social media, which is visually led, is enormously influential" (Mangla 2015).

Among our survey respondents, 51 percent think wearing the head covering is fashionable, with only 32 percent agreeing with the statement that "Islamic head coverings should be plain and unadorned." There seems to be no real generational difference in the belief that an unadorned headscarf is necessary. However, the idea that the head covering is a fashion statement is clearly the province of the young, with 56 percent of women under forty asserting that covering is fashionable.[17] Ultimately, hijabi fashion reflects yet another tool and emerging meaning for the headscarf. Ariana, a focus group participant in DC, captures the sense of anxiety about the increasing expectation for Islamic attire to be fashionable in the run-up to celebrations for the holy month of Ramadan: "I have to be in tiptop shape because when you walk in there [family celebration] it's like a fashion show."[18] But most important, hijabi fashion also reflects women's evolving choice as to what the hijab means for them. Mariam in Chicago evokes this poignantly:

> I could see that for a lot of people it just is a fashion statement. On the
> other hand, though, a lot of people also will be particular about making

17. There was no clear consensus on the color preference among our respondents as 66 percent reported wearing black head coverings, while 63 percent wore multiple colors regularly—naturally, the two are not mutually exclusive.

18. Ariana is a twenty-three-year-old covered black native-born American woman living in the District of Columbia.

it fashionable or kind of convey that it is a choice. People who wear colorful things or who tie their scarf in elaborate ways, to make sure that they are also making a fashion statement, to convey that it is a choice. So, if other people feel that they are expressing themselves at the same time, it will kind of silently communicate that it is a choice.[19]

These generational and fashion trends in head covering show that for most Muslim women head covering is a choice through which they perform their personal styles and identities alongside their piety and religious identity. As Mariam emphasizes, in many ways the symbolism underlying the act of head covering functions like a silent communication and communion with like-minded individuals, a sentiment shared by our other research participants.

The socially and politically embedded nature of the choice to wear the head covering is also reflected in the variety of motivations and factors that inform the practice in the United States. In the following section we unpack the different factors informing the adoption of head covering in the United States.

Why Do Muslim-American Women Cover?

The 2011 Pew surveys reveal growth in the proportion of American Muslim women who report wearing the head covering: 36 percent of female respondents wear the headscarf all the time, 24 percent some of the time, and 40 percent never, compared with 38 percent, 13 percent, and 48 percent, respectively, in results for the same question in 2007.[20] In comparison, 77 percent of our survey participants (1,416) indicate that they wear an Islamic head covering, though they do not specify how often they wear it. Of the 400 participants who say they do not regularly wear the head covering, 74 percent report wearing it when attending mosque, and 40 percent wear it while traveling abroad to Muslim countries.

As we discussed earlier, the recent international revival in head covering reflects the complex lives of Muslim women negotiating and reimagining their identities within modern society. As Giddens explains, the current conversation surrounding the hijab is "intense, emotional and truly global" (2004, 10). Far from having a unitary meaning, the headscarf "reflects the diversity

---

19. Mariam is a twenty-year-old covered South Asian foreign-born American woman living in Illinois.

20. Even when one accounts for immigration, the rise in wearing the hijab is discernible over time (Pew Research Centre 2007, 2011b).

of women's experience and aspirations," an observation relevant to the variety of national, historical, social, and political contexts within which these behaviors emerge.

Head covering is associated with a mix of factors, from varying degrees of piety to class mobility, from freedom of movement and from harassment to the neutralization of sexuality. In some cases it reflects peer group acceptance or pressure; in others, compliance with family values; and in yet others, asserting the right to individual choice.[21] Previous scholarship describes piety and religion as primary motives for head covering (Cole and Ahmadi 2003) alongside familial expectations (S. Ali 2005; Hoodfar 2003). Many scholars have also focused on its regulation of social interactions between men and women (Droogsma 2007; Read and Bartkowski 2000) but also its ability to be a source of gender empowerment (S. Ali 2005; Marshall and Read 2003). Scholarship exploring social capital within the Muslim community also finds it to be integral to building communal solidarity (Kopp 2002), to structuring personal identities (Williams and Vashi 2007), and even to fostering political protest against Westernization and neo-Orientalist attitudes toward Muslims (Haddad 2007; Read and Bartkowski 2000; Williams and Vashi 2007).

The religious, social, and political motivations for covering are interconnected and mutually reinforcing.[22] Our research participants provide a profile of the modern fashionable, independent, self-asserting, and educated hijabi, and as we discuss above, she embraces head covering as a reflection of her multilayered identity. Despite the diversity and complexity of the practice, however, head covering remains primarily an act of piety among our research participants. In response to the question "Why did you decide to wear a Muslim head covering?" 82 percent of our respondents indicate "personal piety," and the percentage is consistent across converts and nonconverts.[23] Other responses justify wearing a head covering in order to "express personal identity" (45%), "to spread the word about Islam" (24%), for "individual freedom

---

21. See Franks 2000; Khosrokhavar 1997; Killian 2003; Scott 2007; Williams and Vashi 2007; Wing and Smith 2005; Winter 2008.

22. In our previous work, we unpacked the relationship between these motivations and the choice to cover using the same survey data (Westfall et al. 2016). Using factor analysis, we find that religious lifestyle, religious abstinence, Muslim socialization, and political activity emerge as the main clusters of factors predicting head covering. While all three religious factors predict head covering among our respondents, unsurprisingly, religious lifestyle exhibits the strongest positive relationship with covering. This is perhaps because covering is a ritualistic religious activity embedded in daily life, and it serves a social function in identifying like-minded people to one another. Our findings demonstrate that religiosity is not a monolithic factor, and religious practices interact with and enforce head covering in complex ways.

23. We requested respondents to select their top two reasons for adopting the head covering.

of movement" (18%), for "protection from sexual harassment" (12%), because of "family expectations" (7%), to conform to "societal expectations" (3%), and as a symbol of "political protest" (1%).[24]

The clear dominance of piety as the primary reason for covering affirms the notion that religious faith has become "the dominant social paradigm that transcends racial and ethnic boundaries" across Muslim Americans (Bagasra 2009, 5). Certainly, the designation of personal piety captures a variety of religious sentiments and behaviors. Some of these may manifest in the private, internal lives of religious believers, while others may take a more demonstrative, public role.

Head Covering and Internal Piety

Internal piety refers to the inner spiritual lives of religious adherents. In relationship to head covering, internal piety relates to the ways in which Muslim women debate the merits of covering with reference to their private belief systems. Our focus group participants reveal three main themes in the way they describe the influence of personal piety on their decision to cover: they accept head covering as a command, they view it as a way to please God, and they believe head covering aids in the development of faith, serving as a constant reminder of the need to be pious.

In our survey, those who justify head covering with reference to God's commandment typically do not expand their reasoning. As one survey respondent tells us, "It's a command from God! I have to obey his command without any reasoning or rationalization." Another survey respondent takes it even further and says, "The number one reason [for covering] is that I believe Allah [God] commanded the believing woman to stay covered in public. So it's an obligation, a must! To go against Allah's order is to sin. And Allah does not command something unless there is some benefit in it for the believer." When our research participants expand on their motives, many of them assert that this commandment is their first consideration, to be obeyed "above all others." As our focus group participant Lydia puts it, any other benefits associated with covering are "icing on the cake." [25] These latter research participants acknowledge other reasons for covering but prioritize their understanding of God's will as their primary motive. Not all of our survey respondents explicitly

---

24. Percentages do not add up to two hundred because of rounding (N=1,360). About 5 percent of our respondents selected the "other" category.

25. Lydia is a twenty-eight-year-old covered South Asian native-born American woman in Virginia.

mention head covering as a religious command. However, the vast majority (79%) of our covered and noncovered respondents agree with the statement "covering one's head is mandatory according to the terms of Islam." Among those who cover, the number jumps to 90 percent, while for those who do not cover, only 42 percent believe head covering is mandatory.

Among our focus group participants who discuss head covering as a form of internal piety, many do not explicitly mention any religious commandments, but they provide other descriptions of religious benefit. Several participants describe head covering as a way to grow in their faith or to grow closer to God, suggesting its function in developing certain ethical dispositions as an embodied religious practice. These participants differ from those who explicitly mention covering out of piety, and instead they suggest that head covering makes them more pious or allows their piety to evolve. In other words, our participants' statements often indicated that covering preceded and even guided their full embrace of faith. Jasmin in Boston told us about how she gradually came to appreciate the benefits of head covering:

> The main goal to want to put it on was a spiritual reason. I wanted to get closer to God, one step closer to fulfilling one of the obligations that I had to do. I prayed and I fasted and everything so I have to do this, too. It took me a while before I actually understood the logic completely behind it. . . . When I put it on I didn't even think of all the benefits that I would get from wearing it, but then after a while I'm like "Oh, that's why." It's an obligation. You start to realize "Oh, this is the reasoning behind it."[26]

Jasmin views covering as an obligation—as one of a larger collection of religious obligations—and suggests that she strove to fulfill this obligation before understanding why she was doing it in the first place. The act of head covering helped move her along the process of understanding her faith and spirituality.

A large minority of our respondents agree that head covering "makes a woman more pious" (43.3%). Many of our participants describe this mechanism for increasing piety as an increased awareness and contemplation of faith within the practice, what Tamira in Chicago calls "God consciousness."[27] She explains, "As I grew my understanding of Islam, I decided it was time to start [wearing the headscarf], something I should be doing as a Muslim woman. I noticed as I started wearing it that I became very conscious of myself, my

---

26. Jasmin is a nineteen-year-old covered Arab-American woman, born abroad, and currently in Massachusetts.

27. Tamira is a thirty-seven-year-old covered black native-born American woman in Illinois.

behavior, what I was doing. So it was a consciousness thing for me." Similar to Tamira, Jessica in Detroit describes the way the head covering helps develop her piety in a more practical way: "I felt stronger in my religion [because of the head covering]. I was able to feel like I could pray more and pray the five times a day because I was already in what I needed to wear for that."[28]

For our survey respondents and focus group participants, head covering presents an opportunity to fulfill religious obligations, demonstrate obedience to God, and develop their faith. Many of our respondents recognize the development of piety as a process, and they depict head covering as occurring at different points along this process. For some, it represents a pinnacle of piety, and they suggest that they may not be ready for it. Others report adopting the practice very early in their faith and describe how their practice evolved with their understanding of Islam. Despite these individualized experiences with head covering, nearly all of our respondents connect it with piety and their internal development of faith.

Head Covering and the Public Demonstration of Piety

Though most of our research participants describe their motivations for head covering as coming from internal religious conviction, head covering is an external and visible act, making it a public demonstration of internal piety. For some respondents, the public nature of head covering represents a major motivation for adopting or continuing the practice. This is evident in our respondents' describing the role of their headscarf as a reminder of their faith, a tool to regulate their own behavior in public, and a way of representing Islam to others. For example, Kadijah from Boston says, "I feel like it's a reality check for me whenever I want to do something that's probably not right. . . . I look at myself and I think I'm a Muslim woman representative so it holds me back from sinning or either doing something wrong. . . . [I'm] definitely grateful that I wore it at a young age."[29] Kadijah's testimony walks the fine line between private and public piety, as she describes an internal effort to avoid sin. However, when she thinks, "I'm a Muslim woman representative," it brings her moral concern into the public sphere. Here, she recognizes that a sinful act on her part would carry implications not only for her but for other Muslims as well.

Shakira in Chicago also brings up the role of faith ambassadorship when she tells us a story about how the headscarf is a "protection of my faith—it

---

28. Jessica is a forty-year-old covered Arab native-born American woman in Michigan.
29. Kadijah is a twenty-year-old covered Arab native-born woman living in Massachusetts.

has brought me back . . . I did forget I was wearing it, and then there were things that people will see and think 'This is contradictory.' But I don't want to be that bad representation of Islam. I don't feel like I should take on the entire *din* [Arabic for "religion"] to be the representation of Islam, but I want to think about how people will think about Islam. It has brought that consciousness."[30] Shakira is more hesitant than Kadijah to accept the role of representing other Muslims, but she still appreciates the way her actions reflect on Islam and other Muslims and suggests that her headscarf gives her that awareness. When she forgets she is wearing it, she suspects that she is more likely to do things that may be perceived to be in conflict with her belief system.[31]

Aafreen from Washington, DC, goes even further in emphasizing the public role of the hijab and says, "I think that it regulates the morality of the society. Covering is not only for women, there is a measure also for men in Islam. They have body parts that should be kept covered too. I think in this respect it regulates the society's morality. There is a restriction for both Muslim men and women."[32] By discussing head covering as a practice for both genders, Aafreen gives it significance for the whole Muslim community, not just for women in a public, non-Muslim space, as implied by Khadija and Shakira. She describes the imperative of modesty as informing all Muslim behavior in public whether one is in the presence of Muslims or non-Muslims.

Besides these public demonstrations of piety achieved through the headscarf, our survey respondents mention proselytizing as another explicitly public expression of their piety. Nearly 25 percent of our respondents suggest that they wear the head covering as part of a mission of "spreading the word about Islam." We argue that this is also a function of personal piety, in particular an expression of *da'wa*, an Arabic word meaning "to invite" or "to offer to share." The Qur'an itself instructs believers to practice da'wa (Surah 16:125), though there are various ways to do it. Some Muslims are active in their practice, while others are more passive and wait to discuss their faith until asked for more information. Covered women are more likely to be approached and asked about their faith, since their head covering visibly identifies them as religious practitioners and makes them de facto visual representatives of the faith.

---

30. Shakira is a twenty-seven-year-old covered black native-born woman living in Illinois.

31. The way Kadijah and Shakira describe the headscarf as a reminder of their faith echoes some of the traditions in Jewish clothing, as with the *tzitzit* (tassels) on the *tallit*. The tallit can be either a large four-cornered rectangular shawl worn over one's clothes during worship or a smaller four-cornered undergarment worn daily by Orthodox Jewish males, often with the tzitzit hanging out. The tassels are intended to remind the wearer of the duties and obligations associated with being a Jew.

32. Aafreen is a twenty-six-year-old covered white native-born woman living in the District of Columbia.

Though we consider proselytization a form of piety, there is some evidence that our respondents do not view it as a component of piety more generally, or that they are distinguishing between public and private forms of piety. Among our survey respondents who indicate that they covered in order to proselytize, 19 percent do not select piety as a reason for covering. For these respondents, the public nature of head covering constitutes a reason for covering by itself.

Head Covering Disassociated from Piety

The finding that our respondents are primarily motivated by piety is not surprising. However, 18 percent of our survey respondents do not select piety as a rationale for covering and identify other motivators instead. This population provides us with an opportunity to explore the relative strength of other reasons for head covering.

Figure 1.1 reveals that those who do not identify piety as one of the two primary reasons for covering report other social, identity-based, and political reasons for the practice, more so than those who do identify piety as a main consideration. Among all the response categories in figure 1.1, only protection from sexual harassment is less frequently selected among

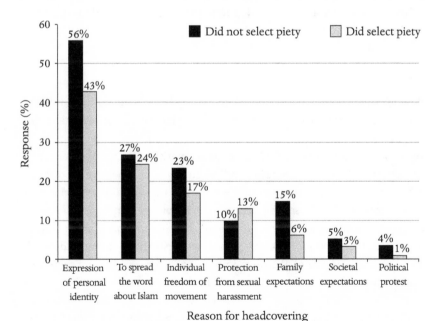

FIGURE 1.1. Response to "Why did you decide to wear a Muslim head covering?" broken down by whether piety was also selected (N=1,116) or not (N=243)

respondents who did not select piety as a primary reason than among those who did select it. Though we discuss below protection from sexual harassment and gender relations as a social motivator for head covering, in the Qur'an gender segregation is clearly discussed as a reason for head covering. Surah 24:31, from the beginning of this chapter, describes the sartorial requirements for women, and it emphasizes chastity and modesty as the primary rationale for the head covering alongside the intent to frustrate male sexual desire. Pious women are likely familiar with and endorse this rationale for the practice.

Figure 1.1, suggests that if the decision to cover is *not* driven by piety, it is most likely an expression of personal identity, followed by family expectations and freedom of movement. Further, Muslims may adopt the headscarf with strategic extrareligious and social reasons in mind, whether it enhances their freedom of movement or fulfills family expectations.

Social Reasons for Head Covering

While most research acknowledges the dominant religious imperative in head-covering behaviors, these religious motivations intersect with Muslim women's social lives. In particular, head covering is motivated by socialization behaviors across family and friend groups, gender relations, and social considerations related to mobility and identity.

Family

Religiosity, especially in a secular state, is largely determined by family life, and recent life experiences do not dull the influence of the parental home (Myers 1996). Traditionally, maternal figures are assumed to be the primary vector for religious practice. Despite the formative role that parents play in determining their child's religion and religiosity, only 8 percent of our covered survey respondents mention their family as motivating their choice to cover. However, for those who did not identify piety as a primary reason for covering, that number jumps to 15 percent. This is not to say that our respondents' families are not important. It only suggests that our respondents do not view them as one of the most important factors influencing their decision to cover. This number can be partially explained by the number of converts in our sample (28% of our covered respondents). These converts are less likely to have been socialized into head covering through their families. In fact, only 6 percent of our convert respondents report having a mother who covers.

Considering the high number of respondents who cover (1,359 respondents, or 77%), the presence of family members who also cover is unexpectedly low, with only 54 percent of covered respondents reporting a mother who covers.[33] In fact, a sizable 25 percent of our covered respondents report being the only member of their family to cover. Our respondents who do not cover report even lower levels of familial covering: 29 percent report having mothers who cover (among foreign-born respondents that number jumps to 37%).

Our covered respondents appear to experience reduced opportunities for religious socialization within the family, a finding that makes our high covering rate somewhat surprising given the expectation in the literature that religiosity is transmitted mainly by one's parents (Myers 1996). Scholarship on the transmission of religiosity through familial socialization mainly shows that parents have a significant role. However, very few studies explore this effect among immigrant groups where society and social institutions do not support their religion.[34] Research on parental transmission of religiosity among immigrants either finds it to be important alongside internally motivated religiosity (Maliepaard and Lubbers 2013) or suggests the effect is dependent on "the larger contexts of the immigrant generation and the institutional location of a particular religious tradition within the broader American religion" (Park and Ecklund 2007, 111).[35] These findings indicate that immigration status and generational differences need to be accounted for across all groups of Muslim women when considering how the family influences their head-covering practices.

As illustrated in figure 1.2, our respondents' birthplaces are highly correlated with the number of family members who cover. The most striking category shows that 39.4 percent of our American-born respondents report no family members who cover, compared with only 17 percent of foreign-born respondents. Converts can explain a large part of this difference: 44 percent of our American-born respondents are converts, compared with 8 percent of our foreign-born respondents (34 percent of converts report having at least one family member who covers).

---

33. Forty-eight percent of our covered married respondents report having a mother-in-law who covers, 49 percent of our total sample of women have an aunt who covers, 48 percent have a cousin who covers, and 45 percent have a sister who covers. Only 30 percent report having a maternal grandmother who covers and 29 percent a paternal grandmother who covers.

34. See Güngör, Fleischmann, and Phalet 2011; Maliepaard and Lubbers 2013; Park and Ecklund 2007.

35. Maliepaard and Lubbers (2013) find that the effect of parental influence and self-ascription on religiosity is contingent on the degree of social cohesion within immigrant groups.

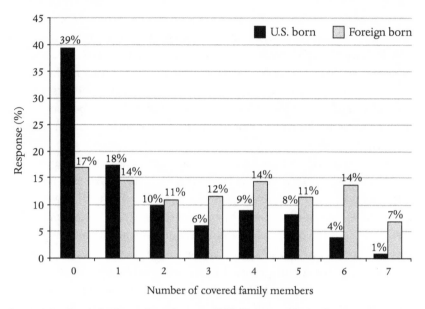

FIGURE 1.2.   Female family members who cover, divided by US- and foreign-born

American-born women coming from Muslim families are also less likely to have a diverse range of family members who cover. This probably reflects a story of immigration and assimilation, during which the women removed their headscarfs when they migrated to the United States. Hence their daughters and granddaughters are rediscovering the head covering outside the family and are embracing it as a part of their personal identity. As Ernest Gellner argues, "Contrary to what outsiders generally suppose, the typical Muslim woman in a Muslim city doesn't wear the veil because her grandmother did so, but because her grandmother did not" (1992, 16). A roughly equal number of American and foreign-born women in our sample who report approximately one or two family members covering may imply the emergence of a new generation of covered women.

The age of the women who report family members covering is revealing in this respect. The average age of American-born respondents who report having no family members who cover is about thirty-seven, and those with one family member who covers average about forty. The average age drops to about thirty-one and continues to fall as more family members cover. This suggests that our older respondents did not come from a familial environment that promoted head covering. Perhaps these women converted to Islam, or maybe they are the daughters of the generation who removed the head covering in an effort to assimilate into mainstream America. For these women, religious and familial networks promoting the adoption of the headscarf were not very present. However, the more youthful profile of American-born women who have two or more relatives who cover suggests that a new generation of Muslim-American women is being socialized into head covering. Their process of religious socialization differs from that of their immigrant grandmothers, who may have rejected our respondents' politically or ethnically defined forms of head covering in favor of American assimilation. This new socialization treats head covering in America as a new expression of Muslim-American identity.

FRIENDS

While family is one of the most influential social forces impacting religiosity, friend groups are also powerful in shaping beliefs and identities.[36] The extent and nature of social learning are often the product of how a person's social networks are constructed. Diverse social networks such as those that contain many people of different beliefs, backgrounds, and ethnicities generally facilitate higher levels of social learning by linking individuals to different kinds of people. Such social networks expose individuals to diverse opinions, forcing group members with conflicting ideas to compromise. They also motivate people to examine sources of conflict between members and increase their efforts to understand viewpoints that differ from their own. Conversely, homogenous networks (those that are made up of people who are very similar) are more likely to reinforce group ideas and practices.

In our survey, we explore the religious homogeneity and heterogeneity of our respondents' social networks. Friendship ties within religiously homogeneous groups are often found to strengthen religious beliefs and levels of religious engagement (Roberts and Davidson 1984; Welch 1981). While the religious homogeneity of a social network matters for the religiosity of its members, the strength of network ties is also an important factor; strong ties may lead to "more enduring, supportive, and intimate" relationships (Cornwall 1987, 47). In our survey, we assess the religious homogeneity of our respondents' social networks by asking them specifically about their closest friends. Their responses are illustrated in figure 1.3.

When we ask our survey respondents how many of their closest friends wear head coverings, an overwhelming 81 percent report a friend network in which at least some of their closest friends cover. Six percent indicate all their

36. See Cornwall 1987; Gunnoe and Moore 2002; King, Furrow, and Roth 2002; Regnerus, Smith, and Smith 2004.

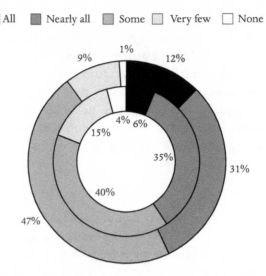

FIGURE 1.3.   The composition of social networks. Inner circle: proportion of close friends wearing headcovering. Outer circle: proportion of close friends that are Muslim.

friends cover, with 90 percent of those being American citizens and only 21 percent having spent their youth in a Muslim country.[37] When we isolate the sample to covered respondents, the percentages remain the same.

We follow up with a question about the religious diversity of the friend groups, and ask how many of our respondents' closest friends are Muslims. Twelve percent of respondents state that all their friends are Muslim, while 10 percent of respondents state that none or very few of their closest friends are Muslims. Among the respondents who state that all their friends are Muslims, 88 percent are American citizens and only 31 percent spent their youth in a Muslim country. When we isolate the sample to the covered respondents, the percentages remain almost the same. However, of the respondents with exclusively Muslim friends, most of them come from states with substantial Muslim populations and Muslim enclaves within larger cities: California, New York, Ohio, and Virginia. Given the nature of the friend networks as well as the religiosity levels of the respondents in our sample, it is perhaps unsurprising that the vast majority of the women in our sample are in romantic relationships with Muslim partners (91.4%).

In general, our respondents' friend groups are predominately Muslim, and the majority of respondents with exclusively Muslims friend networks are

---

37. Forty percent of our covered respondents report that some of their friends cover and 35 percent report that nearly all of their friends cover, with 6 percent indicating that all of their friends cover.

born in the United States. The relative religious homogeneity of these friend groups is striking, given how small the Muslim population is in the United States (only about 2% of the total population). Converts report having only slightly more diverse friend groups than other Muslims, though we would expect their social connections to be more diverse as a result of family and friend networks from before their conversion. Muslim friend networks may also serve a very important function for new converts, as their non-Muslim families are less likely to provide a faith-affirming or religiously educational network.

Many of our survey and focus group participants report actively seeking out and establishing social relationships through their mosques and community organizations and in some cases, forming friendships as a reaction to a social environment that is not supportive of their faith. Some of our focus group participants mention mimicking their friends in head-covering behaviors, and many others mention discussing and dissecting their head-covering practices as well as those of other women with their Muslim friends. Ultimately, the more religiously homogenous friend groups of our survey respondents serve to affirm their faith and the practice of head covering.

INTERACTIONS WITH MEN

Our respondents' interactions with men provide another social motivation for head covering, and here the headscarf is assumed to encourage respect for Muslim women.[38] Wearing the head covering helps Muslim women "cross gender boundaries" (Siraj 2011, 723) and navigate gendered spaces by protecting women from men who might harass or molest them and by desexualizing social interactions between unrelated men and women. Approximately 12 percent of our respondents explicitly select protection from sexual harassment as one of the primary reasons informing their choice to cover.

Many of our respondents use notions of respect to frame the hijab as protective in nature. Thirty-nine percent of our respondents explicitly describe being treated with more respect when they cover and note an effort on the part of both Muslim and non-Muslim men to refrain from sexual conversations, overtures, or physical contact. For example, one survey respondent from Pennsylvania tells us, "I never get cat calls or whistles or other demeaning/sexual attention. . . . Men (Muslim and non-Muslim) tend to respect my personal space and will not bump into me or stand too close in line. If I am

---

38. See Read and Bartkowski 2000; Ruby 2006; Siraj 2011.

walking home late I feel that guys are more likely to offer to walk me home and are very protective (in a good way)." In one of our focus groups in Detroit, Emily mentions that she introduced others to the notion of head covering by emphasizing its protective function: "You look around and you see people not dressed so well and you hear [about] the rise of rapes and sexual assaults and stuff like that. This [headscarf] is a protection for me. I walk outside and I feel like I'm not going to be judged, harassed, or hear comments. You'll be walking around campus and if someone walking by is not dressed too well, guys will whistle; I'm very protected."[39]

Another young survey respondent from Wisconsin stated that the head covering is an implicit request for privacy and personal dignity, both of which require men to refrain from sexualizing women: "Most Muslim men understand Muslim women cover themselves to allow for personal privacy and dignity while out in public. Those who understand this and honor it tend to show me this type of respect and will prevent themselves from eyeing me as they might less clothed women, whether or not it would be intentional." This statement makes an interesting reference to unintentional objectification, which speaks to underlying assumptions about male sexuality. According to this logic, women carry a responsibility to cover in order to protect themselves from assault and to protect men from their male impulses. Men also have a Qur'anic responsibility to protect themselves from lust and are told to "cast down their glances" to prevent any possibility of temptation—a practice known as "hijab of the eyes" (Surah 24:30). Many of our respondents refer to this practice, stating that men "lower their gaze" when encountering a covered woman.

Respondents describe a variety of other physical demonstrations of respect. One survey respondent told us, "Men don't talk to me if there's situation where I'm the only woman in the room," and another said, "Men do not extend their hand to shake hands. I see respect in their eyes." The tone of these comments makes it clear that the women do not interpret these behaviors as problematic or offensive but see them as placing a respectful distance between the genders.

Framing the headscarf as protection from objectification or sexualization might seem to place women in a defensive position, but many of our respondents contradict this assumption by describing the way head covering motivates people to stop assessing the physicality of the covered woman and to focus on the whole person: "I feel like people really respect me for who

---

39. Emily is a twenty-year-old covered Arab native-born American woman in Michigan.

I am not for what I look like." Conversely, a number of our respondents suggest the scarf sometimes serves as a distraction. Unlike one respondent, who says the scarf motivates men to look her "in the eyes more, rather than at my body or hair," another woman observes that "most people will not look me in the eyes," and a third respondent notes, "Some people will only look at my scarf and not at my eyes." These seemingly contradictory claims are understandable within the American context, where the modesty of the head covering and the religious identity it projects may discourage casual sexual objectification. However, the distinctiveness of the practice in a non-Muslim setting can also attract a different sort of attention, often associated with the creation of symbolic boundaries around a gendered religious minority group.

FREEDOM OF MOVEMENT

Eighteen percent of our survey respondents select individual freedom of movement as a primary reason for wearing the head covering. Covering as a mechanism for ensuring mobility speaks to the way Muslims perceive public space as gendered and potentially fraught with moral pitfalls. First, covering is required to allow women to navigate public spaces and to be perceived primarily as persons and not sexual objects. It is intended to create a gender-neutral place for the exercise of their personal agency. This choice is clearly related to avoiding sexual harassment, though freedom of movement is framed as more empowering, while protection from sexual harassment is defensive. Furthermore, as noted earlier, the argument that the hijab is intended to protect women from male sexual desire is also made in the Qur'an, and justifying head covering with reference to sexual harassment therefore becomes a part of religious practice, while freedom of movement is a concept referencing social space. Such a distinction may account for the gap in the number of women who select freedom of movement in figure 1.1, which shows that those who do not identify piety as a primary reason for covering report freedom of movement as a primary reason with much greater frequency than those who select piety.

Second, the headscarf allows for enhanced mobility by signaling the range of acceptable behaviors toward Muslim women. Some activities will be out of bounds for covered Muslim women in public, so the head covering provides ease and comfort in moving between the private and public domains by signaling how others should behave toward them. "Veiling is a mobile form of *purdah* that secludes a woman while at the same time allowing her to move around freely in public" (Werbner 2005, 40). Our survey respondents and focus group participants highlight this aspect of head covering often. For example, Ghazala in Washington, DC, explains,

> When I am wearing the headscarf, I am giving the message that for me religion has priority and I regulate all of my tastes, choices, and daily life according to my religion. This means that someone who sees me wearing the headscarf can definitely guess that I would not go to a bar to have a good time or that I would not be able to go to a beach that is open to public, that I would not be able to choose such a way of holiday or relaxing time. I think it gives this kind of message. I think that the headscarf directly shows my choices to the outer world, to the other people.[40]

For Ghazala, this signal of her values is liberating. It helps her avoid potential social conflicts or compromising situations with very little effort and allows her mobility within a secular society. Ghazala's sense of liberation conveys the sense of empowerment behind freedom of movement as a reason for covering. Head covering hereby enables Muslim women to enter the public domain "without fearing the loss or corruption of their religious identities" and the values associated with these identities (Endelstein and Ryan 2013, 262).

Personal Identity

After piety, the most frequently cited reason for wearing the head covering is that it expresses our respondents' personal identity. Among our covered respondents, 45 percent select the "expression of personal identity" as a primary reason for covering. As indicated in figure 1.1, this explanation is particularly salient for those who do not select piety as a primary reason, of whom 56 percent choose the personal identity option. While converts select alternative reasons for covering at the same rate as nonconverts, among those who do not select piety converts are far more likely to choose the expression of personal identity (71%) than nonconverts (49%). This may suggest that, for converts, head covering is an important signal of their religious identities as Muslims. While the catch-all concept of identity can mean many things to an individual, the women in our sample appear to connect head covering to at least four identities: Muslim identity, American identity, gender identity, and ethnic identity.

---

40. Ghazala is a forty-three-year-old covered noncitizen Turkish woman living in the District of Columbia.

The resurgence in head covering by young, second-generation immigrant women is attributable to the salience of their Muslim identity over their national origin or their parents' identities (S. Ali 2005). Furthermore, younger Muslims in America are collectively redefining what it means to be a Muslim. Rediscovery of Islam is at a new high in the United States, and many young Muslim Americans are taking individual initiative to gain more knowledge about their faith (ibid.). At the same time, these youthful religious adherents are finding the teaching styles and traditions of their ancestors to be unsatisfying and unengaging—this generation does not listen to commands. They want to understand why they are being commanded and seek religious knowledge to reach their own conclusions about their religious obligations. Martha, an immigrant living in Boston, hints at the experience of reinventing Islam in America: "As a hijabi, as a Muslim woman, I feel more accepted here [in the United States] than in my own country. I'm sure that's just my family demographics. I mean, I know friends who have very practicing families, and even my parents do pray, but just in my family Islam is just a bunch of rituals and that's it. I don't think anyone has ever opened a Qur'an and tried reading it and understanding it. That's just not the concept."[41] Young hijabis see head covering as part of this engaged faith. Though head covering is a ritual like other religious rituals disparaged by Martha, our participants decide to cover or not with reference to the Qur'an, the surrounding social environment, and their personal lifestyle choices. These same considerations allow Muslim women to adapt their practice in ways that were not available to older generations. Within a pluralistic America, the diversity of the Muslim population provides numerous cultural interpretations of the head covering, which anyone can adopt or adapt to their individualized practice.

However, the construction of our respondents' identities through the headscarf is about more than embodying a solely Muslim identity; it is also a renegotiation of a distinctly Muslim-American identity. As we will discuss in chapter 2, Muslims who immigrated before 1960s were focused on assimilation into the American mainstream, but the dawn of multiculturalism led to a greater celebration of difference within informal and formal American life. As Syed Ali recounts,

Whether one likes the idea of multiculturalism or not, this effective shift towards it allows more space for the public display and practice of ethnicity. Where once it was not "cool" to be anything other than white,

---

41. Martha is a twenty-four-year-old covered South Asian noncitizen living in Massachusetts.

black or Latino, a wide array of "otherness" is now valued. In the recent past, nonwhite ethnic culture was not something that second-generation immigrants admitted to liking or performing. But a transformation has occurred. Ethnicity is not only acceptable, it is often chic. (2005, 522)

This trend toward embracing difference has opened public space to outward religious identification and has created opportunities for a hybridized Muslim-American identity.

Questions of identity are particularly intense in the Muslim-American population, especially for covered women. Because of their visibility, they are not allowed to function purely as individuals, but they have become often-involuntary standard-bearers of Islam. The head covering became important for this very reason—it is a way for Muslim-American women to telegraph a shared identity to the external non-Muslim world (Kopp 2002). Any construction of identity through the headscarf has consequences beyond the individual and can influence perceptions of the Muslim community at large. This reality also leads to a reassessment of Muslim-American identity, as women must negotiate their identity as faith ambassadors. Some of our participants, like Zeynab, are fully conscious of this role:

> I have always kind of just lived in this world where there is a stigma against Islam, or a misunderstanding. So, when I decided to wear the veil it was kind of a sense of ambassadorship, in a way. You kind of get to be the smiling face of Islam and invite people to ask questions. My background is in Catholic school, so I tell them that this is my cross to bear. This idea that it is my little sacrifice, my little contribution to the community. My way to serve by offering some sort of educational source. Instead of Wikipedia-ing Islam, you can come and ask me about it.[42]

Zeynab acknowledges that in the secular context, the headscarf is effectively a uniform for religious ambassadorship.

The headscarf is a vector for the portrayal of the many changing identities of modern Muslim-American women. Women explicitly use the headscarf to express their identities in the space created by American multiculturalism and pluralism, and the ease with which the headscarf can communicate identity is a large part of the appeal of wearing it. At the same time, not only is the headscarf a tool for the expression of identity, but it also creates identities for the wearer, as with the often-external assignment of roles of ambassadorship to covered women by Muslims and non-Muslims alike.

---

42. Zeynab is a twenty-one-year-old covered native-born Arab-American woman living in Texas.

Political Reasons for Head Covering

In many cases outside the United States, head covering has taken on a political meaning. In some, this is because covering has been regulated and women don the scarf as a form of protest or to express solidarity with other Muslims in the face of Islamophobia.[43] In other cases, covering has been tied to Islamist political influences, under which it is conceived as an act against the secular, imperial state. In the United States, head covering was politicized among African Americans as an activist symbol through its association with the Nation of Islam. The practice has never fallen under governmental oversight, and perhaps this lack of government regulation accounts for the relative absence of politicized head covering as a form of protest among our respondents. Political protest is the least common reason for adopting the head covering reported in our survey. Only 2 percent of our respondents report covering primarily as a form of political protest, even though 99 percent of them agree that policies banning Muslim head covering are discriminatory.

Though very few of our respondents suggest that politics motivated them to cover, many of our focus group participants describe an iterative process in which head covering informs their politics, which further informs their head-covering practice, which ultimately informs their politics. For many of our participants, this process started with September eleventh, when they became sharply aware of their status as a controversial minority. Semra describes her experience from when she was a teenager: "September eleventh was really my first exposure to the broader global context of wearing hijab. When it happened, a friend came up to me and she was like, 'Do you think that the people were Palestinian?' It was so shocking to me. I didn't even realize how politicized my hijab was until that moment."[44] In reaction to this experience, Semra adjusted her head-covering behavior to blend in better with American society.

Other participants discuss how being a Muslim and covering makes them feel like a member of a global community and gives them a sense of belonging that reinforces their practice. Many describe reacting to the increasingly discriminatory social environment in the United States by becoming more dedicated to their practice, but some also shed their headscarves. Perhaps this is why 10.1 percent of our (covered and uncovered) survey respondents agree that "wearing or not wearing a headscarf expresses my political opinions and beliefs," a larger percentage than the 1.6 percent who report political

---

43. In some cases, even men participate in head covering as a show of solidarity with covered women, as we have seen in Iran and Afghanistan. See Sanghani 2015; Saul 2016.

44. Semra is a thirty-year-old covered South Asian native-born woman living in Illinois.

protest as one of the two primary reasons for covering, or the 3.6 percent of covered and uncovered respondents who agree that "wearing or not wearing a head covering represents belonging to a political movement." Ultimately, while head-covering behaviors are imbued with political meaning, for the vast majority of our survey respondents, political considerations are not a central reason for adopting the practice.

Overall, there may be no single reason for and no one meaning of head covering for Muslim-American women precisely because of the choices they enjoy and have the ability to enact in the United States. In the post–September eleventh context, many Muslim women adopt the practice in an effort to represent Islam, to assume a public Islamic identity, or to define what it means to be a Muslim living in a pluralistic society.[45] These manifestations of religious agency are embodied through head covering and intersect with Muslim women's social lives in myriad ways, making it an effective symbolic boundary marker used to index their social and religious identities. Although covering is not regulated in the United States, the practice is clearly influenced by the larger social and political environment. Our respondents underscore the choice behind adopting and adapting the headscarf as well as the choice behind continuing to cover. They consider all three socially and politically embedded decisions. Yet despite the complexity underlying covering behaviors, for our participants head covering is primarily an enactment of their piety and their belief in God.

Furthermore, we observe strong generational trends in covering behaviors whereby younger Muslim women are adopting the practice at higher rates and with more sartorial diversity and flare. Peer groups impact the decision to cover, and the women who do so often turn to their Muslim friends to model good Islamic practice in a non-Muslim setting (S. Ali 2005). In the United States "there is a new trend among younger Muslims to define collectively for themselves what it means to be a Muslim" (521). Chapter 2 explores how the complex symbolic function of hijab fosters intra-Muslim interaction and what role it plays in constituting a more unified *ummah*—community of believers— across a very diverse Muslim-American population.

---

45. See S. Ali 2005; Peek 2005; Haddad 2007.

CHAPTER 2

Unity amid Diversity?

> I move through this world as a person of color. I
> think the scarf helps you say that as well, how you
> move through this world, your behavior. . . . We are,
> I think, a special set of Muslims who happen to live in
> America, in a very special place and time. It is a very
> interesting context where race, culture, religion start
> to have different meanings in this American context
> and so our experiences in many ways can't really be
> understood by other Muslims in other parts of the
> world because they can't really understand what it is
> like to live here and to be Muslim.
>
> —Tamira, a covered American Muslim

In this chapter, we explore the diversity of the
Muslim-American population and the community's historical development as
a minority group in the United States. Muslims are one of the most ethnically,
racially, and denominationally diverse religious publics in America. Adopting the head covering as an enactment of faith symbolically unites the many
pious women within the community itself, but this choice also has important
implications for Muslim identity politics.

Muslim-American women may use the head covering for a type of identity production that can bind together but also distinguish and even create
rifts between ethnicities, races, and denominations in the United States with
consequences for group cohesion. Thus the headscarf emerges as a symbolic
boundary marker around which women often orient their integration into
religious, racial, and ethnic Muslim social networks. The exclusivity of these
groups varies according to the nature of their collective identities and the historic experiences of the groups themselves. As Tamira vividly illustrates in the
opening quote, the experience of being a practicing Muslim in a non-Muslim
country with such a diverse Muslim population is unique.[1]

Most of the focus groups we conducted in the summer of 2013 reflect this
diversity. While the overwhelming majority of our participants wear the head

---

1. Tamira is a thirty-seven-year-old black covered native-born American living in Illinois.

covering, they are still a very ethnically and racially diverse group, often coming from South Asian or Middle Eastern backgrounds. We also occasionally encounter white, Hispanic, and African-American converts in our interviews. Our participants are usually young with a college education, which aligns with demographic statistics showing the Muslim community to be younger, better educated, and slightly better off than other minority groups in the United States (Johnson 2011). The conversations mainly focus on head covering and the experiences surrounding the practice in the United States, often gravitating to contemporary topics such as the treatment of Muslims by the mainstream media and the politics of everyday life after September eleventh.

Of all the focus group interviews we conducted that summer, the most politically and socially charged was an interview we held in inner-city Chicago. The participants were exclusively covered African-American women, born in the United States, and from different socioeconomic backgrounds. All were university educated. This focus group had the distinction of being our most racially and culturally homogenous group of women. The stories that emerge from these women in Chicago are not strikingly different from the rest of our interviews except in one way: the participants focus heavily on internal divisions within the Muslim community itself and perceive an especially tense relationship between African-American Muslims and what they termed "immigrant" Muslims, referring to Muslim-American citizens of South Asian or Arab descent who had immigrated to America since the 1950s.

While many of our interviews cut across racial and ethnic lines, and participants occasionally mention cultural differences, this particular group in Chicago adamantly points out the difficulty of negotiating intersectionality as a black, Muslim female in the United States. One of the participants, Shakira, notes, "A lot of times we try to portray to the outside and to ourselves that Islam is perfect, and therefore Muslims are perfect. But we do not deal with the issues that Muslims have with each other: I'm talking about how you just treated your brother or your sister. That is not Islam, the way Muslims are treating Muslims. There are two different conversations about what should be in Islam versus the way we are treating each other right now."[2] Our Chicago interviewees' discussion of intracommunity divisions all but overshadows the more typical commentary relating to escalating tensions between Muslims and non-Muslims (which we will explore in chapter 3). This discussion of internal divisions is not completely unique to the Chicago group, however. For example, Eliza, from our Washington, DC, focus group, says, "You walk

---

2. Shakira is a twenty-seven-year-old black covered native-born American living in Illinois.

into the *masjid* [mosque] and there are different groups. Pakistanis do not talk to the Americans, the Americans do not talk to the Africans."[3]

These comments reflect the cultural divisions in the American-Muslim population. The cultural identities communicated through the headscarf can further entrench such differences and amplify preexisting tensions. Alternatively, the headscarf can also provide the opportunity to transcend the differences across diverse Muslim groups because it is a simultaneous expression of individual and collective identity. Either way, the head covering plays an important role in mediating belonging and social interaction within and between Muslim communities. Furthermore, the headscarf allows us to track the evolving norms of piety and Muslim identity projection within the community itself. It draws symbolic boundaries between covered and uncovered women and between Muslims from different generational, immigrant, and ethnic groups, often with varying head-covering practices.

While exploring the bonding potential of the headscarf, this chapter tracks the historical emergence of a distinct Muslim collective in America and considers its in-group dynamics. The historic use of religious and cultural "invisibility" as a strategy for Muslim political inclusion into the American mainstream in the past makes women who choose to cover an important political group to explore in the present. Covered women are visible as a religious minority and often as an ethnic and racial minority as well. Thus, they are easy targets for discrimination. Their visibility created an increasingly fraught environment for them from the 1980s onward, when many Americans began to associate Muslims with Islamic fundamentalism in the aftermath of the Iranian Revolution. In the public eye this fundamentalism is often linked to notions of the headscarf as indicative of female oppression or women's sympathies for Islamic radicalism (Ghanea-Bassiri 2010). Consequently, the ability of covered women to actualize their identities as American citizens is often dependent on current understandings of American and specifically Muslim-American collective identity, especially whether it is more or less inclusive.

In this chapter we document the diversities represented by Muslims as a multiethnic group and consider how Muslims negotiate them through intracommunal institutions such as the mosque. In particular, this chapter examines the specific challenges associated with cultural interpretations of Islam and how they raise the question of Islamic authenticity for a community that is still finding and claiming its collective identity within a nominally secular state. Finally, we investigate the role of head covering in creating a complex

---

3. Eliza is a fifty-year-old black covered native-born American living in Maryland.

system of symbolic boundaries across the Muslim community through its representation of the cultural, ethnic, and religious diversity of the Muslim-American population.

The Development of the Muslim Community

Muslims have been part of the American social landscape since colonial times and, according to some academics, perhaps even earlier. A minority of scholars suggest that Islam was the second religion introduced to the New World after Christianity (Diouf 2013); some argue it arrived even earlier based on classical Arabic sources contending that Muslims visited the Americas before Christopher Columbus (Nyang 1999a).[4] It is also possible that Islam was first introduced to America through the beliefs and practices of African slaves brought to the country (Gomez 1994). Despite the presence of Muslims in the United States since its founding, the development of the Muslim community itself within the United States was largely determined through changes in formal immigration and citizenship policies, and by the emergence of homegrown Muslim-American social movements such as the Nation of Islam in the early twentieth century.

Muslim Invisibility

The inclusion of Muslims in the early American population was contingent on their ability to blend into the then-dominant modes of citizenship. Historical attempts at Muslims' inclusion into a colonial American mainstream saw light-skinned Muslim men assimilating or "performing whiteness" as part of citizenship within a largely Protestant America.[5] European Muslims and often Arab and Indian Muslim populations were visually indistinguishable from the larger white population. The fact that they belonged to what were deemed white ethnic groups with origins in the Ottoman Empire and South Asia rendered many American Muslims of the 1800s visible white citizens yet invisible Muslims: "The stigma around Islam at this time would not have allowed for its inclusion within this national identity paradigm, immigrant Muslims who sought inclusion did so primarily through an ethnic and economic rather than a religious mode of self-identification" (Ghanea-Bassiri 2010, 137).

---

4. Sulayman S. Nyang cites the doctoral work of Abdullah Hakim Quick (1998) on the travels of Khashkhash Ibn Saeed Ibn Aswad in tenth-century Spain.

5. The Naturalization Act of 1790 limited citizenship to free white persons determined by the court to have a "good moral character" and who had been living in the United States for at least two years (Al-Sheikh 2016, 30).

Many Middle Eastern men sought citizenship in the United States by claiming whiteness toward the end of the nineteenth century (Beydoun 2013; Prewitt 2013; Tehranian 2009). Muslim litigants of Arab, southern European, and South Asian descent were expected to successfully demonstrate "evidence of whiteness in character, religious practices and beliefs, class orientation, language, ability to intermarry, and a host of other traits that had nothing to do with intrinsically racial grouping" in their defense during criminal cases (Tehranian 2009, 5). Thus, performing whiteness would play an integral part in how Muslim immigrants advocated for themselves in citizenship hearings during the nineteenth and early twentieth centuries, as it did for other groups deemed nonwhite such as the Irish and the Italian communities (Al-Sheikh 2016; Said 1979).[6] All these ethnic groups in the precolonial and colonial era sought to pass as white through assimilating into and performing the dominant white, Anglo-Saxon, Protestant culture.

The potential to assimilate for Muslims who were ethnically white or who could pass as white cannot overshadow the simultaneous experience of many West African Muslims, both male and female, who had fewer possibilities for assimilating because of skin color (see Austin 1997; National Public Radio 2005). While some scholars note that approximately 10 percent of the slaves brought to the United States were most likely Muslims (Austin 1997; Nyang 1999a; Turner 2003), others estimate that the number might be as high as 30 percent (Diouf 2013).[7]

Shift to Visibility

The Immigration and Nationality Act of 1952 changed the way the United States considered immigrants for citizenship and rendered race an ineligible factor, which moved the country away from prioritizing whiteness and promoting de facto assimilative policies. The civil rights movement also ushered in new expectations of American identity, shifting them away from monolithic conceptions of race or religion (i.e., Caucasian and Judeo-Christian) and centering them on ideas of accommodating diversity and inclusion. Later, the Immigration and Nationality Act of 1965 spurred the largest wave of Muslim immigrants to the United States. It repealed a long-standing national origins quota that favored European immigration and offered citizenship to

---

6. See Roediger 2005 and Jacobson 1998 for discussions on other immigrant communities in the United States that perform whiteness.

7. Muslim slaves were often more literate than their animist or Christian counterparts as many had learned at least rudimentary Arabic (Diouf 2013).

individuals with preferred skill sets. These immigrants become the corner-stone of future migration based on family reunification policies. Such changes attracted Muslim professionals mainly from Iran, Pakistan, and India, and they shifted the ethnic and labor composition of Muslim-American citizens over the next half century (Haddad, Smith, and Moore 2006). The provisions of new refugee laws in 1980 and 1990 led to an influx of Muslims from formerly communist and other war-torn countries, especially the former Yugoslavia.[8] Immigrants also came from Egypt, Algeria, Sudan, Somalia, and Morocco, further diversifying the existing Muslim population (ibid.).

These changes in the immigration and nationalization laws corresponded with greater acceptance and even celebration of cultural difference and, most important, a shift in how minority groups viewed and agitated for themselves vis-à-vis the state. There was also a corresponding push that communities and not just individuals be recognized and provided with a share in the benefits conferred by the federal government (Prewitt 2013; Thernstrom 1980).

In the post-1965 era, the United States began to reflect the Muslim dias-pora of Europe while hosting homegrown, heterodox Muslim communities and sects from earlier in the twentieth century such as the Moorish Science Temple of America and the Nation of Islam (Ghanea-Bassiri 2010; Simmons 2008). The negative experience of colonialism and the participation of many new immigrants in nationalist movements in their home countries almost ensured that most Muslims who came after the 1960s were less willing to assimilate by changing their name, religion, or cultural practice. Performing whiteness became less desirable and even unacceptable (Ghanea-Bassiri 2010). This reticence and its coincidence with ever-increasing cultural and religious pluralism in the post-1965 era resulted in a dramatic increase in the number of mosques and organizations with a particular ethnic or denominational affili-ation in the United States.

During this period, the Arab-Israeli conflict, the oil crisis, and the Iranian hostage crisis were also influencing the way mainstream Americans viewed Arabs and, by extension, Muslims. Even though Arabs constitute only 20 per-cent of the world's Muslim population, they became emblematic of the faith in the eyes of the American public. The increased prejudice from the American mainstream as a by-product of activist foreign policy in the Middle East, along-side a growing sense of ethnic Arab pride, inspired many Arab Americans to

---

8. In the 1980s (Public Law 96–212), the refugee act raised the number of accepted refugees from 17,500 to 50,000 for each fiscal year, and revisions to immigration law in the 1990 (Public Law 101–649) also allowed up to 700, 000 immigrants to annually enter the United States.

claim minority status after centuries of passing as white and thus to reclaim their Arab and Muslim heritage and identity (Ghanea-Bassiri 2010).

The Race and Ethnicity of Muslim Americans

It is difficult to decisively track the growing diversity of the Muslim population, at least in part because the classification of a Muslim in the United States is not standardized or included in demographic data. As with the size of the Muslim-American population, the numbers vary on the exact ethnic and racial composition of the community (Bagby 2012; Mohamed 2016; Simmons 2008).[9] Table 2.1 shows some of these inconsistencies in establishing the ethnic and racial parameters of the Muslim community across multiple studies (including our own survey and focus group populations). A 2011 Pew survey found that 30 percent of Muslims described themselves as white, 23 percent as black, 21 percent as Asian, 6 percent as Hispanic, and 19 percent as mixed race. In stark contrast, other scholarship claims 40–42 percent of Muslims are black, placing South Asians as the next largest group at 29 percent, with Arabs making up some 12–15 percent of the total US Muslim population (Ahmed 2014). The remaining 17 percent of Muslims reflect a truly global range of ethnicities with no group explicitly identified as white.

Earlier studies of American Muslims posited a roughly equal split across the Arab, African American, and the South Asian population. The use of the Census's racial categories (white, black, etc.) in the Pew survey, as opposed to the ethnic categories (South Asian, Middle Eastern, etc.) preferred by the Ba-Yunus and Kone (2004) and Ahmed (2014) studies, likely makes a difference

Table 2.1   Racial and ethnic demographics of American Muslims

RACE/ ETHNICITY	OUR FOCUS GROUPS	OUR SURVEY	PEW (2011)	AHMED (2014)
White	26%	47%	30%	NA
Black	20%	8%	23%	40–42%
Arab	22%	15%*	21%	12–15%
South Asian/Asian	28%	39%	21%	29%
Hispanic	4%	NA	6%	NA
Other/mixed	NA	7%	19%	NA

* Self-identified in open-ended part of the survey's US Census question (292 survey participants).

---

9. The latest Pew estimates (January 2016) put the number at 3.3 million, approximately 1 percent of the US population (Mohamed 2016). However, the number of Muslims has been variously estimated from between 2.5 and as high as 8 million.

in the estimated breakdown of the respective ethnic groups. It is much more difficult to infer ethnicity from a category labeled and self-reported as white in the Census and the Pew survey. In fact, the Pew study also found that self-reported racial breakdown varied generationally, by region of origin, and according to whether citizens were foreign-born. For example, the majority of Pew's survey participants born in the Middle East and North Africa described themselves as white (60%).

Regardless of the exact ethnic breakdown of American Muslims, this diversity is still emblematic of the quintessential American melting pot. In the words of Malcolm X, "Only Mecca during the *hajj* brings together such a range and variety of Muslims as now reside in the United States" (as quoted by Ahmed 2014, 159). This trend is likely to persist as the 2016 Pew estimates show that around 10 percent of incoming American immigrants are Muslim, while the number of Americans who convert to Islam is similar to the number of those who leave the faith (one in five) (Mohamed 2016). The United States today is racially, ethnically, religiously, and culturally more diverse. This evolution coincided with a broader era of identity politics, which emerged in the late twentieth century inspired by the civil rights movement (Heyes 2016), which we discuss in more detail in the following section.

Black Muslims and the Nation of Islam

Muslim Americans actively participated in the multicultural politics inspired by the civil rights movement of the 1950s and 1960s alongside other cultural and religious minority groups. Most prominently the African-American Muslim community aligned its interests with the civil rights movement directly through the activities of Malcolm X and other Muslim activists. However, not everyone in that African-American community embraced a culturally pluralistic vision, as the tensions between the Nation of Islam and other racial and ethnic communities illustrate.

The Nation of Islam formed in the 1930s, and up until the 1975 death of its leader, Elijah Muhammad, it remained the most prominent voice of African-American Islam. The movement arose in reaction to the racism and the exploitation of the Jim Crow era as an alternative Islamic lifestyle for African Americans. As one of the most prominent Islamic political groups in the United States and a well-known symbol of black nationalism, the Nation of Islam embraces a largely syncretic religious life that draws heavily from Islam and more recently from Scientology (Gray 2015). While the primary theological roots are Islamic—followers profess, "There is no God but Allah— the messianic message differs from orthodox Sunni Islam in that the founder,

Wallace Fard Muhammed, was believed to have been both the Islamic *Mahdi* and the Judaic Messiah. The "Nation" refers to the black community, or the purportedly ancient African "tribe of Shabazz," which was reconstituted in contemporary times through the Atlantic slave trade in the Americas. According to Wallace Fard Muhammed, it was then marginalized, disenfranchised, and kept downtrodden and undereducated in fulfillment of the prophecy of Genesis 15:13–14: "Then the Lord said to Abraham, 'Know for certain that for four hundred years your descendants will be strangers in a country not their own and that they will be enslaved and mistreated there. But I will punish the nation they serve as slaves, and afterward they will come out with great possessions.'"

In the early twentieth century, Elijah Muhammad, the cofounder of the Nation of Islam alongside Wallace Fard Muhammed, consolidated many of the beliefs of the movement into a ten-point platform for action and a twelve-point doctrinal explication. These doctrinal points were often only peripherally about Islam and more about reconstituting the black nation and embracing and promoting blackness across the political, social, and economic sphere (Simmons 2008).

The Nation of Islam has been the most overtly political of the very few homegrown American Islamic groups and movements, whether with its past goal of overthrowing the system or, in more recent years, mobilizing African-American Muslims to participate and reform it. It was and is more a "black nationalist protest organization" than a religious community per se and is therefore also more politically controversial than other Muslim-American organizations, which toe a more patriotic line (Simmons 2006, 174). In particular, the Nation of Islam's glorification of blackness along with historical references to whites as "devils" has made it difficult for the group to mobilize within formal institutions of politics, since the latter are dominated by white Americans.

In late 2016, Representative Keith Ellison (congressman for Minnesota's Fifth District and the first Muslim elected to Congress) ran a fraught campaign for the Democratic National Committee (DNC) chairmanship, which he ultimately lost, partly because of his past ties to the Nation of Islam (Sheffield 2016). The Nation of Islam–organized Million Man March in 1995 inspired legions of African-American men like Ellison to agitate for their civil rights, but it was also deeply divisive in its scapegoating of other minorities, such as Jews and homosexuals and projecting what Ellison would publicly later call "a chauvinistic model of manhood" (Detrow 2016).

The Nation of Islam has never had a substantial female membership, possibly because of its focus on "masculine self-realization" and the largely secondary status of women within the organization (Simmons 2006). In fact, in the time of Elijah Muhammad, men still outnumbered women five to one in membership (ibid., 175). Our focus group participants also referenced the chauvinistic tendencies of the Nation of Islam and most frequently connected this to their treatment of women. In one of the Chicago groups, Lara notes that when the organization initially emerged, their women wore uniforms and head coverings: "They had to cover. But I think that was just part of it. They belonged to an organization called MGT—that was Muslim Girls Training (MGT). I'm saying, "Why you all calling these women girls? I'm not a girl." It was MGT . . . all this is man-made. All this is Elijah Muhammad's organization because for the most part any black person that you saw covered, they were part of the Nation of Islam."[10]

Despite the modern criticism, the internal messaging of the group was powerful and rooted in achievement ideology, which translated into its own distinct code of ethics and conduct. African-American Muslims became symbols of "uprightness, immaculate appearance, discipline, high regard of self, self-determination, strong families, strong men, obedient women, cultural refinement, education and self-improvement" (Simmons 2008, 269). This was the opposite of stereotypes perpetuated in the mainstream about African Americans and represented a transition "from the burden of acting white to the honor of being black" (Akom 2003, 313). The achievement ideology of the Nation of Islam encouraged women specifically to continue their education and defy cultural stereotypes within their own communities: "rigid morals, self-determination, non-traditional Islam, and black nationalism" were key elements in constituting the ideology and lifestyle of Nation of Islam members (307). With the leadership struggle after Elijah Muhammad's death in 1975, the organization has been largely defunct. Most African-American Muslims have turned to mainstream Sunni Islam, with a few holdouts in Louis Farrakhan's revamped version of the organization that emerged in the 1980s.[11]

Negotiating Diversity through Islamic Organizations and the Mosque

The Nation of Islam's adamant promotion of absolute ethnic and racial differences stands in stark contrast to the notion of a color-blind American Muslim community—essentially an American *ummah*—which is an idea vital to

---

10. Lara is a black covered native-born American woman in her sixties living in Illinois.

11. More recent membership in the Nation of Islam has ranged from twenty thousand to one hundred thousand individuals (Simmons 2006, 174).

mainstream Sunni Muslims and immigrant South Asian and Arab communities in the United States. *Ummah* is an Arabic term for the Muslim population worldwide. The term can also carry the more utopian connotation of "the global Islamic sisterhood and brotherhood united across racial and ethnic differences" (Karim 2008, 3) or more conventionally, the "worldwide Islamic community" (Curtis 2009, 104). The American iteration of the ummah is in many respects a microcosm of the concept in light of the diverse nature of the Muslim community in the United States, which includes both recent immigrants (South Asian and Middle Eastern) and domestic believers (African-American, white, and Hispanic converts) (Karim 2008). The academic notion of an American ummah has evolved as an analytical tool for unpacking the internal divisions among Muslims specific to the American context (Karim 2005, 2008).

Even in the modern American setting of cultural and religious pluralism, racial and ethnic identity is fraught among the domestic and immigrant Muslim-American populations. This tension is expected given the history of political Islam in the United States, thoroughly analyzed in Jamillah Karim's book *American Muslim Women: Negotiating Race, Class, and Gender within the Ummah* (2008). Karim explores the ethnic and racial dynamics between African-American and South Asian women in the cities of Chicago and Atlanta, revealing an often tense and racially charged environment. The book introduces an African-American interview subject (Shantesa) in a discussion with a Pakistani (Sanjana) and an Eritrean woman (Husna) about whether Chicago's Muslim community is racially divided (Karim 2008, 2). Husna and Sanjana see their experiences in local mosques as being color-blind, since they perceive Islam as a religion that is not racially divisive. However, Shantesa argues that there is a difference between the theory and the reality of the Muslim experience for African-American Muslim women. According to Shantesa, the attitude of many immigrant women could be summed up with "Yes, you are Muslim, you are welcome here [to the mosque], but you are African American." In Shantesa's view, a pluralistic ummah seemed to still be distinguishing ethnic and racial groups and tracking Muslims into ethnically specific mosques and communities.

In Boston and Chicago our African-American research participants report experiencing overt discrimination based on their skin color. In particular, members of the focus group in Chicago—a key site of the Nation of Islam in the past—were very cognizant of the tensions between different races within Islam. Shakira claims an "in-between" status of African-American Muslims due to the discrimination they faced by non-Muslims because of their race and religion but also the overt discrimination they faced by racially prejudiced

Muslims. She observes, "In the Muslim community there is a racial hierarchy. There is [sic] Arabs, then South Asians, anybody in that world and then black people down here." Shakira also confirms that African-American Muslims were often guilty of the same kind of racial prioritization, and she hints at why African-American mosques tend to be less inclusive of other groups: "I just don't think they [African-American Muslims] would see themselves as all-inclusive. I don't think we're there yet. Much of that is because we want so badly to maintain our [African-American] culture. Our community is having its own struggles about what it means to be African, black, in America. We are still dealing with that and on the other hand how do people view African Americans. . . . We are also dealing with an in-between status."

In addition, Shakira speaks of the matter-of-fact way immigrant Muslims discussed her racial heritage and its socioeconomic implications, citing how another Muslim woman had derisively implied that black people would be maids or servants in her home country. In Norfolk, Virginia, Abeera, who is also African American, mentions how the discrimination against African-American Muslims dovetailed with their political affiliation, socioeconomic status, and whether or not they were converts: "The converts though, the black American Muslims, they are Democrats, because they always were the poor ones. . . . They were a subclass, the subgroup."[12] Abeera concludes that as a black woman, her experience as a Muslim was not the same as that of others who were of a different race.[13] While it was generally our African-American participants who most often raised the issue of intracommunity conflict, these tensions did not apply within the African-American community itself, which tended to be very cohesive.[14]

The larger Islamic organizations such as the Council on American-Islamic Relations and the Islamic Society of North America attempt to bridge these divisions through community and identity building, but they may not engage all communities equally. In the case of these latter organizations, and Muslim student associations, much of the membership tends toward first- and second-generation immigrants of South Asian and Arab descent. These groups are

---

12. Abeera is a sixty-four-year-old covered black native-born American living in Virginia.

13. More generally, the African-American Muslim community has reported feeling marginalized by both American mainstream culture and the immigrant Muslim community. See Elliot 2007; Karim 2008; McCloud 1995.

14. We coded any mention of intergroup conflict in the focus groups; 35 percent of the instances coded were attributable to our black respondents, a disproportionately high number considering that only 20 percent of our focus group participants were black. See Ghanea-Bassiri 2010; Gibson and Karim 2014; Haddad and Smith 1994; Haddad, Smith, and Moore 2006; and Karim 2008 for more details on the relative homogeneity and cohesion of the African-American Muslim community.

the original founders of ISNA, CAIR, and many of the existing MSAs (Ahmed 2014). This means that the African-American Muslim community may not be mobilized through existing or even conventional political channels catering to Muslim Americans. In fact, since the transformation of the Nation of Islam into a more orthodox Sunni organization under Louise Farrakhan, a social movement geared at politically mobilizing African-American Muslims has yet to emerge—with the partial exception of Black Lives Matter. However, Black Lives Matter is oriented more around reinvigorating the struggle for African-American rights than around agitating for intersecting communities, even though many on the group's steering committee are African-American Muslims.[15]

These considerations speak to the complexity and challenge of achieving cohesion in the broader American ummah across race and class, especially at a time when America's political and social institutions are regularly accused of Islamophobia and racism. There are many who wish to prioritize the concerns of one group over another, making it a difficult time for Muslim Americans and especially African-American Muslims. The response of organizations such as CAIR and ISNA, as well as the newly established Emerge-USA Political Action Committee, has been to lobby for civic justice across the board, and we see some of that same cross-cultural vision emerging in the broader mosque community as well. One of EmergeUSA's founders, Khurrum Wahid, discussed the difficulties inherent in agitating for the Muslim community as a whole and commented on the challenge of mobilizing young Muslims to vote with the American ummah in mind (Chideya 2016). "We're seeing a lot of younger Muslims thinking about voting for a third party even in swing states." Wahid suggested that Clinton was the obvious candidate for Muslims and saw millennial Muslims who were planning to vote for a third party as "selfish," explaining, "You are voting for your own interest, not the [Muslim] community."

Despite these divisions and tensions in the American ummah, there have been attempts to transcend them—most successfully through the mosque (S. Ali 2005; Peek 2011). Our own research as well as other scholarship reveals that the mosque is the locus of the most active and crosscultural community

---

15. Black Lives Matter is an international activist movement that emerged in the wake of the 2013 acquittal of George Zimmerman for the shooting of African-American teen Trayvon Martin. The movement focuses on combating violence and systemic racism in the United States against African Americans (especially police-based violence) and originated in the African-American community, using the hashtag #BlackLivesMatter on social media to coordinate protests and events related to the movement. The movement has over thirty local chapters and expanded rapidly between 2014 and 2016.

and identity building among Muslims in the United States.[16] Mosques unify and mobilize Muslims toward greater engagement among themselves but also toward engagement with non-Muslims.

In general, American mosques and Islamic centers cater to socioculturally diverse communities.[17] At the beginning of the new millennium a mere 7 percent of American mosques had completely ethnically homogenous populations, while some 70 percent of surveyed mosques promoted that the Qur'an should be interpreted in ways downplaying denominational differences (Bagby et al. 2001). By 2011, that number had further decreased to only 3 percent of mosques hosting only one ethnic group (Bagby 2012). In fact, more than 90 percent of mosques have some Arab or South Asian congregants, while 81 percent reported also hosting African-American attendees (ibid., 12).[18] For many of our focus group participants, the inclusive stance of particular mosques helps to build community across race and denomination. This is possible precisely because many Muslim Americans see themselves as "purely Muslim" rather than denominationally distinct. Approximately 24 percent identify as "just Muslim" rather than Sunni or Shiite in a 2011 Pew Survey. In our survey, 15 percent of respondents identify themselves as having "no sect" or denomination. The role of the mosque in facilitating ties between members of the Muslim community across racial and/or denominational background makes mosques an important venue for political mobilization, as we discuss in chapter 5.[19]

There are certainly many mosques in the United States that define themselves as ethnically specific. We encountered Bosnian, Somali, Nigerian, Ethiopian, Turkish, Persian, Afghan, Kurdish, and Albanian Islamic centers and mosques while recruiting research participants.[20] African-American mosques are more likely to be ethnically and racially homogenous than are the mosques of other communities—these are often referred to as "immigrant mosques" by our African-American survey respondents. Our research suggests that the social networks and bonds of immigrant as opposed to African-American mosques may be distinct, which may affect the ability of a collectively engaged

---

16. See Djupe and Calfano 2012; Haddad and Smith 1994; Haddad, Smith, and Moore 2006; Karim 2008; Peek 2011; Westfall et al. 2016.

17. See Bagby 2012; Bagby et al. 2001; Barreto and Dana 2009; Lotfi 2001.

18. Some of this diversity can be attributed to the convenience of attending mosques for prayer during work hours that are not as close to home as those attended with family (Bagby 2012, 12).

19. See Granovetter 1973; Putnam 2007; Westfall et al. 2016 for discussion of bridging or weak bonds that facilitate social cohesion.

20. Out of the 1,015 institutions we contacted, only 34 explicitly identified themselves as ethnic, though there has been a greater trend toward building exclusively Shiite mosques over the last twenty years (Haddad and Smith 1994; Sacirbey 2012).

American ummah to emerge (Bagby 2001, 2011). Interestingly, African-American mosques also tend to be the best at recruiting new converts, although most African-American participants actually reported converting in immigrant mosques (Bagby 2012, 12). The relatively small size of the Muslim population in the United States has meant that many Muslims of different ethnicities, races, and denominations are praying together, especially within smaller communities. The mosque we visited in Reno, Nevada, is an interesting example of this in that it includes Hispanic and white converts alongside many South Asian and Arab congregants.

Big cities have been sites for building larger Muslim communities and experimenting with community innovation. The emergence of more heterodox forms of Islamic practice in urban American centers in the 1920s was partially due to the urban migration of African Americans (Simmons 2008). In New York City, Fadia notes, "I don't think I've come across any issues within the religion because the masjid that I go to is so open. I don't know people's backgrounds, their religious backgrounds, because it doesn't necessarily come up."[21]

Some of the mosques in Chicago are cultivating a reputation for inclusivity even though our Chicago research participants mention intracommunity tension. Hawa', a lawyer and activist, is hopeful: "I think that this masjid is different than my other masjid experiences. Maybe that is what has driven all of us to participate [in this focus group]. I think that more than any other masjid I have seen, the woman's perspective is heard, taken into account, accommodated for. I think we attract a diverse ethnic background because most of the programs are conducted in English."[22] This is a very important observation since many immigrant mosques tend to invite imams from abroad to lead *khutba* (Friday sermon), while African-American sermons tend to be conducted in English by local imams (Wilson 2008).

Some of our participants also mention concerns about denominational differences affecting Muslims' attitudes toward one another. In New York City, Haarisa explains,

> I wish every Muslim institution had that model of being very inclusive and open-minded because I don't want us to go down the path of trying to police what is Muslim and what isn't Muslim like what's happening in other places . . . I'm Sunni myself . . . and I've heard so much [sic] negative things about the Shi'ite community from Sunnis and I have to challenge them on that. I'm like, you need to educate yourself and they are Muslim and we need to respect anyone that calls themselves a Muslim

---

21. Fadia is a thirty-year-old black uncovered native-born American living in New York.
22. Hawa' is a thirty-four-year-old covered South Asian native-born American living in Illinois.

and just leave it at that. We're not the ones to judge other Muslims. I am part of the majority and Shi'ites they are the minority. As the majority I have the privilege of the majority, I need to be in solidarity with the minority, which is the Shi'ite community, and which is so oppressed not just in other places but in this country as well.[23]

Other participants note that the focus on religion in America beyond cultural specificities allows them to transcend some of the prejudices of their parents, who were often first-generation immigrants. Farah, another South Asian New Yorker, observes, "When I think of American culture . . . of American Muslim culture . . . what I was thinking was that it's made religion purer because it's weeded out things from our parents' culture."[24] Similarly, Zia, a covered participant from Detroit, asserts, "Religion gives you freedom, but culture limits you."[25] As will be discussed in the following section, many of our participants raise concerns regarding what is considered authentic Islamic practice versus traditional practices rooted in culture, and naturally head covering becomes part of that discussion.

Cultural Islam: Authenticity and Head Covering

Cultural differences present challenges to building a coherent Muslim-American identity, and one of the sharpest points of conflict is due to varying notions of religious authenticity in Islamic practice. Much of the debate centers on questions regarding the religious versus cultural notions of what constitutes authentic Islamic practice and social behavior. Many of our focus group participants note there are significant differences between the theory and the reality of religious practice in a non-Muslim state. Furthermore, the heterodox interpretations of Islam present among American believers—ranging from the influence of the Muslim Brotherhood to the spread of Sufism—have made the evolution of an "American" Islam more complex.[26] Head covering is

---

23. Haarisa is a twenty-six-year-old covered South Asian foreign-born American living in New York.

24. Farah is a twenty-five-year-old covered foreign-born South Asian American living in New York.

25. Zia is a forty-seven-year-old covered foreign-born Arab American living in Michigan.

26. Sufism (or *tasawwuf*—derived from the word "mystic" in Arabic) represents a mystical branch of Islam in which Muslims seek truth and divine love through a more personal and direct relationship with God. This branch seems to have evolved from early ascetic practices of the Islamic faith in the ninth and tenth centuries. In the modern era, it has also readily absorbed elements from non-Muslim beliefs. Conversely, Salafism (derived from the word *salaf*, or "devout ancestor" in Arabic) is a reactionary, fundamentalist, and extremely conservative tradition in Sunni Islam, which emerged in the early eighteenth century on the Arabian peninsula. Salafists reject religious innovation, focusing on the lives of pious forefathers and requiring the adoption of Shari'a in everyday life. In the modern era, the most extreme iteration of this belief system has been Wahabism.

necessarily part of this debate. However, as we will see further in this chapter, the discourse around head covering among Muslim women is not necessarily centered on cultural difference or a backward "cultural Islam" as much as on differing levels of presumed piety between women who do and do not cover.

In our interviews, cultural Islam—ethnically or nationally determined Islamic practice—is often shorthand for the religious norms of Arab Muslims from Muslim-majority Arab states where the faith has mingled with a millennium of local traditions. According to Lara, a participant in one of our Chicago focus groups, "Immigrants brought a peculiar focus. . . . [They brought] a focus on women's bodies, gossip, what women could not do." A very common refrain across all of our focus groups is the observation that religious practice is often culturally determined and that, in some cases, vaguely heretical tendencies crept into American Islam as a result of Muslim immigrants' cultural interpretations. Other participants note that immigrant Muslims did not follow the faith appropriately or that they followed it superficially and should be chastised for non-Islamic behavior.

Among our participants there is discussion of an extemporaneous or universal "authentic" practice of those who solely rely on the holy texts and words of the Prophet and his companions to guide their religiosity. In particular, our African-American participants often see their immigrant counterparts' religiosity as tainted by cultural or even national traditions that have little to do with what they perceive as "true Islam." Sometimes nonconverts share this perspective: Elinor inherited the faith from her immigrant parents and jokingly recounts the following words of advice on converts from a covered acquaintance: "I used to have a social studies teacher who said to me, 'Marry a convert. Don't marry anyone else. Everyone else comes with too much cultural baggage. At least the converts learned the religion before they decided to become Muslim. You can't have that guarantee—[nonconverts] might have a Muslim name but that is not any guarantee of knowing Islam at all.'"[27]

Conversely, significant research has shown that immigrant Muslims of Arab and South Asian descent look upon the homegrown African-American social movements inspired by Islam with distrust and accusations of blasphemy.[28] A covered Arab participant in Virginia is shocked that some African-American Muslims cover their daughters' hair before they are menstruating,

---

27. Elinor is a twenty-four-year-old covered native-born Arab American living in Texas.

28. These are largely African-American organizations or movements such as the Garvey Movement, the Moorish Science Temple, the Nation of Islam, and the American Muslim Mission.

scoffing at what she deemed to be an excessive practice born of religious ignorance and cultural backwardness. Xara, a covered African-American participant from Chicago, notes, "There have been many times I have been in a conversation but been told, 'You are not really Muslim . . . you don't have the authentic experience.'"[29] Yet she also observes that the need for projecting Islamic authenticity seemed universal across both immigrant and nonimmigrant Muslims in America, especially when they invoked Islamic dress as part of that projection:

> We have a vast community of people from different backgrounds [in Chicago]. . . . But there is this desire for the authentic. I find it among the immigrants. . . . When you saw the women they were in full black abaya, full black niqab. I mean at one point I remember thinking, "Oh, they're Arab." . . . But they were talking about how they wanted to be closer to the *sunnah* and this was closer to the sunnah, the most authentic and a subtext was, "Oh and you need to get with it, or you are not getting close to Allah."

The practice of head covering is never invoked as heretical or inauthentic, though some styles of covering are occasionally deemed "foreign" in our focus group interviews. Tamira illustrates this point: "I perceived myself wearing the *khimar* as a foreign thing. I thought *I'm not wearing it like that*. It was foreign at that time, but when I first took the *shehada*, I was more concerned with my behavior and dressing modestly." One of our survey respondents, however, notes that she does not believe the hijab is tied to Islam; rather that it is "an Arab cultural idea." Another uncovered Egyptian-American survey respondent maintains that the Qur'an does not require head covering and that it is the by-product of "propaganda and pressure exerted by [Islamic] fundamentalists."

The underlying diversity of the Muslim-American community is represented in head covering. Muslim-American women create and re-create complex, overlapping identities as Muslims, as women, as cohorts of a particular generation, as immigrants, as members of a specific ethnic group or race, and as citizens of other countries through the headscarf. We especially see this through some of the different covering patterns across ethnic groups in the United States. Many of the styles of head covering illustrated in the introduction are culturally bound, and the practice itself varies across demographic groups. For example, African-American Muslims tend to cover at higher

---

29. Xara is a thirty-seven-year-old black covered native-born American living in Illinois.

rates than Muslims of other races in the United States. Conversely, South Asian Muslims are less likely to cover than their white and African-American counterparts. To some degree, this could be the byproduct of a substantial proportion of our survey respondents' having been born abroad. They may still face the pressures of being first-generation immigrants and reject the head covering in an attempt to integrate into mainstream American society. Members of the African-American community, on the other hand, feel marginalized by both American mainstream culture and immigrant Muslims and may enact this difference by embracing head covering with much more zeal than other Muslims (Elliot 2007; Karim 2009; McCloud 1995). Embracing the headscarf is a way to further set themselves apart and elevate what is essentially a Muslim identity marker into an emblem of African-American Muslim group consciousness (Wong, Lien, and Conway 2005). Ethnic identities can be achieved socially and relationally through head-covering practices, as they can demarcate "differences between groups as well as within groups, one woman's adoption of particular veiling habits will have an effect on the perceived and experienced identities of other women both in her vicinity and in all the spaces discursively touched by her actions" (Lewis 2007, 437). The practice can even signal class and education level within certain communities, as does the advent of "hijab couture" (*Economist* 2014; Moors and Tarlo 2007; Williams and Vashi 2007). Moors and Tarlo capture this point well in their work on global Islamic fashion:

> The same item of dress, however, may have quite divergent resonance and meanings in different contexts. Some women in south India, Yemen, Indonesia, and Mali look to Saudi Arabia for sartorial inspiration, leading to the spread and popularity of the *abaya* (an all-enveloping black cloak) in different locations. Whereas in Saudi Arabia the *abaya* can be considered a form of state-enforced national dress, in Yemen and south India it takes on different connotations and is perceived by many Muslim women as a sophisticated, cosmopolitan, and fashionable alternative to local varieties of covered dress. In contexts where the introduction of the *abaya* is linked to labor migration, it may indicate a claim to a higher status and standard of living. However, when introduced by students of religion, the same garment may acquire more conservative or radical religious and political connotations. (2007, 135)

While the style of head covering may accentuate ethnic specificities, it identifies Muslims to each other and breaks down superficial and often cultural barriers across different Muslim ethnic groups. Therefore, the religious practice of head covering often translates into a personal politics of intracommunity integration within the United States. In fact, for a few of our convert focus group participants, the hijab is the gateway to Islam as well as a mechanism to find or identify other community members upon embracing faith. Naja speaks excitedly about this:

> It's [the headscarf] an encouragement, and in our area where you can go out for three days, four days, five days, and not see a Muslim, when you do, it's like "Salaam!! How are you doing?! Who are you?! It's so nice to meet you!!" I get so excited when I meet a Muslim in my neighborhood. That happened last week. I was at the park and a man came up to me and greeted me with salaams and said he and his wife lived in the neighborhood, and that's how he knew I was Muslim, from how I looked.[30]

Several of our covered survey respondents report similar experiences, and observed they were more likely to be greeted by *"assalamu aleykum"* (peace be upon you), especially from other covered women. Responding to our survey, a white convert in Cincinnati proclaims, "I think the best part of hijab is that it alerts all the Muslims in the area to watch out and look out for their Muslim sister."

These respondents emphasize how head covering is necessarily a visual cue that can potentially open or circumscribe the social networks of Muslim women. It identifies members of the ummah to each other, creating opportunities for bonding relationships among those with similar values. However, it can expose the wearer to a degree of religious judgment from other Muslims, because it is believed to signal a particular type of religious lifestyle. A covered survey respondent from Ohio complains that both Muslims and non-Muslims essentialize her identity because of the headscarf: "Muslims and non-Muslims are polite to me for the most part, but both groups put me in a box. Muslims have said things like I am a better Muslim because I wear a headscarf, which I don't believe. Non-Muslims think I am more like a catholic nun, which I am not. So if I do something or act in a way that seems outside their box they are surprised. If I did not wear a headscarf I think my actions or words would not be as noticeable."

Many of our respondents resent the social pressure to live up to the expectations created by the headscarf, even as they recognize its ability to elicit respect and even reverence among Muslims and non-Muslims alike. A survey respondent from Pennsylvania echoes this sentiment: "When I am with people who aren't Muslims, they treat me with respect and dignity. When I'm

---

30. Naja is a thirty-seven-year-old white covered native-born American living in Virginia.

with Muslims who are more practicing, I feel as if all my actions are being scrutinized and feel pressured into being this so-called ideal *Muslimah*."

Our covered survey respondents also complain about how uncovered Muslims expect them to be "excessively" or even "judgmentally" pious—to be the enforcers of the faith in their surrounding communities. Covered survey respondents across Texas, California, and New York all observe that noncovering Muslim women tend to be on edge around them and often try to act more pious around them. One focus group participant from Cincinnati maintains "the hardest parts [of wearing a head covering] are when it creates barriers for you with other Muslims, who think, because you wear a scarf, that you somehow walk around judging all those girls who don't wear a scarf."

Similarly, the survey respondents who choose not to cover report feeling judged by those who cover. Many uncovered women elaborate that they were waiting to wear the headscarf until they felt "ready" or "strong enough" to adopt the practice. These statements would imply that uncovered women perceived those who cover as both spiritually more mature and pious, though descriptive statistics from our survey in table 2.2 tell a different story. Only 24 percent of uncovered women in our survey thought the headscarf contributed to the piety of its wearer, and only 50 percent of covered women agree with the idea that "wearing the head covering makes a woman more pious." These sentiments appear despite the dominance of piety as the primary reported reason for covering, as discussed in chapter 1. In the words of one of our uncovered survey respondents, "Beside saying prayers, I do not think covering the head makes anyone better or worse, pious or non-pious. I believe any woman can be strong and practice good morals if she wants to." Another respondent comments, "Modesty is in the heart and not in attire."

The diversity represented by the headscarf goes beyond demographic identity markers into different religious meanings within the Muslim community, which are often difficult for our focus group participants to navigate. For example, Martha highlights how her fiancé's family rejected her because she chose not to wear very conservative Islamic attire: "The guy I was engaged to, he decided to pursue Islamic scholarship, but suddenly I was someone who

Table 2.2   Opinions relating to head covering (% responding affirmatively)

OPINION	COVERED	NOT COVERED
Covering one's head is mandatory according to the terms of Islam.	89.8%	42.9%
Wearing a head covering makes a woman more pious.	49.7%	23.5%
Covering one's head makes one's ideas and opinions count more than one's sexuality.	79.3%	30.7%

was not good enough because I didn't wear an abaya. I didn't wear a [face] veil like his mother and his sister did. Suddenly I felt no matter what I did, it was just not good enough."[31] Conversely, Elmira, a successful programmer in Houston, describes how the Pakistani community ostracized her precisely for wearing the headscarf, calling it a sign of her "backwardness."[32] One of our survey respondents succinctly illustrates the many conflicting expectations of covered women across both Muslims and non-Muslims: "Muslim pious people see me as a respectable person while I am a human and can do [sic] mistakes. . . . Muslim non-pious see me as a sexual object and I want to give them a nice big slap for it. . . . Non-Muslim conservatives see me as a fanatic and I don't care about crazy people. . . . Non-Muslim liberals see me as a Muslim and only as a Muslim as if I don't have any other interest and my whole life revolves around religion."

While our research participants express frustration with the conflicting expectations associated with the headscarf, many engage in the mixed messaging themselves. Our respondents trust their own motives for covering, but they do not necessarily trust the motives of other Muslim women, which may pose challenges to inclusion for Muslim outsiders such as recent converts or rival ethnic groups even if they cover.[33] At the same time, converts use the headscarf and other forms of Islamic attire as one of the ways they communicate a pious Muslim identity to their new community in order to facilitate social inclusion (Ajrouch 2007; Droogsma 2007).

The high levels of agreement among covered women in their responses to the two questions in table 2.2 as to whether head covering is mandatory (90% of covered respondents) and whether it makes one's personality count more than her sexuality (79%) hint at the coherence of our covered respondents' Islamic values. In contrast, there is more disagreement across all three questions among uncovered Muslim women. Less than half of them agree with each statement, and over 70 percent of uncovered women reject the notion that the headscarf makes a woman more pious. Consequently, we assume that Muslim women can and do use the headscarf to cultivate a general Muslim identity and build community. However, many other cultural meanings are embedded in the choice to cover, which engender symbolic boundaries across Muslims.

---

31. Martha is a twenty-four-year-old South Asian covered foreign national living in Massachusetts.

32. Elmira is a thirty-two-year-old covered foreign-born South Asian American living in Texas.

33. Earlier research on gender segregation in voluntary associations has shown that women tend to be more insular in social networks than men (McPherson and Smith-Lovin 1982; Popielarz 1999).

Ultimately, for most Muslim women in our research the decision to wear the headscarf is personal and predominantly rooted in piety, as discussed in chapter 1. The headscarf is also an important part of Muslim identity projection, which makes Muslim women a visual representative of their own minority group within the Muslim community and beyond. Many of our participants describe positive and respectful reactions to their head-covering practices from other Muslims, and this respect often allows young Muslim women to navigate the identity debates within their own communities.

The history of Muslims in America is complex. Muslim Americans are going through the same process that many other nationalities and religions have historically experienced upon immigration into the country. However, their path to inclusion is conditioned not just by their religious but also by their ethnic and racial identities. Groups such as the Jews, the Irish, and the Italians were racialized and stereotyped at the turn of twentieth century and were often tasked with performing an Anglo-Saxon variant of their whiteness similar to what was later expected of many Muslim Americans of European or South Asian descent. In his 2006 Johan Skytte Prize lecture on diversity, Robert Putnam vividly traced this process, one that foreshadows the tensions and social upheaval that represent the growing pains of yet another new immigrant group:

> At the turn of the last century inter-marriage was "castelike for new ethnics from east and southern Europe," whereas by 1990 only "one-fifth [of white Americans] have spouses with identical [ethnic] backgrounds.". . . The cultures of the immigrant groups permeated the broader American cultural framework, with the Americanization of St. Patrick's Day, pizza and "Jewish" humor. In some ways "they" became like "us," and in some ways our new "us" incorporated "them." This was no simple, inevitable, friction-less "straight-line" assimilation, but over several generations the initial ethnic differences became muted and less salient so that assimilation became the master trend for these immigrant groups during the twentieth century (2007, 162).

Some of the growing pains Muslims face may be a by-product of this slow mainstreaming process and their own attempts at bridging social, ethnic, and religious divides within their own communities while simultaneously attempting to close the distance between themselves and non-Muslim Americans. Symbolic boundaries such as those enacted through the headscarf are employed to reframe the meaning of social differences between men and women and Muslims and non-Muslims as well as between various ethnic communities (Lamont and Molnár 2002). By shifting the narrative around the headscarf toward its multidimensional uses from an object of religious expression for some to a tool for personal and collective empowerment for others, Muslim-American women become active representatives and advocates for their personal Islam in their own communities and beyond. They are also unwitting ambassadors for the mainstreaming of difference into the public arena, where they become the living embodiment and the vanguard of an emerging intersectional American identity.

The goal of unifying religious identities can be overshadowed by cultural and even socioeconomic differences between immigrant and African-American Muslims, allowing identity politics to undermine the unity of the American ummah. This can impede the ability of Muslims to act as a defined and unified interest group in the United States. Head covering could and should conceivably unify coreligionists, and yet it seems to often create hierarchies of piety that reflect women's different interpretations of what it means to be a pious Muslim woman. Again, quite a few of our survey respondents challenge the notion that head covering is the only way to display modesty and piety or that it is even religiously mandated.

In general, our research has not found that the act of head covering exacerbates any racial or ethnic tensions within the Muslim community itself. The intracommunity tensions that the head covering does intensify arise from presumed judgment from other Muslims surrounding levels of piety. These tensions underlie the question of authenticity in religious practice and the headscarf's role in the boundary work of cultivating historical and evolving Muslim-American identity. Islamic dress more generally plays into common performative and ritualized aspects of Islam, many of which have become more publicly prevalent as the United States openly embraced a more multicultural ethos from the 1960s onward. Muslim women can present an alternative future through their head-covering behaviors by potentially privileging their Muslim identity over their ethnic identity and "displaying that 'Muslimness' by wearing *hijab* and *jilbab*" (Ali 2005, 516). But, as noted earlier, this identity prioritization also carries costs: Xara worries that "there is this whole thing about trying to wash away race [in the Muslim-American community]."

The conception of the American ummah as color-blind has been especially prevalent among second-generation immigrant women and has now even been taken up by African-American women sympathetic to Muslim black power movements (Karim 2005, 2008). A unified Muslim identity appears to be an objective for many Muslims, especially with creeping Islamophobia in the United States. While the American ummah is still very much an emergent concept, the increased social marginalization, alienation, and Islamophobia faced by Muslim Americans may yet politically bind the community across differences in ethnicity, denomination, and even levels of piety. In fact, our focus group participants generally perceive the Muslim community as more cohesive than conflictual, providing a stark contrast to their interactions with non-Muslims, which were overwhelmingly cited as conflictual.[34] We discuss these experiences with non-Muslim othering and their implications for the Muslim community and head-covering practices in chapter 3.

---

34. In the focus groups there were seventy-three occurrences of positive or "cohesive" discourse about the Muslim community and sixty-one occurrences of negative or "conflictual" discourse.

CHAPTER 3

Visibly Different

> Sometimes, people treat me as an "other," different, foreign. I feel that when people see me, they don't see me as a peer or another individual with her own beliefs and ideas, but as a Muslim and a poster child for Islam. When I answer questions, I must be answering for Muslims.
>
> —Arab-American survey respondent

In the statement above, one of our Arab-American survey respondents from Ohio describes her experience with being treated as the "other." She believes that most Americans automatically assume she is different and that her difference overpowers her individuality. Such experiences are common among individuals from minority groups. This chapter examines Muslim-American women's experiences with "othering" in the United States. Othering involves the development and affirmation of social difference in relation to oneself and treating the other as if they are intrinsically different or alien. These differences can involve many identities including class, race, gender, culture, and/or religious practice. The concept of othering also consists of defining another person or group's difference and converting it into "otherness." We examine the wide range of othering behaviors toward Muslims in America. We also focus on our respondents' perception of their acceptance within American society and explore questions associated with social belonging as a backdrop for cultural integration. While othering does also occur within the Muslim community as discussed in chapter 2, this chapter focuses on covered women's experiences of being othered by non-Muslims.

When Omar Mateen, an American Muslim claiming affiliation with ISIS, killed forty-nine people at the Pulse nightclub in Orlando, Florida, in 2016, the then-Republican presidential nominee Donald Trump proposed enhancing surveillance of American mosques. He suggested creating an exclusively

Muslim national database to aid in profiling terror threats, and potentially even banning Muslims from entering and immigrating to the United States. Despite Trump's implications about Muslim otherness, survey research shows American Muslims are one of the most hardworking groups when it comes to integrating into mainstream American culture. A 2011 Gallup poll reports that American Muslims exhibit high levels of loyalty to the United States and are more optimistic than other faith groups about their future (Gallup 2011).[1] The same survey reveals that American Muslims also embrace their religious and American identities at roughly equal levels (Younis 2011). Furthermore, while they are less likely to be registered to vote than adherents of other religions (Gallup 2011), they vote as frequently as non-Muslims in American elections (Kohut, Lugo, and Keeter 2007) and are on par with the rest of the US population in average income and education (Johnson 2011; Golshan 2016). In short, the civic behavior of American Muslims is not exceptional relative to other Americans.

Nevertheless, many American Muslims (and other minority groups) experience systematic injustices and social discrimination. In 2010, Gallup found that more Muslims (48%) said they experienced discrimination than any other religious group.[2] Even non-Muslims recognize pervasive prejudice against American Muslims: according to the 2015 American Values Survey administered by the Public Religion Research Institute, seven in ten Americans say there is "a lot" of discrimination against Muslims. However, even as they identify Muslims as targets of discrimination, a majority (56%) of Americans in the same survey believe that Islam contradicts American values and the American way of life (Cooper et al. 2015). Sometimes these beliefs manifest in direct violence against Muslim Americans or their religious institutions. After the religiously motivated 2015 terrorist attacks in Paris and San Bernardino, California, the rate of hate crimes against Muslims tripled to thirty-eight in one month (Lichtblau 2015). These crimes included arson attacks and vandalism, death threats, shootings, and assaults against women wearing the headscarf.

---

1. This finding is particularly interesting considering that the timing of this survey was well after the 2001 passage of the USA PATRIOT Act and the 2004 incident when the Census Bureau illegally shared data on Middle Eastern households with the Department of Homeland Security. These caused considerable alarm among these communities and civil rights experts and resulted in comparisons to the unethical use of Census data in locating Japanese Americans for forced placement in internment camps during World War II (Clemetson 2004).

2. Interestingly, the percentage of Muslims reporting discrimination does not vary substantially by race, though Arab Americans report the highest rates (52%). Mormons report the second-highest rates, with 31 percent claiming to have experienced racial or religious discrimination (Gallup 2017).

Muslim women who wear the head covering are particularly vulnerable to these types of assaults because the head covering unambiguously identifies them as members of a religious minority. The headscarf serves as an identifier of difference, establishing a symbolic boundary marker between Muslims and non-Muslims and rendering Muslim women vulnerable to othering on the part of the non-Muslim mainstream. While difference is a more or less factual attribute that distinguishes an individual from another person or group, its conversion into otherness requires the construction of sameness and difference through categories of us versus them. Differentiating us from them, in-group from out-group, requires construction of symbolic boundaries that conceptually differentiate people into separate groups using some boundary criteria (Lamont and Molnár 2002, 168). The head-covering practices of Muslim women present one such symbolic boundary. The reactions of non-Muslims and the resulting experiences of Muslim women being treated as different create new and altered possibilities for exchange, understanding, and misunderstanding within a context where the symbolism and the meaning of the headscarf is negotiated and contested.

The events of September eleventh produced an environment of fear and threat for Muslim Americans in the United States. The Muslim community has witnessed aggressive acts rooted in fear or bigotry and sometimes both. However, othering is a much more complex social phenomenon than a quick reaction to a frightening trigger such as the September eleventh terrorist attacks. Othering does not always result in experiences that our respondents consider negative—instead, they sometimes see themselves as beneficiaries of exceptionally courteous treatment as a result of their visible faith. Consequently, in this chapter we also consider whether constructs of "the other" can have positive social benefits and to what extent othering can be used to correct inequalities without reinforcing them.

The Headscarf and the Spectrum of Othering

No matter the target of othering behavior, the process of othering is associated with the creation and maintenance of symbolic boundaries, particularly when the value judgments implied by the otherer are shared largely across society. Symbolic boundaries are essential tools in creating categories of us versus them, in the formation and transformation of group identities, and in establishing firm conceptions of self-worth. When the symbolic boundaries created by othering become institutionalized, individuals and minority groups may find themselves in conditions of structural inequality, social degradation, and subordination (e.g., boundaries defining global colonialism or race in the

United States), which is why othering has often been associated with socially destructive behaviors that contribute to prejudice and discrimination. However, the evidence provided by the women in our survey and focus groups encourages the construction of a more expansive conception of othering that captures the varied realities of these "others" living within American society.

Othering is related to discrimination, which in its most basic form constitutes the recognition of difference between people or things and carries a negative connotation. It is commonly associated with unjust prejudice, which is an action or opinion rooted in a negative bias or predisposition.[3] However, our data on Muslim women's experiences suggest that othering does not always issue from a negative construction of difference or prejudicial thinking. As we conceive it, othering includes the recognition of differences between people and actions that follow from it. Sometimes a group is provided with special benefits based on their difference. But even if an action is beneficial, if it is prompted by the perception of difference, it carries implications for the creation and maintenance of symbolic and social boundaries.

Judging partly on the evidence we consider here, we believe othering occurs on a spectrum ranging from social inclusion to social exclusion. This includes more benevolent forms of othering in which individuals might receive special treatment on account of their "otherness" and hate-motivated exclusion othering, which seeks to remove the "other" from mainstream society. All these categories represent a clear construct of a "them" in an us-versus-them conceptual framework and therefore promote the formation of symbolic and potentially social boundaries.

Figure 3.1 illustrates the variety of othering experiences described by our research participants, falling along a spectrum of social exclusion. Along the spectrum we identify five categories of othering behaviors, which do not necessarily correspond to fixed points on the spectrum and are not mutually exclusive. An advantage of conceptualizing a more fluid spectrum is that it allows for some degree of overlap between categories or ambiguity in specific instances. Furthermore, though the categories offer discrete descriptions of the intent behind the othering, methods of othering can span the spectrum.

---

3. Gordon Allport is credited with the foundational study of prejudice, which he defined as "an antipathy based on a faulty and inflexible generalization" (1979, 9). In recent years, the academic treatment of prejudice has expanded to allow for a much more complex reality of discrimination in which prejudice is not necessarily tied to antipathy and can be based in truth at the group level, and in which the ideas are flexible across context (see Dovidio, Glick, and Rudman 2005). The modern understanding of prejudice corresponds closely to our conceptualization of othering. As we define it, "other" is a verb, while "prejudice" is a noun and is typically the product of othering.

	Benevolent othering	Condescending othering	Avoidance othering	Assimilative othering	Exclusionary othering
Definition	Differentiating between groups with the intent to advantage the "othered" group, potentially in an attempt to compensate for inequalities	Differentiating between groups and (implicitly or explicitly) highlighting a perceived deficiency in the "othered" group	Differentiating between groups with the intent to avoid the "othered" group whenever possible	Differentiating between groups with the intent to require the "other" to conform to some generalized standard	Differentiating between groups with the intent to exclude or expel the "other" group from mainstream society
Intention	To benefit minority group	To demonstrate superiority	To avoid minority group	To assimilate minority group	To exclude minority group
Example	Affirmative action, Quotas	Benevolent sexism	Segregation	Cultural assimilation	Ethnic cleansing

FIGURE 3.1. The spectrum of othering

For example, microaggressions can manifest in any of the categories as tools of social exclusion, as can verbal communication.[4]

While we do not expect this spectrum to apply universally to the experiences of all othered groups, it does correspond with observed behaviors toward many minority groups in American society, especially racial minorities and women. Figure 3.1 provides examples of documented behaviors that may exemplify types of othering. In what follows, we unpack these categories and the associated examples with reference to the testimony of our survey and focus group participants.

Covered Muslim women's experiences are a special case for illustrating the multidimensional nature of othering because they are often at the intersection of multiple systems of cultural difference, including gender, religion, and sometimes race and/or ethnicity. The multiple dimensions of othering have been well documented with reference to race and sex. In particular, research on intersectionality suggests that addressing the social reactions to race and gender as separate categories is insufficient because individuals at the intersection of these systems of inequality experience unique and cross-cutting forms of discrimination. Further, inequality is an issue not only of intergroup relations but also of intragroup relations. For example, while women of color are often disadvantaged vis-à-vis men of color, they are also disadvantaged by comparison with white women. Muslim-American women who cover regularly occupy, or are perceived to occupy, at least two of these intersections in especially visible ways, making the exploration of their othering experiences particularly evocative.

Benevolent Othering

As we conceive it, "benevolent othering" is the most inclusive form of othering because it seeks to support members of minority or historically disadvantaged groups. Individuals who engage in these practices recognize the construction of difference and alter their behavior to be more accepting and inclusive to members of the othered group than they might otherwise be. Benevolent otherers may be motivated by a number of considerations: they may favor the othered group; they may be trying to correct or compensate for personal or societal biases; or they may simply recognize and appreciate diversity.

---

4. Microaggressions are everyday intentional or unintentional snubs or insults that communicate bias to targeted populations exclusively on the basis of their marginalized group membership (Sue 2010).

The idea of benevolent othering is mainly developed in studies on positive action or positive discrimination.[5] Positive action describes efforts to encourage and support underrepresented groups. Positive discrimination is the recognition that certain characteristics have disadvantaged a group of people through no fault of their own, and involves an effort to compensate by providing a particular benefit based on those same characteristics. Positive discrimination distinguishes between equality of provision and equality of outcome, and it suggests that identical treatment in circumstances with social structural differences may sometimes serve to reinforce or preserve inequality in outcomes.[6] Benevolent othering may manifest as positive discrimination, but we define benevolent othering as including behavior that would not normally be considered prejudicial toward anyone. For example, any benevolent othering that does not involve the zero-sum distribution of resources (e.g., positive feelings, admiration, kindness) does not necessarily have a negatively prejudicial intention, even if a benevolently othered individual may feel discomfort as a result of preferential treatment.

With our focus group participants and survey respondents, we observed that othering can take a benevolent form when covered Muslim women are treated with more respect, greeted with compliments, or provided with more personal space in an effort to accommodate their difference. Many survey respondents mention receiving compliments about their scarves from non-Muslims: "I have had people in stores and public places admire my scarf and say it looks beautiful or ask me what my heritage/background is." This statement reflects the way stereotypes can manifest in benevolent othering, in which non-Muslims are complimentary and friendly but simultaneously enact stereotypes, as revealed by questions into the background of this (white and US-born) hijabi.

Some of our focus group and survey respondents report being treated with more respect because of their head covering. The word "respect" is explicitly mentioned 168 times in the 451 descriptions of positive othering behavior within the survey: "They show more respect. They approach me differently than they approach everyone else, in a good way." Many of our respondents

---

5. See Noon 2010 for an argument justifying the use of positive action and discrimination in the workplace.

6. Positive discrimination is implemented in policy platforms such as affirmative action and electoral gender quotas. See Crosby 2004 for a thorough examination of affirmative action in the United States and Krook 2009 for a thorough discussion of gender quota implementation worldwide. Positive discrimination is sometimes labeled affirmative action or reverse discrimination, with the suggestion that a majority group is being unfairly discriminated against through the efforts to advantage a minority group (typically in an attempt to discredit the effort).

describe how non-Muslims alter their behavior in order to accommodate Muslim sensibilities. Most often they mention that many non-Muslims engage in self-censorship ("They don't curse or talk about their sexual relationships with me"), that they desexualize social interactions (Ghaliya does not experience men rubbing against her in the subway anymore and instead encounters "a lot of respect" since starting to cover), and that they provide more personal space (Hafeeza says "people keep their distance").[7] These testimonies suggest that either actual or perceived positive stereotyping underlines behaviors of benevolent othering. As one of our older survey respondents describes, "I am recognized throughout the world and often greeted as a Muslim woman. I find this quite marvelous."

Our participants seem to interpret all these acts as examples of respectful treatment by which non-Muslims are making an effort to accommodate Muslims living within their community. Assuming that our participants are correct in their attribution of positive intent, these actions also enforce an awareness of difference, which is sometimes accentuated by apologies if non-Muslims fear they have insulted a Muslim nearby. This awareness is also often coupled with stereotypical thinking about Islam or the head covering. For example, Shakira tells us that she will frequently have conversations about her headscarf with well-intentioned non-Muslims.[8] She believes that people want to know whether she is forced to wear the head covering and that they often have an interest in liberating her: "When people ask me questions about covering or wearing the headscarf, almost in that same conversation they tell me, 'I believe women should wear what they want.'" While the questions about her head covering practice reflect commonly shared assumptions among non-Muslims that the practice is imposed, Shakira's endorsement of women's freedoms also supports her own right to wear the headscarf. She also recognizes that right as one of a larger set of freedoms within the United States.

When discussing their diverse experiences with benevolent othering, our respondents will frequently generalize about a particular demographic group's response to the head covering. We discuss in chapters 1 and 2 the perception that non-Muslim men and Muslims generally respond to the headscarf with increased respect. Many of our survey respondents extend the perception of respect to explicitly non-Muslim groups and attribute increased respect to a common experience with religion in the United States, not limited to

---

7. Ghaliya is a thirty-seven-year-old covered white native-born American in Massachusetts. Hafeeza is a thirty-one-year-old covered white native-born American in Massachusetts.

8. Shakira is a twenty-seven-year-old covered black native-born American living in Illinois.

experience with Islam. These respondents connect their head-covering practice to similar practices within Christianity and Judaism.

Eleven of our survey respondents explicitly refer to Catholic nuns as a frame of reference for non-Muslims when they encounter covered women in public, with sometimes entertaining outcomes. Ghaliya in Boston tells us, "When you see a nun or you see a Jewish woman covered or dressing modestly, it's basically the same idea." And one of our survey respondents notes, "For some people it makes them curious to ask questions, which also gives me an opportunity to talk about Islam. . . . For example, I say, 'In every statue, drawing, painting, have you ever seen the image of Virgin Mary without her long cloak or uncovered?'" In this way, our respondents actively participate in the consolidation of communal religious identity and use it to confront discrimination and create community cohesion. Sometimes the connection is made for them: one of our survey respondents tells a story about a woman in California who exclaimed to her, "You look like the Virgin Mary!"

In addition to these interreligious associations, the religious nature of practicing hijab primes Muslims with a set of expectations about how people (and Muslims, especially) should react to the head covering. The practice of hijab is rooted in modesty and is associated with decency, propriety, and self-respect. Some of our respondents attribute their treatment to a general culture of respect around religious practice. When describing her experiences of othering, one of our survey respondents from North Carolina suggests, "If it's a Muslim, they treat me with more respect and are nicer around me. If it is a non-Muslim, most of the time I actually get respect because most people have come to be educated that I practice hijab due to religious or piety reasons." Similarly, a forty-six-year-old from Missouri observes, "People of other faiths have told me that they really respect that I choose to follow my religion despite so much negativity about it." A sixty-four-year-old from Maryland suggests a correlation between respectful treatment and knowledge of and experience with religion: "I receive greetings of *salaam* [peace] from those who respect Islam but are not Muslim—Christians and Jews who understand show polite respect."

These respondents may be picking up on a distinctive feature of American culture that values religion as a unifying social bond and moral enforcer and "allows people of one faith [to] see themselves as similar to people from another faith by virtue of their common participation in 'religion'" (Gordon 2008, 48). As we discuss in the introduction to this book, Gordon identifies cultural religion as a key feature that prevented the creation of a French-style headscarf "affair" in the United States. The testimonies of our survey respondents affirm the continued relevance of this construct within the American public sphere.

Overall, benevolent othering behaviors come from a good-willed intention to accommodate diversity. However, the goodness of this intention often serves to reinforce the essential difference of the other. Even as our respondents are grateful for the accommodation they receive within society, they simultaneously recognize that these behaviors set them apart from the mainstream. Awareness and emphasis of difference can reinforce a sense of alienation for the othered, even if they benefit from their distinctiveness. Further, if mainstream society is generally hostile to the othered, the acts of benevolent othering could be viewed as accommodating a group with some sort of presumed negative difference and so reinforce inequality.

Condescending Othering

Condescending otherers may also be well-intentioned toward the othered group, and the subsequent actions may appear to be friendly or accommodating. However, condescending othering distinguishes itself though the assumptions that lead to the othering. While benevolent othering comes from a desire to celebrate or accommodate, condescending othering assumes that the person or group in question is somehow inferior.

The idea of a condescending form of othering is mainly developed in studies on sexism. Benevolent sexism involves holding positive attitudes toward women while simultaneously holding more stereotypical views about women and their restricted roles in society (Glick and Fiske 1996). Women on the receiving end of benevolent sexism may perceive their experience in a positive light, but since these behaviors are still grounded in common assumptions about women's restricted roles, they eventually serve to justify differences between the sexes. According to Glick and Fiske, "Though the stereotypes of women contain many positive traits, the positive traits relate to social-emotional, not agentic dimensions, so women are portrayed as being nice but incompetent." They elaborate further on this idea, stating that the ideology of benevolent sexism combines "notions of the exploited group's lack of competence to exercise structural power with self-serving 'benevolent' justifications" (ibid., 492). Unlike our category of benevolent othering, which is intended to capture moments when the difference between groups is accentuated in order to promote ideals of fairness and equity, benevolent sexism is based on assumptions of inequality, even if kindly intended.

The condescending othering reported by our covered focus group participants and survey respondents exemplifies the multifaceted nature of the othering confronted by our participants as women, as Muslims, and frequently as ethnic minorities. The othering they describe is typically related to assumptions about their religious faith, language skills, educational achievement status, and in some instances their ability to be independent agents who can think, speak, and act for themselves. Dilshad summarizes some of the condescending assumptions about covered women:

> When someone wears a headscarf people tend to think "Oh how sad it is, what a pity, she's oppressed, she doesn't have rights," but being an independent woman and going to a top college in the United States and still choosing to wear a headscarf shows that I'm not oppressed and I choose to cover my body because it helps people not to objectify me. When men talk to me they don't see my physical features, they tend to focus on what I'm saying, on my opinions. This shows the other side and how a headscarf protects, provides modesty, and is not oppression.[9]

Behaviors and attitudes representing condescending othering toward covered Muslim women neither constitute affirmative responses to head covering, as in the case of benevolent othering, nor demand a change from covered Muslim women, as with more aggressive forms of othering like assimilation othering. Rather, condescension elicits either explicitly or implicitly patronizing or disrespectful actions.

One of the most ironic demonstrations of condescending othering relates to the mainstream assumption that the headscarf signals oppression. Many of our survey respondents and focus group participants have been told that they need not wear the head covering anymore because they are in America and have the freedom to shed their headscarf. These comments are usually grounded in the assumption that wearing the head covering is not a choice outside the United States, particularly in Muslim-majority countries. Although these comments may be well intended, they are based on the presumption that the headscarf is essentially an imposition and that given the choice and relevant information about the constitutional protections regarding religious expression in the United States, women would not follow the practice. For example, a survey respondent reports being told, "You know, you live in America now. You are free. You don't have to do that." Similarly, other respondents report comments such as "You are in America now. You can take it off." Other people will tell them that because America is a free country, covered women "can take the liberty" of removing the headscarf. Though these statements acknowledge that the constitutional protections and freedoms provided in the United States give Muslim women the right not to cover, they

---

9. Dilshad is a twenty-year-old white covered noncitizen living in Virginia.

ignore that freedom of religious expression also protects the practice of covering as a personal act and as a form of religious expression.

Sometimes religious beliefs appear to encourage condescending othering. Samar reports the religiously patronizing behavior she experienced in the subway when she recalls that "sweet little old ladies" on the train would say to her, "Darling, do you know that you are going to burn in hell?"[10] Samar continues to explain that she used to sit down and talk to people about her faith and explain why she wore the head covering, but after a while she got tired of justifying herself and her beliefs and chose to ignore these condescending and hurtful comments. Another survey respondent had a complete stranger tell her that she would "pray for [her] and people like [her]," while yet another respondent laments, "People talk to me as if I need to be saved from my religion." These instances of condescension express attitudes of religious superiority—often that Christianity is morally superior to Islam—and disrespect Muslim women's faith and religion, even though the desire to "save" covered women may be genuine.

Condescending othering toward covered Muslim women is also sometimes grounded in assumptions about their ability to speak English. Our survey respondents frequently report instances when non-Muslims speak to them loudly or slowly or even address comments or questions to their husbands. One survey participant recounts an experience when she tried to register for courses in her doctoral program: "People at registration kept speaking in overenunciated words that were slow and spaced out with many hand motions. 'English test that way, English test that way.' So I smiled and put my transcripts, which include a master's in linguistics, into the window box. I have two bachelor's and two master's and two doctoral degrees. The registrar said, 'Oh, I guess you can enroll.'"

Assumptions about the ability to speak English build on prior assumptions that Muslim women are ignorant, uneducated, oppressed, and/or foreigners who do not know that head covering is not required in their new social and political environment. For example, one of our survey respondents observes, "People talk to me like I've been forced to wear my scarf like an oppressed woman. I don't speak with an accent, but when I am covered, I am always asked where am I from. Others in the street will tell me, 'Welcome to America!' like I just landed, when I've lived most of my life here."

Many of our participants find condescension to be offensive and demoralizing, regardless of the original intentions of non-Muslims. One native-born

---

10. Samar is a covered thirty-year-old South Asian American living in Illinois.

survey respondent in Maine notes, "People are very rude to me. They often assume I don't speak English. Though I have three degrees and eight and a half years of education, even when I use perfect English, they assume I'm stupid. I had such a hard time as a teacher that parents came to conferences just to tell me they don't respect me. So I left."

The implications of condescending othering are in some ways more serious than the implications of benevolent othering. While both serve to accentuate difference, condescending othering may reinforce forms of hostile othering. For example, research shows that indicators of benevolent sexism and more hostile forms of sexism are positively correlated, which suggests that both types of sexism are components of a discriminatory or sexist ideology (Glick and Fiske 1996, 507). We would expect similar correlations between the assumptions underlying condescending othering and those motivating the more exclusionary forms of othering directed at Muslims, suggesting that these forms of othering are all rooted in prejudice.

Avoidance Othering

Avoidance othering is exclusionary and typically nonverbal, involving physically avoiding interactions with those perceived as the "other," or reacting with distaste or hesitancy when contact is unavoidable. Avoidance othering has been implemented politically through policies of segregation, such as the 1896 *Plessy v. Ferguson* decision allowing for "separate but equal" provision of public facilities for African Americans. It is possible for avoidance othering of this type to be rooted in benevolent intentions if the otherer genuinely believes that the othered group is better off in its own homogenous communities or that this guarantees mutual security. However, the latter belief has been discredited by the clear inequalities in application. The 1954 *Brown v. Board of Education* ruling declared that separate facilities are inherently unequal and therefore cannot be constitutionally supported. More recently, questions about segregation have reemerged with reference to gender and sexuality. The most controversial debates have centered on toilet facilities, single-sex institutions, and religiously based discrimination in the service industry. These examples illustrate the persistence of structural segregation justified with reference to physicality, vulnerability, or personal preference, which the practice of head covering can fall under fairly easily.

While structural segregation can be legislated against, social or interpersonal segregation is simultaneously more pervasive and less explicit and therefore more difficult to confront politically. Social discrimination typically results in de facto segregation, but it is based on underlying economic conditions or relational preferences rather than on formalized rules and institutions. For the average person, social segregation would be reflected in distinctly homogenous friend groups, even when the surrounding environment may be very diverse.

American Muslims are not immune to notions of avoidance othering, even within their own communities. As we discuss in chapter 1, through the mechanisms of the headscarf and gender segregation in the mosque, Islamic belief systems can promote symbolic, social, and structural segregation between the genders. The headscarf is meant to separate men from women, but it is also a mobile form of segregation that allows women to navigate society and interact with others from a protected place. Essentially, the headscarf is a way for women to emerge from a segregated environment into an integrated environment and to avoid extreme exclusionary othering such as the practice of *purdah,* or female seclusion. Within non-Muslim societies, however, Muslim women experience avoidance on a regular basis from men and women alike.

For example, one survey respondent described how she feels othered when "sometimes people will not make eye contact, or they will give you a three-finger [hesitant] handshake when you wear a scarf or hijab. They don't realize they are scrunching up their face and not fully extending their hand to shake your hand. Often, they will turn up one side of their face in a scowl." Similar instances of avoidance othering include the perception that "people are often wide-eyed and stiff when they have to speak" and "some people pull their children closer, give a wider berth when passing."

Avoidance othering can be either a passive or an active activity, which distinguishes it from the other types of othering on the spectrum. The consequences of avoidance othering can be as severe as those associated with the other forms of othering, as avoidance signals discomfort and distaste, which suggest that the "us" and the "them" cannot interact normally in public or belong to the same community.

Assimilative Othering

While benevolent, condescending, and avoidance othering do not necessarily demand a change in the behavior of the "other," assimilative othering is characterized by a demand for assimilation from covered Muslim women. This demand is sometimes reflected in verbal attacks that offend or insult them for being different. Assimilative othering assumes that there is an ideologically coherent mainstream to which the other does not belong and that in order to become a member of mainstream society, the othered must shed their otherness. These assumptions are most commonly articulated with reference to immigrants through the policies and expectations of immigrant assimilation. Historically, assimilation has been associated with nativism, ethnic conformity, and the assumption that Anglo-American culture and values are constants that minority groups must adapt to.[11] By the 1990s, formal expectations of assimilation began to recede and were replaced by multiculturalism, a philosophy much more sensitive to and encouraging of difference.

By the early 2000s, however, concerns over moral relativism, fragmented identities, and equality called multiculturalism into question, and signs of a "return of assimilation" appeared (Brubaker 2001). This new form of assimilation transforms the concept to a multigenerational and disaggregated process of integration, which often prioritizes assimilation in certain areas of civic and economic life rather than focusing on cultural conformity. Brubaker argues that this is because "the notion of a universally acknowledged 'core culture' has lost all its plausibility since the late 1960s" (ibid., 540). However, we find that the cultural conversation has shifted since 2001, and while the American core culture may remain ambiguous, there seem to be emerging understandings about what American culture is *not*: American culture is apparently not Muslim. The majority of the respondents in the 2015 American Values Survey reflect this sentiment and believe that Islam contradicts American values and the American way of life. As a result, in the social sphere, Muslim Americans face demands that they assimilate, and the nature of the assimilation—including the erasure of Muslim religious and cultural life from the public eye—resembles that from the early twentieth century.

Assimilative othering often directly targets the headscarf as an object deemed to be offensive, un-American, or merely inappropriately different. One survey participant references this sentiment herself when she describes her head covering as "obviously anomalous garb." Dorcas recounts a story of strangers approaching her and telling her to "take this shit off your head!"[12] Similarly, one of our survey respondents reports that among the other negative reactions about her head covering, a stranger approached her and told her "to take off [her] fucking garb."

---

11. Assimilation was defined in the American interwar period as "Americanization," which is a philosophy that expected ethnic groups to unlearn their cultural traits in order to relearn the values of the host society and become fully integrated. The theory was most clearly articulated by Milton Gordon (1964), who proposed a multidimensional formulation that allowed for variance in the processes and outcomes of assimilation in the United States, ranging from acculturation to civic assimilation. Despite the variance in process, Gordon perceived acculturation and assimilation as a unidirectional acceptance of Anglo-American culture and values.

12. Dorcas is a thirty-five-year-old Arab covered noncitizen living in Virginia.

By viewing the head covering as an imposition or offense, assimilative othering demands Muslim women shed the head covering. The emphasis that they are "now" in America and must uncover, symbolically constructs the headscarf as an abnormal practice in the United States. As a result, assimilative othering serves to maintain the symbolic boundaries between "us who are free" and those "others who cover" and hence are not free. One of our survey respondents reacts to this binary symbolic categorization, calling out its double standard: "The lawyer told me to take it off for a divorce trial. I refused as it is my right as an American with freedom of religion and dress. Others wear miniskirts; why can't I wear a scarf and cover my body as I like?"

On occasion, the perceived contradiction between the American and Muslim lifestyles manifests in open assumptions that visible Muslims are in some way associated with terrorism. Haarisa experienced an offensive and casual form of assimilative othering, which clearly illustrates the pervasiveness of the bigotry.[13] She recalls, "I was snowed in so I went to the airport really early and I'm just sitting there, nothing to do, so I went to get something to eat. I ask this guy if he can watch my luggage and he's like 'It's not going to blow up, is it?' . . . Stuff like that has happened quite often."

The generalization of the terrorist threat to include anyone who looks recognizably Muslim is especially alienating. Not only do these types of comments question whether Haarisa or her hijab belong in American society, but they also frame covered women as potential enemies of American society. As Semra phrases it, "Being hijabi or being of a certain ethnic background almost means that you are in a state of presumptive guilt. You are almost criminalized."[14] Through the presumption of guilt, those who engage in assimilative othering on the basis of security concerns effectively punish covered Muslim women for being different. The only way a Muslim woman can seemingly atone for this is by shedding her difference (i.e., removing the headscarf) as it is embodied in the head covering.

These experiences demonstrate a partial public acceptance of the ethnocentric expectations of assimilation that were more commonly expressed (and politically affirmed) in the early twentieth century. American public institutions do not conform to these standards of assimilation today, but the symbolic boundaries created by the social understandings of American identity may play a more important role in the daily lives of Muslims living in

---

13. Haarisa is a twenty-six-year-old South Asian covered foreign-born dual citizen living in New York.

14. Semra is a twenty-seven-year-old South Asian covered American living in Illinois.

the United States than the public institutions and legal protections of diversity do. Even if those pushing cultural assimilation are a vocal minority, their expressed beliefs deny the reality of a Muslim-American identity. Further, they make Muslim Americans aware that a segment of the American population is unlikely to ever see them as equal citizens unless they erase every sign of their religious beliefs.

Exclusion Othering

Exclusion othering is the most extreme form of othering on our spectrum, typically involving hate-motivated verbal and nonverbal abuse that unconditionally rejects Muslims as members of American society. Different from assimilative othering, which represents demands for acculturation, exclusion othering represents outright refusal of difference and the insistence that it be removed. In this sense it is the most dramatic and aggressive type of avoidance othering.

In the most the extreme instance, the intent behind the exclusionary othering that our research participants experience is identical to the rationale behind ethnic cleansing: it is to remove the "other" from mainstream culture.[15] The most common example of exclusion othering in both our focus group and survey data is the comment "Go back to your country!" This is an uncompromising discourse forbidding the head covering within American society. For example, one of our survey respondents mentions being shouted at with calls of "Muslims out of America! Go back to your country!" and other racist comments such as "sand nigger." Another respondent reports being told to "Go back to Afghanistan, Osama!" These comments reflect the belief on the part of some non-Muslims that the head covering is unconditionally un-American, that it represents a threat and must be removed, and further, that the women wearing the head covering must be removed, regardless of whether they are citizens. One of our US-born Arab survey respondents reports that she had been stopped a couple of times to be told that she is an "abomination" to America and that she should just go "home," a suggestion she describes as "ironic, because I am home." These instances of

---

15. While exclusion othering does not always result in ethnic cleansing, ethnic cleansing will always be executed with reference to exclusion othering. Ethnic cleansing seeks to systematically remove an undesirable population with the aim of creating a more homogenous population, and it includes a number of tactics ranging from forced migration to rape, murder, or genocide. Cleansing is the "dark side of democracy" because democracy "always carried with it the possibility that the majority might tyrannize minorities, and this possibility carries more ominous consequences in certain types of multi-ethnic environments" (Mann 2005, 2).

othering unequivocally exclude covered Muslim women from American society, rejecting the women's own feelings of belonging and American identity.

On occasion, exclusionary othering behaviors move beyond words and into physical violence. Our respondents report assaults ranging from being spat on to run over or charged by a vehicle. One of our respondents describes being physically attacked by a Spanish tourist in the United States blaming her for the Madrid bombings. Fortunately, our respondents report personal experience with physical violence infrequently, but most of them suggest that they either directly know or know of Muslim women who have been assaulted.

Though the majority of forms of othering challenge the notion that Muslim women have a place in American society (benevolent othering is the exception), exclusionary othering unequivocally says "no." Moving beyond assimilative othering, which demands that Muslim women adapt to fit into the mainstream, exclusionary othering either insists that they be removed or results in violent behaviors intended to encourage the women to remove themselves. The existence of these behaviors and the underlying symbolic boundaries that encourage (or at least do not dissuade) them have very worrying implications for sustaining peaceful, pluralist, and ultimately democratic society. Generally, these more severe forms of othering have not been officially tolerated within the United States. However, should the state overlook the issue, exclusionary othering could cement symbolic boundaries into social boundaries with serious consequences for democratic pluralism.

The Frequency of Othering

While Muslims have encountered othering and discrimination throughout the history of the United States, the frequency of hate crimes against Muslims has increased in the twenty-first century. Figure 3.2 reveals the total number of anti-Islamic hate crimes reported to the Federal Bureau of Investigation (FBI) by year since 1996. In the United States, hate crimes against Muslims spiked in 2001 in reaction to the September eleventh attacks and subsequently stabilized to between 100 and 200 crimes per year. A second spike of 257 hate crimes in 2015 was associated with the Paris terrorist attacks on November thirteenth and the shootings in San Bernardino on December second of that year (Lichtblau 2015).[16] According to data collected by the Southern Poverty

---

16. According to a special report by the Center for the Study of Hate and Extremism, in the wake of the Paris attacks and San Bernardino mass shootings, the monthly rate of hate crimes against Muslims in the United States has nearly tripled, including an increase in assaults against Muslim women wearing the hijab (Levin 2015).

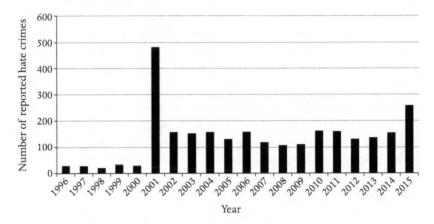

FIGURE 3.2.　Reported hate crime incidents against Muslims

Law Center, 867 hate incidents were reported in the ten days following the 2016 presidential election, and 49 of these incidents were explicitly anti-Muslim. Muslim-American women were also likely to experience the vitriol directed at immigrants, with 280 incidents of harassment reported against women (Miller and Werner-Winslow 2016).

The growing frequency of anti-Muslim hate crimes reflects an association between Islam and terrorism, which moved to the center of public awareness as a result of the generalization and racialization of the growing terrorist threat. The generalization of the terrorist threat to include anyone who might look Muslim deeply affects the daily experiences of covered Muslim women. In comparing how nuns are perceived as religious and representing the church while covered Muslim women are considered terrorists, Zia from Detroit shares her experiences in confronting discrimination and stereotyping in the post–September eleventh context: "Before . . . we never had any experiences before. I did not have an experience that someone would look at me [and wonder] why I am wearing this."[17]

The association of Islam with terrorism defines Muslim religiosity as essentially negative and even highly dangerous, thereby creating a particularly threatening version of the "othered." This process of othering invariably requires the mental construction of a monolithic Muslim identity in order to sustain the distinction between "us" and "them." It also reflects the workings of Orientalist discourses that juxtapose a civilized and rational image of the

---

17. Zia is a forty-seven-year-old covered foreign-born Arab American living in Michigan.

West against a violent cultural image of the East. Since these encounters take place within a Western domain, they lead to a situation in which covered Muslim women become targets of grievances against Islamic terrorism because they are seen as willing embodiments of a fundamentalist religion.

As a result of the backlash after September eleventh, some Muslim-American women decided to take off their head covering out of fear for their security. While discussing her experiences of stereotyping after September eleventh, Zia reports hearing about Muslim women getting "attacked for their hijab" and many of them taking off their scarf "because they were afraid," even though she herself never considered removing her headscarf. Conversely, Safia explicitly took her headscarf off "right after 9/11" after ten years of wearing it: "I had a little newborn and I had a little three-year old. I just did not feel safe walking around because I used to get all of these glares and nasty looks and it was not very comforting going to the grocery store, especially with two little kids. So I took it off."[18]

While Safia is in the minority—most of our focus group and survey participants did not remove their head covering in reaction to September eleventh—she is not alone. Of our 402 survey respondents who do not regularly wear a head covering, 272 (68 %) have covered at some previous point in their lives. When asked why they stopped wearing it, 76 people express fear of or an experience with a negative form of othering. Eighteen respondents (less than 5% of our overall sample) explicitly mention "discrimination" as the reason they stopped covering.

The increasing politicization of the Muslim head covering in the United States led some of our participants to modify their practice rather than remove the headscarf all together. For example, Semra, a South Asian woman from Chicago, explains how she became exposed to "the broader-global context of wearing the hijab" after the events of September eleventh. At the age of fourteen Semra started wearing a jilbab and recalls being "über-conservative" until September eleventh, when she was sixteen and one of her friends at high school came up to her and asked, "Do you think that the [terrorist hijackers] were Palestinian?" Semra observes, "It was so shocking to me. I didn't even realize how politicized my hijab was until that moment. It was my junior year that I actually stopped wearing the jilbab and just started dressing normally, wearing American clothing." Like Zia and Semra, many of our participants in focus group interviews perceive the events of September eleventh as a turning point in their awareness of the implications of head covering.

---

18. Safia is a thirty-six-year-old covered South Asian native-born American living in Illinois.

Some of our focus group participants report being in downtown Manhattan on the day of the September eleventh attacks. Among them, Samar was a couple of blocks away from the twin towers and was among the people who walked to Brooklyn that day. She remembers the reactions from non-Muslims as they were walking away from Manhattan: "There was this one lady on Brooklyn Bridge, she kept telling me, she kept following me, 'You need to take it off! They're going to kill you! You need to take it off!'. . . There were actually some other people saying, this one guy saying 'You did this! You Arabs did this!'" Samar mentions feeling "really anxious" and came to realize the personal security implications of being covered: "That was actually the first time that kind of brought to light that there might be a danger in wearing [the headscarf]. Even before we even knew what happened! All we knew was that the towers were on fire. Even then, I never considered taking it off."

The association of Islam with terrorism places covered Muslim women in a perpetually defensive position. Because of their visibility as members of the Muslim community, breaking down the monolithically constructed images of Islam has become the covered Muslim woman's burden. This burden to explain Islamic practice and faith to non-Muslims takes the form of a moral and religious obligation for many of our participants. While these themes will be taken up in chapter 4, it is important to note that some of our covered participants link the unique burden of faith ambassadorship to the negative stereotypes resulting from September eleventh. For example, Shakira resents the association of terrorist attacks with her faith and the subsequent expectation that she needs to continuously defend her head-covering practice: "I think we are constantly having to defend. . . . The association that they make between 9/11 to Muslims and that my people did it. Islam doesn't teach that. That is not the rhetoric. That's not the way we do it. Islam means peace. Don't kill innocents."

While spikes in hate crimes and discrimination are clearly associated with specific events, the general increase in anti-Islamic hate crimes over time is at least partly attributable to the growing size of the Muslim population in the United States. In fact, the share of Muslims in the US population is expected to double by 2015 (Mohamed 2016). That said, the post–September eleventh context presents a particular kind of social environment for Muslim women, where interactions between Muslims and non-Muslims seem as if they are "the work of an invisible hand or collective behavior of individuals acting in patterned responses" (Fiske 1998, 233). The pattern is one of exclusion and even sometimes violence: figure 3.2 shows a sharp surge in anti-Muslim hate crimes after September eleventh, and our respondents clearly identify these events as conditioning the social responses of non-Muslim Americans. In return, Muslims take a socially defensive position, which results in patterns of withdrawal from and engagement with non-Muslims and presumably more frequent instances of othering along the spectrum.

While only a few of our survey respondents report experiencing violent hate crimes, a vast majority experience more mild to moderate forms of othering. Figure 3.3 reveals the percentage of our survey respondents who believe they have experienced some form of othering. The survey first asks whether the respondent believes people behave "differently toward you when you wear your head covering." This question was asked only of covered women, and its phrasing deliberately requires the respondent to identify her headscarf as the trigger for any experience of othering. If the respondent suggests that she does perceive a difference in behavior, she is asked to describe an example of how people behaved. This open-ended response allows our respondents to determine what "behaving differently" meant for them and to individualize their responses.[19]

Our respondents experience othering in varied and diverse ways. The categories in figure 3.3 are the result of our analysis and coding of the open-ended

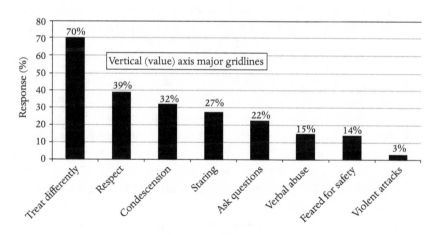

Type of othering

FIGURE 3.3.   The percentage of covered survey participants experiencing othering

---

19. Our question phrasing contrasts against questions like those in the Gallup polls, which ask about personal experiences with "racial or religious discrimination." We deliberately worded this question with the value-neutral phrase of "behave differently" to allow our respondents to interpret the question as relating to both positive and negative experiences. We argue that "discrimination" is contextually defined and may have different meanings in different countries.

responses to our questions about othering behaviors, with categories arising from these responses. Nearly 70 percent of our covered respondents report that they perceive some form of othering while wearing head coverings, and these reported experiences reflect the full spectrum of othering from benevolent to exclusionary.

Two different women sharing the exact same experiences might understand the events in seemingly contradictory ways depending on the context, the tone of speech, personal characteristics of the speaker or the recipient, or personal experience. There is an added layer of complexity through which we, as the researchers, attempt to make sense of our respondents' experiences. In several instances our respondents describe something that we could consider discriminatory or negatively prejudicial (e.g., men do not shake my hand, people cross over to the other side of the street) but that our respondents appear to regard as a positive outcome. In our analysis, we make every effort to convey the intent of the respondent rather than our own perception of the experience. We also classify responses according to whether our respondents report positive or negative experiences, relying on the tone in which they describe the experience. Positive othering is reported by 49 percent of our covered survey respondents and was usually signaled by words such as "respect," "support," "friendly," or describing personal enjoyment in the encounter. Negative experience, reported by 68%, were associated with words like "rude," "discriminate," "fear," or descriptions of unwanted, intimidating, belittling, or aggressive behavior. Many times individual women describe both types of experiences simultaneously. Nearly 28 percent of our respondents provide examples coded as both positive and negative. A survey respondent provides this assessment: "It depends on different people. Mostly people who are [respectful towards any] religion have a positive reaction, even though they themselves don't believe in any special religion. On the other hand, people who disagree with religious beliefs usually don't have positive behavior."

Many of the experiences described by our respondents are easy to fit into the spectrum of othering. Positive and respectful experiences reflect the benevolent forms of othering, while acts that make Muslim women fear for their safety or actual violent attacks are clear examples of exclusion othering. Other experiences are more complicated. Verbal abuse described by our participants could be classified as assimilative or exclusion othering, depending on what is said and the intent behind it. For example, one of our respondents provides a wide array of verbal abuse that she has experienced: "Told to take off my fucking garb, told to go back to my country, given the finger." Being told to remove the head covering is assimilative othering, while the command to go back to her country and the rude gesture qualify as exclusion othering. Notably, this respondent was a thirty-six-year-old, white, US-born American citizen.

Staring is similarly difficult to fit into the othering spectrum. It may reflect simple curiosity or friendliness but may likewise be malevolent. In addition, asking questions can take on a different meaning depending on the content of the question. For example, many of our respondents are asked whether their head coverings make them physically uncomfortable. We would consider this a form of benevolent or condescending othering, assuming that the question is asked out of concern. Others encounter questions like "Does your culture make you dress like that? You know there's freedom of expression here?" In a certain tone, these statements could be exclusionary, but in another, they could reflect condescension or even simple ignorance. We classify this specific example as condescension because the respondent reported that these people "felt bad" for her.

As previously mentioned, more of our respondents describe negative (68%) rather than positive (49%) experiences with othering. There are both physiological and psychological reasons why our respondents might be able to recall negative experiences with more clarity and why they might not think to recall positive instances when asked to describe how people "behave differently." Negative experiences have a greater psychological impact and are processed more thoroughly than good experiences, largely because people are highly motivated to avoid bad experiences (Baumeister et al. 2001).

In all likelihood, our respondents will regularly have positive or benign interactions with others but may not typically ascribe positive reactions to the headscarf, since the behavior does not stand out. Conversely, any negative behavior might be attributed to the headscarf as Muslim women attempt to process why they are being singled out for discrimination or differentiation. Even if our respondents are predisposed to notice and remember instances of discrimination, the frequency of reported negative behaviors among our respondents signals a threat to the inclusion of Muslim women in American society. Although a woman might generally be treated well, one negative experience can be enough to make her question the intentions of those around her and her own place within American society. Research on the psychological effects of ostracism finds that even brief episodes result in personal sadness and anger and can threaten fundamental needs like a sense of belonging, self-esteem, control, and recognition of one's meaningful existence (Williams 2007). These feelings then stimulate complex behavioral responses that could include prosocial, antisocial, or socially avoidant behaviors (Richman and Leary 2009). The effect of even occasional rejection can therefore have serious personal and societal consequences.

Many of our respondents who describe negative othering mention that the experiences are relatively rare and that most of the time they are treated well.[20] One of our survey respondents suggests that a deliberate effort to highlight positive experiences would reify the positive behavior and set an example for others to follow: "I think the people who don't treat me differently because of an extra cloth on my head are underrepresented because there are a lot who treat me equally. I believe if the positive people of society are given attention, other people will follow suit and be understanding of any and every religion."[21]

Vulnerability to Othering

The testimonies above suggest ways in which our survey respondents generalize about how non-Muslims react to Muslim women. Our respondents also reveal insights about how their own personal characteristics like race, nationality, or experience with Islam may influence the way they perceive other people's reaction. In their testimonies we can detect patterns showing whether our respondents readily perceive othering behaviors and also what types of othering they perceive. We infer that those who belong or belonged to a socially privileged group (racially white, American citizens, converts) should report both negative and positive othering associated with their head coverings more frequently. This is because those who belong to otherwise privileged groups within American society are likely to notice instances of othering and particularly negative othering as deviating from how they expect to be treated as individuals born in the United States, as white Americans, or

---

20. Unfortunately, we did not explicitly ask about the frequency of othering experiences in the survey.

21. This respondent's perspective is affirmed by the media attention paid to the #illridewith youth movement in Australia. The movement was started on Facebook by Rachel Jacobs in the wake of the violent hostage situation perpetrated by a Muslim gunman in Sydney in December 2014. Rachel described seeing a women remove her hijab on the train as the news of the Sydney siege was breaking. Assuming that she was reacting with fear to the hostage situation, Rachel started a social media campaign to express solidarity with and provide companionship for Muslims who fear Islamophobic backlash (BBC News 2014). Similarly, in the wake of the Orlando shootings in 2016, a man seen abusing a Muslim woman in the New York subway was met with immediate condemnation from other passengers (Mannarino 2016). In response to the Paris shootings the same year, a French artist created a comic depicting how to respond to anti-Islamic behavior in public (Donovan 2016). These examples illustrate the bright spots in othering responses and demonstrate that hostility can be confronted by empathy and acceptance.

as former non-Muslims. Judging from previous research on the perception of discrimination (e.g., Weitzer and Tuch 2002) and on evidence provided by our focus group participants and described in chapter 2, we also expect that individuals with prior experiences of discrimination in the United States such as African Americans should more easily perceive discrimination. However, they might not automatically attribute it to the headscarf, expecting discrimination based on race instead.

The Experiences of Converts

The most marked difference in the perceptions of discrimination motivated by head covering is between those who converted to Islam and those who were born or socialized into the religion through their families. Converts are well positioned to notice a change in other people's behavior based on their Muslim identity and particularly relative to their adoption of the headscarf because they have a concrete before-and-after experience. In other words, converts—particularly white converts—have moved about American society as a member of the non-Muslim mainstream and have enjoyed some degree of social privilege. After they convert and begin to cover, their experiences often contrast starkly with their previous life.

Figure 3.4 illustrates the percentages of convert and nonconvert covered women in our sample who report experiences of othering. Converts report all forms of othering, both positive and negative, with greater frequency than do nonconverts. This result is not very surprising since conversion is a deliberate decision, and converts may be highly motivated to notice positive othering as affirming an important and transformative life choice.

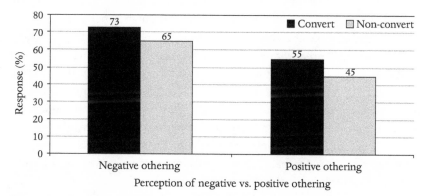

FIGURE 3.4. Comparison of perception of othering experiences among covered respondents between converts and nonconverts

The experiences of converts may vary on the basis of other personal characteristics or life events. Nearly 50 percent of our white respondents are converts, while only 12 percent of our converts are nonwhite. Forty-seven percent of our black participants are converts. Similarly, 44 percent of our native-born participants are converts, compared with 8 percent of our foreign-born participants. White converts are the most likely to notice othering in any form and are especially likely to notice negative othering, with 70 percent reporting negative experiences; the black converts in our sample report negative othering at 62 percent. This corresponds with our theory that previous experiences and expectations set a standard of treatment and a basis of comparison for converts. African Americans already report extremely high levels of discrimination because of their race (Pew Research Center 2016a), and an additional layer of religious othering may not be as noticeable for them as for white converts.

Of course, descriptive statistics like those displayed in figure 3.4 tell only part of the story. Any individual respondent could simultaneously be foreign-born, white, and a nonconvert. Furthermore, she might be highly educated and relatively young. All these factors should influence how and whether a person might be more likely to experience and perceive othering. In an effort to disentangle the way individual attributes may increase the probability of experiencing othering while taking other relevant attributes and conditions into account, we use a simple logistic regression analysis to predict the probability that our covered respondents might experience othering. For example, they may perceive that they are being treated differently while wearing the headscarf. We did this while controlling for simple demographic characteristics including race, age, education, employment status, citizenship and whether they converted (see appendix E to view the results of the analysis). On the basis of our models, we estimate the average probability that a covered woman in our sample will experience othering is a high 70 percent regardless of her demographic characteristics. However, some characteristics increase the likelihood that the women in our sample experience othering.

When we hold all the other demographic characteristics at their mean, nonconverts have a 66 percent probability of reporting othering, while that number jumps to 76 percent for converts. This result is likely a product of the convert's ability to explicitly compare experiences before and after adopting the headscarf. Interestingly, when we run the same models on whether othering is perceived to be negative or positive, being a convert significantly increases the probability of perceiving positive othering from only 45 percent to 55 percent. It does not significantly predict negative othering. This does not mean that converts do not experience negative othering in condescending, discriminatory, or exclusionary forms. The average probability that they perceive negative othering is still 68 percent and fairly sizable. But it indicates that their convert status makes them neither more nor less likely than nonconverts to perceive negative othering. No other attributes significantly increased or decreased the probability that our respondents will perceive particularly positive or negative experiences.

Most strikingly, our rough measures of race among nonwhite respondents and status as foreign-born do not significantly increase the probability that they will perceive othering, despite previous research suggesting that race is one of the most important predictors of the perception of discrimination (Weitzer and Tuch 2002).[22] In our sample, participants of all races and nationalities are likely to perceive othering in roughly equivalent amounts when we control for whether the respondent is a convert, as well as her age, education, and employment. As members of minority groups that normally experience discrimination and profiling for reasons associated with race and citizenship, our nonwhite and foreign-born respondents may perceive little difference when they add yet another layer of differentiation. The effect is moderated by education and age and conversion background. For white respondents, perhaps the shock associated with going from a nondescript member of a majority to a targeted member of a minority group is captured in the process of conversion in our statistical model.

Education significantly increases the probability that our survey respondents will perceive othering; the likelihood of perceiving othering is 50 percent for those with a high school diploma, 70 percent for college graduates, and 75 percent for those with an advanced degree. Age negatively impacts the probability that our respondents will perceive othering. The likelihood that an eighteen-year-old respondent perceives othering is 79 percent, while the probability drops to 70 percent for thirty-four-year-olds (the average age in our sample) and into the fiftieth percentile for respondents aged sixty. These findings speak to existing work exploring the role of demographics and social class on the perception of discrimination, which suggests that educational attainment is associated with increased awareness of discrimination and is therefore positively correlated with the perception of discriminatory practices and disapproval of profiling practices (Weitzer and Tuch 2002). For younger women, their higher rates of sensitivity to discrimination may be linked to modern campaigns raising antidiscrimination awareness and educational

---

22. This nonfinding could be attributable to the way we measure race in the regression as a dummy variable capturing nonwhite respondents. This blunt measure likely dilutes the effect of a particular racial identity.

training in schools. Conversely, older generations may still be more focused on assimilating to the mainstream and less on othering behaviors.

Contextual Determinants of Negative Othering

Thus far, the examples of variation in exposure to othering behaviors ascribe othering experiences to certain personal characteristics like conversion, age, and education level. Some of our respondents mention the importance of the general context in predicting whether one will be socially accepted or treated with hostility. In particular, our respondents often notice an urban-rural distinction:

> When I am in a more urban area like Philadelphia, people tend to open the door for me more often. (Muslim and non-Muslim) people also tend to use more terms of respect (Ms. or ma'am). When I am at home in my rural community it's quite the opposite. . . . I get stares, people pointing at me (Amish tend to stare at me . . . the irony—ha, ha) I get people yelling "go home" or "nice hat" and laughing. I've had people tell their children not to play with mine. I have also had some positive feedback where another Muslim from another rural community sees me and practically cries because they're so happy see another Muslim. In the county we have discovered thirty-two Muslims.

Even though this respondent describes the rural community as her home, she feels less accepted than when she visits the city. She also hints at a special effort to recognize the other Muslims within the area, presumably with hopes of forming their own community within a generally hostile environment.

Another respondent reports a similar experience of feeling rejected by her home community: "I haven't been able to get a job in my rural community and hope to move to a larger city which is more diverse. I have also had racist epithets hurled at me while I am out and about. I don't like to venture out very often as a result. I strongly feel that because of the close-knit nature of my community, I would still be 'the Muslim' if I uncovered." This respondent elaborates on what makes the rural community more hostile to Muslims and suggests that the close-knit community binds similar kinds of people together while highlighting difference and often marginalizing those who are different. This is why she feels she would still be "the Muslim" even if she were not physically distinguishable from other community members. She suggests that the othering is severe enough to motivate her to withdraw completely from society. Richman and Leary venture that this reaction is most likely in situations like those the respondent is describing: "When there is a low expectation of relationship repair, the relationship is not highly valued, there are possibilities for alternatives, and the rejection is chronic or pervasive" (2009, 18).

Other respondents attribute their negative experiences of othering in rural areas to the lack of exposure to diversity rather than to social cohesion within a close-knit non-Muslim community that is resistant to Muslim outsiders. One thirty-five-year-old survey respondent from Ohio tells us that she has had overwhelmingly positive social interactions while covered, but she qualifies her statement:

> I live in the Midwest where most people are friendly and polite and in a college town where people are educated. If I am out of the college town, people give me sidelong glances and are deeply curious. I am always open to talking about it. I taught [college] courses in a small town for many years, and most of the students had no idea I was a Muslim. I knew they would likely not know, so on the first day of class, I would open the subject by asking if they knew why I was wearing a scarf. Out of a class of twenty, there might be one or maybe two students who knew I was a Muslim.

An eighteen-year-old from Philadelphia similarly perceives othering in non-diverse settings to be a product of inexperience and ignorance: "I am fortunate to live in a diverse and open-minded city where people accept the hijab as a means of practicing of one's faith. However, I have traveled and oftentimes people who have never seen a hijabi tend to get hostile." The main differences between these two anecdotes are the feelings associated with othering in a more rural environment. The first respondent attributes the different reactions in her small town to a mere lack of experience with or knowledge of head covering. She also sees othering behaviors such as "sidelong glances" as a sign of curiosity rather than malevolent motivation. The latter respondent, however, identifies hostility and goes on to describe "outward expressions of hate."

Though othering is a common experience reported by our respondents, they do not necessarily perceive it in the same way or in the same contexts. This diversity of experience speaks to the complexity inherent in confronting instances of discrimination. In some instances, women react to the complexity of othering with equally complex methods of covering, walking the line between blending in and distinguishing themselves as Muslim. They do this by removing the head covering only in contexts where they fear discrimination. This allows them to mitigate othering while still maintaining their practice in nonthreatening contexts. For example, Tamira has concerns about the consequences of covering in a job interview, and believes that she will most likely not get the job if she goes to the interview wearing her *khimar* (cover for head, neck, and shoulders).[23] She responds innovatively: "When I go to the interview, I try to trick them. I wear a scarf turban-like." In adapting her covering behavior, Tamira is camouflaging her headscarf as a fashion accessory to escape scrutiny. Yet while wearing the turban camouflages her Muslim identity, as it is relatively common in African-American communities, her turban could also accentuate her identity as a black woman, potentially subjecting her to racial instead of religious othering.

Denying Othering

Though the vast majority of our respondents describe some experience with either positive or negative forms of othering, 30 percent of our covered survey respondents report never experiencing othering of any type. This is improbable, especially since othering can include microaggressions, which are defined as *everyday* occurrences against individuals who are members of marginalized groups (Sue 2010). Furthermore, according to our conception of the spectrum, othering can include benevolent behaviors as well. There are several possible reasons for underreporting othering. Those who report no othering may have a higher threshold when it comes to identifying different behavior or simple microaggressions. Alternatively, these respondents may have deliberately or subconsciously made themselves oblivious to discrimination in order to minimize the cost and pain of feeling othered. Evidence has shown that minorities might minimize, suppress, or deny personal discrimination even while they generally acknowledge discrimination against their minority group (Allport 1954; Crosby 1984; Ruggiero and Taylor 1997; Taylor et al. 1990).

Overlooking or denying discrimination occurs when the cost of rebelling against the source or cause of the discrimination is high. In the case of discrimination against Muslim women who cover, complete rebellion would involve removing the head covering. For women who believe the head covering is religiously mandated and that their salvation is in some way tied to this act of piety, removing the head covering would be extremely costly. This may psychologically incentivize a denial of discrimination. Indeed, when we factor in whether our participants believe head covering is mandatory according to the terms of Islam to the statistical model predicting perceptions of othering (see appendix D, column 4), it is a significant predictor. In other words,

---

23. Tamira is a thirty-seven-year-old black covered native-born American living in Illinois.

someone who does not believe head covering is mandatory is 12 percent more likely to report experiences with othering.

Some of our respondents suggest that they may be perceiving othering where it does not exist. Kadijah observes that she used to be self-conscious and anxious about wearing the headscarf in public places.[24] She recalls that she would be constantly aware of herself and primed to experience othering: "I have a hijab on. What am I doing, what are people seeing right now?" Over time, she got used to wearing the headscarf and says that she now forgets that she has it on. She believes that her own self-consciousness exaggerated the extent to which she perceived othering. "You think people are looking at you weird, and they're actually not, it's just all in your head." Whether or not Kadijah did experience othering, her point illustrates the complex psychology of being a visible member of a marginalized, defensive group. In being hyper-aware of their own difference and experienced in dealing with discrimination, our participants are more likely to attribute racism or discrimination to a negative action. However, the fact that there is an experiential or psychological component to their perceptions of discrimination does not mean that Kadijah is correct in her assessment that an othering experience was "all in her head." Prejudices are buried within our psyche, and implicit biases and the resulting subtle discrimination may be difficult to detect, especially in ambiguous scenarios (Mellor et al. 2001). The ambiguity of the situation does not mean that the initial feeling that one was othered is questionable. Rather, given the frequency of perceived othering and discrimination among the women in our sample, it appears that being a victim of othering is a daily experience for Muslims in the United States and may in fact be normalized.

Covered Muslim women are easily identified as the "other" in the post–September eleventh United States, and this precarious status was highlighted further during the 2016 US presidential election. However, not all Muslim women experience othering in the same way. Perceived variation in othering along the spectrum of social exclusion speaks to the way head covering functions as a symbolic boundary within different communities. Within the Muslim community, the boundary delineates the head covering as emblematic of a certain type of piety or even ethnic group. Within the American society at large, it builds community around religious people, binding together those who appreciate religious practice in any form. Alternatively, the symbolic boundary may function as a barrier in communication between covered Muslims

24. Kadijah is a twenty-year-old covered Arab American living in Massachusetts.

and those who view the practice as emblematic of what they perceive as anti-American values. The general perception of othering experiences reveals how the headscarf can simultaneously delineate multiple symbolic boundaries to varying effect, both bringing people closer together and distinguishing them from each other. However, the act of differentiation has important implications for the individual other and for society in the way it is enacted—whether in a benevolent or exclusionary manner.

Othering profoundly affects how minorities form their personal or group identity. Identity is not based on a given condition; it is formed through relationships and the perception of sameness and difference within a social context—through the construction of symbolic boundaries: "Identities are defined in relation to how others identify us, and they do so in terms of groups which are always already associated with specific attributes, stereotypes, and norms" (Young 2011, 46). Where social values are negatively predisposed toward a specific group, they impact the formation of identity in particular ways (see Everett et al. 2015). Muslims in the United States confront a variety of negative stereotypes; they are assumed to be terrorists or chauvinists, and Muslim women are simultaneously stereotyped as disempowered, submissive, and uneducated. The risk of reinforcing these stereotypes through othering is not only that they will gain credibility among the non-Muslim population but that individual Muslims may react to social discrimination with societal withdrawal.

Those who are othered do not always capitulate to stereotypes, however, and sometimes they can engage in counterstereotypic coping strategies. Many Muslim-American communities are sensitive to the fear and insecurity that drove the Islamophobic rhetoric of the 2016 presidential elections and recognize the assimilative and nationalistic undertones beneath the calls to "make America great again." Members of these communities have engaged in outward and internal efforts to reconcile their faith and ethnic identities with their American identities. They argue that their religious life is an integral part of their identity as Americans and assert that it reinforces their confidence in democratic values and practices, as we discuss in chapter 4.

✋ CHAPTER 4

Islamic Ethics and Practices of Head Covering in American Political Life

> It's because you're Muslim in America a lot of times people might want to distinguish religion and politics, but for me it's who I am. It's a mixture of both. It's combining the two. They can't be separated. Religion and politics, they can't be separated. People try to separate them, but I don't think they can be separated. Islam, in particular, is very open-minded. Islam wants people to engage. If you look at the politics that happened during the Prophet Mohammed's time and the whole idea of rulers and caliphs that came after him and how that system was set up, that is a whole governing system.
>
> —Aamira, a covered American Muslim

Covered Muslim women in the United States must make sense of the relationship between their religious and political lives within a secular and democratic political system and do so in light of their head-covering practices. In order to understand the complexities of engaging questions of politics by covered Muslims, we examine both the theological arguments and the Islam-derived ethics our respondents invoke in describing the complementarity of their faith with politics. In particular, we focus on our respondents' understandings of political activity and the Islamic justifications for political engagement through the lens of their experiences wearing the head covering, experiences that typically involve instances of othering. This chapter demonstrates that the relationship between head covering and politics—experienced as both discrimination and engagement—is interrelated and mutually reinforcing with important implications for Muslim women's sense of themselves as American citizens.

Many countries outside the United States have witnessed a growth in political Islam, which is the formalization of a role for Islam in politics (see, for example, Kepel 2006; March 2014; Roy 1999). In the American case we see something different. Rather than political Islamism, scholars now point to an era of "post-Islamism" in the United States (as spearheaded by Bayat 2013).

Recent trends in Muslim-American political activism reflect post-Islamism as they have "begun to accommodate aspects of democratization, pluralism, women's rights, youth concerns, and social development with adherence to religion" (Bayat 2007a, 188–89). Rather than calls for strict interpretations of Shariʿa (Islamic law), post-Islamism uses Islamic ethics and morals to call for democratic reform that supports equality and liberty (Bayat 2013, 35–37). It is this accommodation and integration of everyday, secular, and democratic political engagement with Islam that best characterizes the ways covered Muslim women in our study understand political life.

As the opening quote indicates, Islam and politics in the United States are intimately intertwined for our respondents. Beyond issues of definition—for example, what is "political"—their discussions tap into important identity questions about being both American and Muslim within our political structures. Our respondents' hyphenated identities (a concept we pick up in chapter 6 since our use of "hyphenation" is both figurative and literal) challenge them to assess the role of Islam and religious practices like head covering in reflecting or even galvanizing political activity. Compounding factors such as their status vis-à-vis conversion, sexuality, and gender also condition personal activism.

This chapter demonstrates that understandings of religion and politics enacted through head covering are flexible and dynamic. They are also responsive to a swiftly changing and highly contested environment in the United States. The ways covered women understand and justify their political actions as part of their religious world are not static, nor are they predetermined by theological prescription. This dynamism makes current political and social trends all the more potent in contemporary America.

Religious Obligations of Political Action: Theologies of Politics

Many of our participants connect their understanding of Islam both to wearing the head covering and to an obligation for political action that references the state, its leaders, and its populace. Being a faithful person, in this interpretation, requires both the hijab and engaging in political action. Respondents such as Aamira, who opened this chapter, turn to the examples and models set forth in the earliest days of Islam to understand the relationship between religion and politics.[1]

---

1. Aamira is a twenty-nine-year-old Hispanic covered foreign-born American from Washington, DC.

The Prophet Mohammed became both the spiritual and political leader of the earliest Muslim community in 622 CE. In the Medina Charter he put forth the first constitution or agreement for the nine tribes in and around the city of Medina.[2] The document established Mohammed as the mediating authority and leader and forbade the waging of war between the tribes. It provided for equality between Jews and Muslims, guaranteed some protections for women through the institution of the family, explicated a taxation process, and rendered Medina a "sacred space" to be free of bloodshed. This document often serves as a model for a multireligious, Islamic state. In fact, the early marriage of religion and politics represents a model for many Muslims today.

Beyond such historical precedents, debates about Islam and politics dominate many scholarly and lay discussions. On one hand, there is a strong argument that Western encounters with Muslim lands resulted in powerful and often deleterious political and economic influences on native Muslim populations. On the other hand, diverse Muslim perspectives and theologies have proven durable, even reemergent, on issues of political rule and regime type.[3]

One common thread found in native Muslim analyses is that Islamic theories of governance promote antirevolutionary perspectives and an abstention from a more antagonistic or competitive political engagement (Moaddel 2002, 363). "In classical Islamic political theory, the emphasis is to find and install the rightful caliph. After he is installed, following his order is binding to all Muslims" (ibid., 365). These scholars often highlight a conception of a leader (za'im) that pushes toward authoritarianism in its calls for submission in this model of governance (ibid., 363–65). Such an argument has been used to establish and maintain hierarchy, to legitimize power seized through a military coup or established through hereditary monarchies, and as part of Orientalist understandings of the so-called nature of Islam (see also Vatikiotis 1973, 310).

Many Muslims and non-Muslims criticize this viewpoint and instead emphasize the ethical and technical compatibilities between modern democratic, secular societies and Islam (Moaddel 2002, 365). Islamic concepts such as *shura,* or consultation between the decision makers and those who would be impacted by such decisions; *ijma,* or consensus or agreement by Muslim scholars especially on religious issues; and *maslaha,* or serving the common good, are also understood as both fundamentally Islamic and democratic

---

2. See, for example, Ibn Ishāq 1955, 231–35; Lings 1983, 125–31. See also Islam Project 2017.
3. For an extended discussion of the history of these lines of thought see, for example, Moaddel 2002.

principles.[4] They are deemed integral to bringing alternative and less powerful voices into decision-making processes, and in the modern era they have most often been invoked to create a space for women in politics. In fact, Islamic governance can be more democratic for women since—at least in theory—they are shorn of the "modern" state institutions such as personal status laws often codified in the colonial era that officially treat women as second-class citizens and wards of their male brethren (Charrad 2011; Jamal 2010).

Our data reveal that there is significant support for democratic and inclusive processes and institutions among our respondents. This is consistent with global trends. Public opinion polls in the Middle East show that a majority of Muslims support both democratic institutions and Shari'a , and they do not necessarily see any contradictions between the two (Esposito and Mogahed 2007; Jamal 2006; Jamal and Tessler 2008). In fact, according to Gallup's global public opinion survey across thirty-five Muslim-majority states, Muslims seemed to admire the freedom and self-determination of the West and also preferred Shari'a as a source of legislation (Esposito and Mogahed 2007). Islamic texts and traditions are seen as an ethical source for guidance in the wake of the perceived failure of secular regimes to ensure welfare.

Our own survey and focus group participants often report suspicion of the United States' political leadership, which can also be justified in theological terms. This both represents support for liberal democratic views on politics in Islam and demonstrates a resistance to what is at times viewed as a corrupted, but redeemable, political system that promotes and encourages accountability. For example, when discussing political leadership, respondents in Boston assert that "politics is a scam" or "a dirty method" in which bribery and the profit motive dominate. They suggest that the leaders of the United States, whether Muslim or secular, could benefit by emulating the example of the Prophet Mohammed. Per Malika,

> Back then [during the time of the Prophet Mohammed], people had to be pious individuals to be able to make decisions and that was just based off of their actions. Nobody knows other people's intentions but when you see somebody who is really invested in something because they're passionate about it or because they love or because they want something good for you. That's when you put them in that position of power. You know? Nowadays if you have a degree and you have the

---

4. *Maslaha* can also be interpreted as the common good or public welfare.

resume, you can do what you want, but it doesn't mean you're a nice person. It doesn't mean that you care about America at all.[5]

Other respondents connect their political participation to religiously affirmed notions of equality by seeking to embrace the community as a whole and to make sure the less fortunate are cared for. Furthermore, they object to negative ideas such as materialism and classism, which they perceive in American political culture. They appeal to the need for politicians to be there for everybody, not just the rich and famous. Our respondents easily utilize both theology and ethics in their responses.

From Theology to Ethics

It was easy for our respondents to articulate both an Islamic theology of political action that references the state, its leaders, and notions of public welfare and one that promotes engagement in the informal politics of everyday life. Many, if not most, of our respondents point to several key means of integrating Islamic ethics into their political life by moving beyond the Qur'anic and historical references common for understanding the more formal politics described in the previous section (Eickelman and Piscatori 1996). Islam, they assert, demands a reconciling of the political language, ethics, and interpretations of Islamic texts with the myriad examples and analogies of injustices and inequities found throughout society at all levels, not only in formal politics (ibid., 38).[6] As Aamira states in our introductory quote, to be a Muslim is to be engaged both politically and also more broadly with society.

Another way by which Islam plays out politically in everyday life is through the assertion that Islamic knowledge has been, for lack of a better term, "democratized," and authority for interpretation resides in all Muslims, not only the *ulama*, or the trained Islamic scholars. Religious authority in Islam, in contrast to the papacy of the Roman Catholic Church for example, is without a central structure. This enables our respondents to understand Islam for themselves as relevant and conceivable, even actionable, for political engagement. As a participant from Boston emphatically notes, "As Muslims we're not supposed to live as monks. We're supposed to be involved and informed."

---

5. Malika is an eighteen-year-old black covered native-born dual citizen living in Massachusetts.

6. "Islam" here is often understood as an objective body of knowledge and point of inquiry that can be assessed and understood in conscious ways and shapes both discourse and practice. This is consistent with other works that discuss the objectification of Islam and the ways that that is used more widely. See, for example, Tobin 2016.

Beyond questions of leadership and large-scale political organization or ideology, the idea of being involved in government as a necessary part of one's Islamic duty has extended into political participation within local municipalities for some. Part of what makes local politics compelling is that Islamic ethics can be enacted through immediate, timely, and useful political actions that benefit both Muslim and non-Muslim communities. As Khalifa observes, "When it just comes to the city council or just public work, parks, roads, investment in public infrastructure, I feel like it's fair and it's very Islamic. I mean, that's what you should be doing. That's what Shari'a is. But Shari'a is another misunderstood word. But that's what it is, you establish a welfare system. . . . You know there are a bunch of things you do for the town, there are a bunch of things you do for the country."[7] Other respondents connect it to the idea of service to one's community. Jasmin observes, "I think someone may think just by virtue of doing community service you're doing it because you're Muslim and you want to fulfill that religious aspect of it and so you might go into it with that kind of mind-set."[8]

While the influence of religious values on community involvement should theoretically exert an equal effect on both Muslim men and women, our participants describe how community involvement is affected by expected gender roles within the Muslim community. In particular, they draw attention to the ways gender role expectations constrain Muslim women's civic engagement. Some of our participants view active involvement in informal politics, particularly community involvement, as an uphill struggle in a male-dominated social environment. They emphasize that women are generally expected to fulfill community service tasks related to family, children, and other women. For them, the uphill struggle they face in convincing Muslim men that they can take on responsibilities for other issues is discouraging. Tamira decided to remove herself from active community engagement, and she explains her decision in these terms:

> I have a friend who is lobbying for me to come back to the community because women do not want to get involved. . . . There is going to be back fighting and infighting and I don't want my husband or children to have to deal with it. So, getting women in any position of governance, is you have to fight them to make a slot that isn't about the women. They always want to make them the Women's Business Coordinator, something with the kids, education committee. So you can be in charge

---

7. Khalifa is an eighteen-year-old Arab covered native-born American living in Massachusetts.
8. Jasmin is a nineteen-year-old Arab covered native-born dual citizen living in Massachusetts.

of the ladies. There is always the issue of people not wanting to get involved with the drama that happens with the brothers, unfortunately.[9]

While many respondents link politics to their local environs, our interviewees also speak in the abstract about the importance of justice and knowledge within the Islamic tradition. Khalifa remarks, "Islam is definitely for justice and I think to be involved in politics is also to support justice. . . . You have to know your information, you have to know who you're voting [for], and what are you going to do, because you're living in this country and you're not just going to be complacent and not know. You know every vote does make a difference. You know every opinion does help. I think I would definitely emphasize the justice aspect in terms of Islam."

Our respondents often engage in discussions about political activity and ethics that are not based explicitly on the Islamic texts but rather are derived from Islamic values. In those moments, Muslim Americans have to turn to their own understandings of what Islam means and its ethical implications for guiding their own actions. This is an Islamically derived approach that is consistent with our participants broadly defined politics. It is also consistent with the ethos and fragmentation of Islamic authority: without a single guide in the Qur'an or the *hadith* (sayings attributed to the Prophet Mohammed) or *sunnah* (records of the Prophet Mohammed's daily life and companions), Muslim Americans are able to amplify the more "American" values that they hold in order to best engage their spiritual selves. For example, on ethics of dress and comportment, our interviewees defended fiercely the wearing of the hijab as a distinctly American value. Hawa' contends, "I think my biggest struggle is explaining that there is nothing un-American about it. . . . Having a hijab is American to you, but how do I get the rest of the world to [understand]. Hijab is American."[10]

These Islamic ethics of political action are dynamic, and they include widely differing justifications and understandings of appropriate forms and topics for public engagement. As one of our interviewees in Washington, DC, points out, native-born and foreign Muslims prioritize different political concerns.[11] "For the latter, the priorities are domestic issues such as homelessness, civil rights, elections, social justice, and social security reform, whereas the pertinent issues among the immigrant students tend to be foreign policy concerns, gender interaction, and the position of women" (Haddad, Smith, and Moore 2006, 122).

---

9. Tamira is an eighteen-year-old black covered native-born American living in Illinois.

10. Hawa' is a thirty-four-year-old South Asian covered native-born American living in Illinois.

11. Some of these differences are explored in chapter 2.

Larger challenges also affect Muslim social and political identity in a non-Muslim, secular state. There is no "outside society" to support one's faith, and there is strong pressure to conform to an often less religious template. "There is now a gap between one's inner identity as a member of a Muslim cultural community and one's behavior *vis-à-vis* the surrounding society," which makes political action required, expansive, and diverse in its expressions (Fukuyama 2006). This demonstrates that Islam and political action are dynamic and responsive to differing experiences and contexts.

Islamic Ethics after September Eleventh

Some of the most challenging contexts for Muslims in the post–September eleventh era are what they perceive as threat-rich environments (e.g., airports, large public gatherings). Global terrorist activity in the last decades has made it more relevant than ever for Muslim Americans to engage in expansive politics that reference and utilize the ethics of Islam. Cultivating an American Islam that points to expansive politics is one method of diffusing mainstream fears that Islam is a religion of violence. It also justifies one's values as American and combats othering. This is especially prominent for the many women who must explain their head covering to the public and deflect the fearful glances of non-Muslims in public settings.

We conducted our focus group interviews in the summer of 2013 and found the respondents reeling from the Boston Marathon bombings. Many of our participants observed that Islamophobic sentiment had already escalated in the short time between the bombing and our interviews. Hafeeza notes that she felt that wearing the headscarf drew an inexplicable level of attention and hate for what should be considered a very "normalized" and protected form of religious expression. She tells us, "I do not understand: it is OK to be homosexual, it is OK to be whatever, to tattoo your body, it is OK to do what people want. But then when it comes to us, it is like we get slandered, we get spit at."[12]

Many of the women we interviewed spoke out against attacks in the United States and abroad motivated by Islamic fundamentalism from Al-Qaeda, the Islamic State (ISIS), or independent actors espousing fanatical ideas related to Islam. Furthermore, they all emphasized that Islam is a religion of peace and does not condone the senseless slaughter of Muslims or non-Muslims. This aligns with scholarship on the topic. For example, according to the religious

---

12. Hafeeza is a twenty-seven-year-old white covered native-born American living in Massachusetts.

scholar John Kelsay, "Classical Islam indicates a presumption against the use of lethal force," which is dependent on the religious context of the Muslim community (1990, 124). He continues, "The tongue and the hand are 'first resort'; the sword is a 'last resort'" (126). In the wake of the Boston bombings, many of our interviewees expressed their misgivings at how they were treated, particularly the assumption that all Muslims were terrorists or that terrorism was scripturally justified. Ghaliya in Boston invoked the sense of "just war" within Islam similar to what is found in Christianity, which is in stark contrast with terrorism as a tactic.

> After the tragedy in Boston, it really hurt me for two reasons. First of all, there are innocent people that were hurt. There was a three-year-old boy—a little boy—that was sent to the hospital. I have a three-year-old boy. So, my heart went out to him. Second of all, because supposedly the bomber was a Muslim and, unfortunately, that is not Islam. When the Prophet and his companions went to war there were strict rules. They only went to war when they had been oppressed. They had a code of conduct, they could not cut down trees, they could not hurt a handicapped [person], they could not hurt a person working in the field, they could not kill children, they could not kill women. It was very very strict. These people are claiming themselves as Muslims. They are going against the laws. I think if anything they have more of a political agenda, than are using the religion behind it. After that happened it really bothered me a lot. I got nervous about wearing the hijab a little bit. A little bit, but then I got over it quickly.[13]

Ghaliya, like many of our survey and focus participants, finds that wearing her headscarf politicizes her identity, often with the implication that she is a potential terrorist, terrorist sympathizer, or less patriotic than other Americans. "Accidental yet consistent" profiling at airport security drives the point home that the state engages in some of this essentializing behavior deliberately. Many of the women we surveyed report having been called a terrorist, and one mentions being jeered as "Osama's [bin Laden] wife." Sometimes the threat felt by our respondents is enough to convince them to change their covering behavior. For example, one survey respondent reports that she "stopped after September eleventh. "It [the head covering] brought me much negative attraction and discrimination. I became fearful going out by myself and with my children wearing a hijab."

---

13. Ghaliya is a thirty-seven-year-old white covered native-born American living in Massachusetts.

The press and social media often publish editorials by Muslims expressing their trepidation in the wake of any media-reported mass violence. They relay a fear of reprisals or of increased monitoring of Muslim Americans by the state. Still, the majority of our focus group participants and survey respondents continue expressing their religion in public spaces by wearing the headscarf and often also by actively engaging in social justice efforts and community service. Hafeeza in Boston notes,

> We are making progress. People are more educated about Islam now. They are learning the goods and the bads and just like anything else. When they learn that there are good people and bad people, they will stop blaming the religion and they will start holding people accountable for people's actions and not just the religion. That is why we wear a scarf. That is why we try to educate—because my scarf is partly education too. People will talk about it and they will ask this and that even if it is purely a few questions. Some people are very interested and they will want to talk more. They will want to understand. It is so important the good that we do. I will do a lot of community service; I push that in a community because this is how people are learning about Islam. They are learning about how we care about this country and that we are doing things. . . . We are involved in our communities. We are not segregated.

Hafeeza is right. Polls have shown that Americans continue to learn more about Islam (Pew Research Center 2010a). However, this may not always mean they have a favorable view of the religion. Roughly the same number of Americans believe that Islam justifies violence as those who do not. This statistical proportion has held for the better part of the last decade (Bridge Initiative Team 2015b; Lauter 2015). The longevity of the belief that Islam supports violence points to the work that still needs to be done.

Extending Islamic Ethics to Other Communities

Even as our respondents describe living in a constant state of vulnerability due to their visible religious affiliation, they recognize spaces and patterns that may also similarly marginalize others on the basis of class, race, ethnicity, or gender. Our respondents often construed class, race, and gender as being of "political" importance, necessitating a response guided by the same ethics as those that drive formal political participation. To politically essentialize Muslim Americans under the banner of "Islam" erases the tremendous diversity that exists both ethnically and socially among them and that they use to channel their actions.

Even somewhat unconventional "progressive politics" have been aligned with Islam in these newer constructions of Islamic political ethics. Nowhere did this sense of the obligation of American Muslims for redefining political action come to bear on everyday discourse and practice more than on issues of homosexuality and LGBTQ rights in the United States.[14] After the shooting at Pulse, a gay nightclub in Orlando, in 2016 and the revelation that the shooter was a Muslim, many American Muslims came out in support of the larger LGBTQ community (Durando 2016). From denouncements of ISIS (who took credit for the attack) to donating blood for victims (Council on American-Islamic Relations 2016a), American Muslims stood with the shooting victims rather than denouncing their lifestyle choices and morality, as many conservative Christian groups did in the wake of the event (McPhate 2016). However, the Muslim community in the United States is still deeply divided over the issue of gay rights. As Aamanee in DC observes,

> I think our generation and beyond are starting to get more and more involved, people are realizing the necessity of being politically active, of speaking your mind, but even in the most progressive Muslim-American circles we are still obsessed with Muslim Americans. And I think we have to start caring about other issues, such as LGBTQ rights, such as freedom of religion for people of other faiths, freedom of spirituality, what have you. So, I think we have to start caring about other minority issues as well. We have to start caring about other human rights atrocities.[15]

Dr. Mohammed Fadel (2013) of the University of Toronto, a specialist in Islamic legal history, also points out,

> You're certainly right to say that classical Islamic law does not countenance the legitimacy of same-sex acts under any circumstances, and so the idea that two persons of the same sex could be married is an absurdity from the perspective of Islamic law. On the other hand, if we're talking about same-sex marriage as a matter of civil law, non-Islamic law, it's important to point out that under non-Islamic law like in the United States, at least since the Supreme Court decided *Lawrence v. Texas,* you don't need a marriage to make same-sex acts licit. The purpose of the

---

14. LGBTQ rights are severely restricted in many Muslim-majority states, and most often are punishable by death or extended prison sentences. However, trends in LGBTQ relations are historically contingent and have been changing.

15. Aamanee is a thirty-year-old South Asian uncovered foreign-born American living in the District of Columbia.

marriage is not to make same-sex sex acts licit, rather it's to enable a same-sex couple to obtain certain benefits under public law that are only made available to people who have the status as married. And so I think one can certainly take the view, and I know a lot of Muslims might find this to be controversial, that we can support the idea of same-sex marriage because what we want is to make sure that all citizens have access to the same kinds of public benefits that other people do, so that nobody should be excluded from having benefits that are really quite necessary in a modern society, simply based on their sexual orientation.

Still, Muslim Americans are guided by so-called American or at least localized values to a large degree. In fact, they are more likely to support gay marriage than Evangelical Christians and Mormons, according to a 2014 Pew survey (Pew Research Center 2015; Shackford 2016). Pew's Religious Landscape Survey found some 42 percent of Muslims supported gay marriage while 52 percent opposed it. Compare this with 44 percent of Christians overall who supported gay marriage, 26 percent of Mormons, and 14 percent of Jehovah's Witnesses (Pew Research Center 2015).

In the wake of the 2016 election and subsequent hate crimes, many Muslims crossed symbolic and social boundaries to form protective alliances with other marginalized groups, particularly with Jewish communities. For example, on Sunday, December 4, 2016, nearly five hundred Muslim and Jewish women gathered in Madison, New Jersey, in what was the largest interfaith meeting of the Sisterhood of Salaam Shalom (Goodstein 2016). As they studied the sacred texts, practiced self-defense, and reviewed strategies in how to reach out to nonreligious communities, they also traded stories of discrimination and hate crimes. The sisterhood is one of several groups that are seeking to improve relationships between Muslim and Jewish communities, the most notable being the Muslim-Jewish Advisory Council, a bipartisan council that seeks to influence public policies that target religious groups, practices, and immigrants.

The alignment of American Muslims with causes otherwise perceived to be nontraditional, or with social justice organizations, demonstrates that the ethical and moral understandings of Islam have been reinterpreted and practiced in new ways that expand the political realm into more than just the formal politics of voting and party membership. For many of our focus group participants there is a conscious shift toward focusing on intersectionality across various forms of marginalization.

One of the more important ways our covered respondents merge Islam and political action is through *da'wa*, which is the spreading of the word of

Islam and dispelling ignorance about the faith. Only a few of our focus group and survey participants used the word *da'wa* to describe their activities. However, many spoke indirectly of it, referencing its ethics and practices and connecting it directly to their head covering. One survey respondent maintains that the headscarf is "a form of da'wa, or calling, to Islam. They see my scarf, they wonder, they ask. Which helps me spread the message of my Lord."

Though all Muslims are called to practice da'wa as covered women move in public spaces, the head covering elicits reactions that may require a more active response from them to public curiosity. Semra from Chicago welcomes the opportunity engage with others.[16] For her, the broader societal impact of the headscarf is being identified as a Muslim: "I know that when I enter the room Islam has entered the room. I'm communicating that message. . . . However people interpret from that message, I have to deal with, I have to live with. But I kind of like that. I like the fact that I can control that conversation." Erina from New York mentions that the headscarf "is a good conversation starter for some people who aren't familiar" or "aren't used to seeing anyone or anything that is beyond their same practice or habit or culture."[17] She also describes the scarf as a "disrupter in a good way. . . . I feel like when you have this sort of disruption in the cycle of how people perceive life . . . that's the point when they begin to learn something new."

Martha in Boston favors engaging ignorant comments from Muslims and non-Muslims alike through intellectual discussions that resonate with da'wa:

> So in that context when such ignorant comments come up even from Muslims or from non-Muslims in my vicinity or those who are close to me sometimes I do try to engage them in an intellectual discussion because that's how I got a deeper understanding of my religion. Also, I think it's the kind of work you do, and that also influences the intellectual level of people around you. So they don't often ask you silly questions. They often ask you a deeper question and that also provokes you to think deeper and come up with answers that would satisfy them. So most of those questions aren't per se ignorant, but they are not very informed.[18]

By inviting questions from non-Muslims, our participants move beyond passive representation (illustrating how "normal" Muslims are by living their

---

16. Semra is a twenty-seven-year-old South Asian covered native-born American living in Illinois.

17. Erina is a twenty-eight-year-old black covered native-born American living in New York.

18. Martha is a twenty-four-year-old South Asian covered foreign-born American living in Massachusetts.

daily life) into a more active form of representation in which they position themselves as ambassadors of Islam and lived exemplars of the positive attributes of the faith. The head covering becomes a tool for spreading Islam and practicing da'wa. Semra presents head covering and da'wa as an inseparable package deal: "Being an ambassador of the faith is part of the faith. No matter what, no matter where you are living, even if you are living in a Muslim country, it's just part of the package."

Our respondents also invoked the sunnah as exemplary for good citizenship. Sarah tells us, "I'm constantly trying to learn more about the Prophet's life and just practical aspects of our faith because that's where it helps us to be just good citizens to everyone." [19] We find that Muslim-American women "negotiated their identities in tight spaces caught between civil liberties, US government policies, and social misconceptions . . . playing the role of public educators" (Zaal, Salah, and Fine 2007, 173).

This educational outreach is another area in which Islam and political action merge with Islamic ethics. Sometimes the outreach is targeted at other Muslims or converts. There is a growing cadre of Islamic intellectuals who comment on current issues in and through neighborhood mosques or Islamic centers and who support the wide consumption and production of religious media and literature. Mosques are the focus for much of this activity and are oftentimes staffed by women (see Ahmed 2014). Many educational initiatives have started through the creation of classes dedicated to reading the Qur'an, the hadith, and other scripture and in coordinating topical lectures usually hosted at a home or at the local Islamic center. All this activity is far from apolitical, since it is ultimately predicated on transforming many aspects of social and cultural life, as well as political life. Thus, our covered survey respondents and focus group participants demonstrate dynamic and relevant religious ethics tied to their political action.

Politics and the Head Covering

As the discussion of da'wa illustrates, the expectation and application of demonstrative Islamic ethics often fall on covered women as the most visible representatives of Islam. The head covering links Muslim women to certain types and forms of political activism within non-Muslim democratic societies. Among our respondents, activism linking the headscarf and politics tends to fall into one of two types. Either the activism is related to codifying and

---

19. Sarah is a forty-two-year-old black covered native-born American living in Massachusetts.

securing the right of women to wear the hijab, or it is related to a personaliza-tion of the hijab and the political passions of the wearer. While both forms of activism are important, we focus primarily on the latter here. We find that the head covering plays an important role in the consolidation of democratic val-ues and in motivating mobilization around social justice in the post–September eleventh environment. At the same time, some Muslim women are frustrated by the disproportionate political attention attached to the hijab and suggest that political energy would be better invested elsewhere. Whether our respondents viewed the head covering as a political mobilizer or a distraction, the Muslim ethics of dress and comportment provide a clear example of the flexibility of Islamic values and their adaptability to a non-Muslim context.

Head Covering as an Expression of Democratic Values

As we mention above, our interviewees defined wearing the hijab as part of a set of distinctly American values. Hafeeza explains, "You are practicing your faith. Your faith really, you have that right. For me it is a right. Just like anything else, the right to vote, the right to do anything. It is my right. I can dress how I want." These respondents emphasize not only the free environ-ment that allows them to cover (or not) but also their sense that covering is a proactive and empowered choice enacted within a free context. Some of our respondents extend this empowerment beyond the initial choice to cover: one of our survey respondents describes a "perk of wearing the hijab" as "people, regardless of the circumstance, begin to take you seriously. Even in the most relaxed environment, I have walked into places and men, especially, have straightened up and composed themselves. I love having that kind of a demanding presence."

For our respondents, while the head covering is an act of piety, it is also clearly an embodied representation of autonomy, freedom of religion, and personal expression. Our participants also regularly invoke additional demo-cratic values such as equality in defending their choice to cover. Hawa' dis-cusses the headscarf as an expression of her feminist ideology: "I wanted to wear my Muslim-ness literally on my sleeve or on my head. I wanted to openly identify myself as a Muslim. . . . It was a good emulation of my femi-nism, my 'you are feminist' theory. I thought there was no better way to be a feminist than to be wearing hijab."

For Hawa' and many of our other respondents, the headscarf is a way to embrace and emphasize femininity and womanhood but also a source of empowerment and an expression of their rights as women. This testimony and the description of head covering as a free choice among our respondents directly relates to notions of feminism as a liberating ideology, as do testimonies about the way the headscarf allows women to escape sexual objectification and reclaim personhood (see chapter 1).

Our respondents' understanding of equality extends beyond gender equality and into equal treatment—several of our focus group participants highlight inconsistencies in the treatment of Muslim Americans when compared with other religious minorities. In discussing reactions elicited by her head covering, Sarah notes, "You don't really hear people saying anything nasty about nuns." Sarah is one of several focus group participants to mention the comparable case of habits worn by Catholic nuns and to highlight the similarities in the form and function of both head-covering practices. Continuing her line of thinking, Sarah also compares the Islamic practice of covering to the practice of Orthodox Jewish women wearing wigs and Nigerian Christians covering their heads. She underscores that "the negativity is [directed] towards Muslim women." The purpose of these comparisons is to highlight an inconsistency in treatment across religious groups, and by extension, to document injustice and encourage an adjustment toward equal treatment.

Our survey and focus group participants explicitly connect the practice of head covering to politics of equality, feminism, and democracy. They may do this in an effort to reinterpret the covering, making the practice more relatable for the average non-Muslim American, or as a way for them to reconcile their own contemporary values with a practice associated with traditionalism. Either way, these efforts occur within a non-Muslim context that may be predisposed to assume head covering is motivated by oppression and chauvinism. Instead these women opt to transform the practice into a modern, empowered choice in a politically charged environment.

The Head Covering and Social Justice

As described in the introduction and earlier in this chapter, September eleventh proved to be a watershed moment in the construction and usage of the head covering for political activism. Almost overnight, Muslim women were transformed from "invisible citizens" into "visible subjects" (Jamal and Naber 2008, 2). Covered Muslim women became newly subject to American society's politics of racialization, exclusion, and othering.[20] Muslim women responded by mobilizing antiwar efforts and readily politicized the headscarf

---

20. See also Ahmed 2011; Haddad, Smith, and Moore 2006; McGinty 2012; McGinty, Sziarto, and Seymour-Jorn 2013.

themselves, oftentimes turning it into more than a symbol of Islamic piety. The head covering became "a symbol of resistance and solidarity" (McGinty 2014, 683), and thus it became one of the methods by which American Muslims have united their political interests in areas such as democratization, pluralism, equality, and rights. Further, they have done so with an understanding that pious political life is not solely confined to wearing the hijab but also requires living what it represents.

Negative stereotyping and prejudices against Muslims following the September eleventh attacks strengthened young women's determination to cover in an effort to represent the "true Islam" and set an example of a "good Muslim."[21] Wearing the head covering after September eleventh stemmed from a belief that they could represent Islam more positively in a politically tense environment (Badr 2004). It became a means to attempt to limit or overcome symbolic boundaries by reasserting that the headscarf was a positive representation for all Americans in a new and challenging political environment.

Many of our respondents indicated that the symbolic boundaries prompted by the head covering could be overcome by focusing on a commonly shared American or human identity. Erina expresses her desire to be understood beyond her headscarf:

> I think that my wearing the hijab, by my walking down the street, by my taking the subway, by my working where they may not be necessarily other Muslims or especially you know "obvious Muslims" . . . I think it kind of gives the idea that you're going to have to understand me as a human being and not simply as the first thing you see with the hijab and I think once people come to you and once they get beyond the "hello" and "where you're from" type of thing it opens up the idea of you're just human and sort of the human struggle overall.

Similarly, Khalifa, an American citizen of Arab origin who was called a "terrorist" several times in the past, challenges the notion that covering makes her significantly different from other Americans:

> I feel like a lot of people overplay the hijab and "Oh, like you're a Muslim woman. You're so different," and I'm not. I mean, I don't see myself as different from anybody else. All I have is a scarf on my head. I cover myself a little bit more, and I don't look at myself as any different than any other woman. I feel like I'm the same. I shop the same. I almost dress the same. Like, it's not . . . whenever I enter a public office I don't

---

21. See Peek 2005; Sirin and Katsiaficas 2011; Zaal, Salah, and Fine 2007.

look at myself as like a public woman. I completely forget I'm wearing the headscarf, I completely forget that I pray a different way.

Khalifa emphasizes her similarities with the average American while deemphasizing and even forgetting her differences. Both Khalifa and Erina appeal to the attributes they share with other non-Muslims beyond the head covering in an effort to mitigate aspects of the boundaries created by the headscarf.

As illustrated with Khalifa's statement, the desire to overcome the stigma of covering may be expressed through trivializing and deemphasizing the headscarf. Alesha, an African-American respondent, similarly states, "It is a piece of cloth. Come on. It's like putting a necktie, but I put it on my head. What *is* the big deal? What is the big deal?"[22] Sarah, another African-American respondent, observes, "I just think people have such a fascination about a piece of cloth and it's a piece of cloth that can go either way." The intent of these statements is an attempt to delegitimize the visual cue for othering and effectively trivialize the act of covering, especially in the eyes of non-Muslims.

This desire to be understood beyond their head coverings presents an interesting tension for some covered Muslim women. On one hand, they wear the head covering as a public expression of their personality, values, and opinions; it is a vector for quick communication with others. On the other hand, they want non-Muslims to be able to see beyond the head covering and appreciate their individuality. These women recognize that for some non-Muslims, rather than a form of communication, the head covering is a barrier to understanding their Muslim counterparts. The contradictory roles engendered through the hijab—as both a facilitator and a barrier to communication—show the appreciation and sensitivity of these women to social context and the need for varied strategies to enhance communication across symbolic boundaries. Such symbolic boundaries are enacted across religious and nonreligious communities within a secular state.

The complex social climate surrounding the act of head covering has made it "a symbol of an American-Islamic identity—a public affirmation of trust in the American system that guarantees freedom of religion and speech" even (and perhaps especially) when confronted with societal opposition (Haddad 2007, 254). The head covering is the basis for social justice for many American Muslims, galvanizing and expanding political action (Ahmed 2005; Haddad 2007). Even though women were not always energized by the head covering itself, many found that the hijab led to mobilizing for other ends. As

---

22. Alesha is a black covered native-born American living in the District of Columbia (no age reported).

demonstrated by the response to the Pulse shooting, our respondents internalize this merging of Islamic ethics and mobilization on behalf of other disenfranchised minorities, making them part of their political identity. In fact, this may be the most self-consciously American attribute of the women we interviewed.

The Head Covering as a Distraction

The head covering clearly plays an important role in developing a unique Muslim-American identity while defining politics and political action. However, some of our respondents were frustrated by fellow Muslim-American women who demonstrated piety through the head covering but failed to recognize other politically important issues that also affect the larger Muslim community. Wearing the head covering, particularly in a way that draws attention to oneself, was deemed insufficient in light of other pressing political issues. Respondent Aamanee describes it best: "I mean, haute hijabi, how are you fighting patriarchy. Please explain? Again, if that is your self-expression, then that is you have a right to wear ten pounds of makeup and a headscarf on top. If that floats your boat, then that's your thing. But don't come at me and tell me that is more religious than someone who does not wear it." She continues, "The concept of hijab is becoming increasingly, in my eyes, problematic in the American Muslim context. Because we are not addressing issues of capitalism, patriarchy, materialism." Focusing on head covering in the United States, according to our respondents, does not place proper emphasis on other pressing issues in our society. Furthermore, to do so out of only a narrow sense of piety missed the point for many of our respondents because they have a much more expansive definition of piety, one that entails political action. The excessive focus on head covering is often perceived as a distraction from the real issues by our respondents.

Despite the possibility that the politics of the headscarf may distract from larger societal problems, wearing the head covering and participating in broadly defined political activity are part of meaning and identity production (McGinty et al. 2013). A publicly active and present Muslim woman is rendering visible a variety of modes of political engagement that she may hold important to her faith. As a result, covered women constitute an important force behind a national movement that both embraces an Islamically informed political activism and emphasizes the hijab (Ahmed 2011).

As this chapter reveals, many of our participants engage in informal political activity, broadly defined, as it relates to the head covering. They respond to acts of othering and discrimination, particularly in the post–September eleventh context, by rethinking and reenvisioning the role that the head covering plays in enacting symbolic and social boundaries. They also engage in expanded definitions and practices of politics, emphasizing the importance of activities at all levels of government such as civic engagement, and they consider how issues in public welfare and social justice intersect. As this chapter has demonstrated, our interviewees understand both their formal and informal political participation with reference to their religious life and the head covering. Some look to Islamic histories and theologies, while others look to Islamic ethics in order to inform, understand, articulate, and practice politics in everyday life.

This chapter reveals much about the ways that Muslim Americans are engaging in post-Islamist political life with a view toward creating a new community. Muslim-American women have negotiated the politics and the head covering in such ways that they now fuse political participation and their religious life. These women "represent an endeavor to fuse religiosity and rights, faith and freedom, Islam and liberty. It is an attempt to turn the underlying principles of Islamism on its head by emphasizing rights instead of duties, plurality in place of singular authoritative voice, historicity rather than fixed scripture, and the future instead of the past" (Bayat 2007a, 11).

However, such attempts have not yet come to fruition because of several important challenges. As previous chapters demonstrate, Muslim-American women face durable and important obstacles, often connected to race or ethnicity, immigration status, and convert status. Furthermore, as Muslim-American leaders have demonstrated, mobilizing Muslim constituencies can be difficult because of a historic underuse of the American political system to agitate for their rights. Respondent Hasina suggests that the openness of the American system is a blessing but also a curse:

> That's something that I feel like we are really blessed with is that it is absolutely an open system. I think that is something really nice about America. It is so transparent. Really open. If we want meetings with elected officials, we just request the meeting. We just call up the office, and I think that if people's will isn't being reflected, it is because they are not mobilized and they are not working towards it. You can only have yourself to blame because you are not voting, and we are not giving candidates money for their campaign so that they will support our issues. Really it is a reflection of our own community if we don't feel like our will is being put in place.[23]

---

23. Hasina is a twenty-eight-year-old white covered native-born American living in Texas.

These ambivalences speak to the importance of the role of the headscarf in breaching symbolic and social boundaries. The symbolic boundaries enacted through the headscarf become important in assessing how identities are dynamic and negotiated rather than stable and given. The symbolic boundaries create challenges to both social boundaries and politically motivated discrimination. At the same time, our respondents demonstrate that such symbolic and social boundaries can be and are being overcome across ties that help mobilize their engagement in social justice and public welfare and across other sociopolitical agendas.

However, political agendas emerging from head covering do not encompass the entirety of political action. Our respondents had much to say about formal political participation, explored in the next chapter. In it, we see that the practice of head covering is indirectly associated with Muslim women's formal political participation through its impact on the types of social networks covered women tend to engage in. The nature of these networks facilitates distinct types and levels of political engagement with the formal political system and has important implications for future mobilization.

CHAPTER 5

Head Covering and Political Participation

> I live in America. I'm an American. I vote. I participate
> in everything that every other American does. I don't
> see myself as being different.
>
> —Hawa', a covered American Muslim

Despite the growing size and importance of the Muslim population in America, the factors that motivate Muslims' formal political participation are still relatively unexplored.[1] We expect more attention to shift toward Muslim Americans in future years, as some activists considered them to have been the "real swing vote" in the 2016 presidential election (Hauslohner 2016).[2] The 2016 election challenged Muslims' ideological positioning, engagement, and belonging more than other presidential elections in recent history. Though Donald Trump effectively "segregated Islam from his perception of American identity" during his campaign for president (Beydoun 2016), many Muslim voters were also ambivalent about Hillary Clinton's candidacy because of her foreign policy and antiterrorism rhetoric. In particular, she was lambasted for framing Muslim-American citizens solely in national security terms and expecting them to "identify and prevent attacks" on American soil (Hagi 2016). Engaging the Muslim population was an uphill battle for campaign activists canvassing for the Democratic Party (Hauslohner 2016;

---

1. Exceptions include the work of Ayers (2007; Cho, Gimpel, and Wu (2006); Barreto and Bonzonelos (2009); Djupe and Green (2007); Read (2007); Jamal (2005a, 2005b).

2. Large populations of Muslim Americans in Florida, Michigan, Ohio, Pennsylvania, and Virginia and declining voter turnout among the general population in those states provided Muslim Americans with an opportunity to potentially influence the vote in both the presidential and House races.

Rappeport 2016), and as indicated by the election results, the efforts did not yield the desired outcome. One poll released by the Council on American-Islamic Relations indicated that in 2016 Trump won nearly triple the Muslim votes received by Republican nominee Mitt Romney in 2012 (McCaw 2016).[3] Despite Trump's win and the Muslim ambivalence about Clinton, support for her was quite high among Muslim Americans. Polls revealed that support for Clinton was higher among Muslims than among any other religious group, with 40 percent of Muslims supporting her, while only 30 percent of Jews and 13 percent of Christians backed Clinton (Chideya 2016). Still, Muslim-American millennials were more likely to vote for third-party options than for either Trump or Clinton even in swing states—similar to results reported for the same age groups in Hispanic and African-American populations (Black Youth Project 2016).

As discussed in chapter 3, covered Muslim women are subject to gendered and Islamophobic stereotypes and are vulnerable to othering and harassment. Many Muslim women mobilized after Donald Trump invoked these negative stereotypes in his comments about Ghazala Khan, the grieving mother of a fallen Muslim-American soldier. Khan appeared, silent, on stage with her husband at the 2016 Democratic National Convention; Trump publicly called out her silence, suggesting she "wasn't allowed" to speak because she was a Muslim woman (Turnham 2016).[4] Muslim-American women responded to Trump on Twitter with the hashtag #CanYouHearUsNow, and many others reacted to the electoral climate by taking a more active and visible role in American political life.

In some cases, Muslim women can do more than Muslim men to change opinions. Sarwat Hussein, president of the San Antonio chapter of CAIR, explained this in a 2016 interview: "If you wear a *hijab*, you are much more likely to be harassed walking down the street, but there is also much more to gain by being so highly visible. . . . As Americans and Muslim women, we need to make our presence known so that people will see we are a part of the community, and we love this country. We are not what people think—uneducated, oppressed, and incapable of serving society" (*Atlantic* 2016).

In the following section, we explore patterns of participation across the Muslim-American community during recent presidential elections. We examine formal and informal organizations that motivate their political participation,

---

3. The same poll found that 74 percent voted for Hillary Clinton in 2016, compared with 86 percent who voted for Barack Obama in 2012.

4. Ghazala Khan later clarified that she didn't feel able to speak because she was "in pain" and feared that she would be too emotional.

paying special attention to the role of special interest groups, mosques, and social networks. The head covering plays an integral role in motivating and conditioning political engagement for Muslim-American women. We suggest that wearing the head covering translates into distinct social networks, which condition levels of formal engagement with the American political system.

Muslim-American Political Participation

Formal political participation usually refers to participation within government institutions—such as voting, political party membership, and political representation—whereas informal political participation includes activities related to civic engagement and community activism, as well as political protest and issue-related campaigns to raise awareness (Jamal 2005a; Senzai 2012). Exploring the political activity of Muslim women across both of these types of participation gives us a better idea of how and when, as well as at which levels, they engage the American political system. While we consider faith-based informal participation in chapter 4, this chapter focuses on the formal participation of our research participants.

Voting

Muslim Americans tend to register and vote at slightly lower rates than non-Muslims in the United States. A 2007 Pew Research Center survey found that 63 percent of Muslim-American respondents reported they were registered to vote, compared with 76 percent of non-Muslim respondents; 58 percent of eligible Muslim Americans reported voting in the 2004 elections compared with 74 percent of non-Muslim respondents (Kohut, Lugo, and Keeter 2007). In our own survey, 64 percent of our voting-eligible respondents reported voting in the 2008 presidential elections, while 70 percent voted in the 2012 presidential election.[5] In general, the voter turnout of our survey sample more closely resembles general voting trends in the American population: 62 percent of the general population voted in the 2008 presidential election and 59 percent voted in 2012 (McDonald 2016).[6] We suspect the higher rates of

---

5. In our focus groups 47 percent voted in the 2008 elections, while 64 percent turned out for the 2012 elections.

6. Though the self-reported turnout in our sample in 2008 is very close to general turnout, our respondents report much higher turnout than the general population in 2012. Our data also report an increase in turnout between 2008 and 2012, while the general turnout declined over the same period. This could be a feature of the self-reported data in our survey, with our respondents being more likely to report participation, especially since the data were collected shortly after the presidential elections in 2012.

voter turnout in our survey are likely related to the higher education level of Muslim respondents than in the PEW surveys.

Though Muslim-American turnout is lower than non-Muslim turnout in the United States, Muslim Americans are far outpacing their counterparts in Europe when it comes to voter turnout.[7] In comparisons of voting patterns across eligible Muslims and non-Muslims in France and Germany, Muslim citizens vote at half the rate of their non-Muslim neighbors (Cesari 2014, 176).[8] The higher rate of Muslim-American participation may be attributable to higher levels of trust in national institutions. A 2011 Gallup poll revealed that across all religious groups in the United States, Muslims had the strongest trust in legal and civic institutions and in the fairness of the electoral system (Cesari 2014). Conversely, Muslim citizens in France, the United Kingdom, and Germany had much lower levels of trust in civic institutions than the general population, which is potentially why they exhibit low voter turnout (Gallup 2009).

The increase in voting among our survey respondents between 2008 and 2012 could partially be attributed to growing concerns with the Islamophobia creeping into American political rhetoric after September eleventh, motivating many Muslims to engage more directly in politics. In the five US presidential elections since the turn of the millennium, Islamophobia has increasingly become a strategy embraced by candidates to win non-Muslim voters (Senzai 2012, 11). Thirty percent of Muslim Americans identified Islamophobia as a primary concern in the 2016 presidential election, which is a steep increase from the 2014 congressional elections in which only 15 percent of Muslims rated Islamophobia as a top issue (Council on American-Islamic Relations 2016b).[9] Even previously apolitical Muslim organizations such as the Islamic Society of North America have started actively promoting the political participation of both men and women in a bid to stem the political marginalization and increase the political voice of Muslims (Haddad, Smith, and Moore 2006, 122).[10]

---

7. This is partially due to very strict voter eligibility (citizenship) and registration criteria across countries such as Germany, France, the United Kingdom, and the Netherlands.

8. According to the Open Society Institute (2010) survey of Muslims in eleven major European cities, 51 percent report voting in the last national election, compared with 69 percent of non-Muslim respondents.

9. This was particularly evident in the 2016 presidential election cycle, in which the front-running Republican candidate, Donald Trump, stirred controversy by proposing a ban on Muslims traveling to the United States and a registry of Muslims (Council on American-Islamic Relations 2016c).

10. In the past, ISNA promoted the idea that Muslims should participate no more than necessary in the secular state.

The call for Muslim Americans' political involvement has been heard: a 2012 study by the Institute for Social Policy Understanding (ISPU)—the largest Muslim think tank in the United States—reported that 95 percent of polled Muslims believed that "Muslim Americans should participate in the political process." In fact, Islamophobia may be "accelerating a group consciousness" that was dormant prior to September eleventh (Senzai 2012, 59).

Though the majority of our survey respondents and focus group participants reported voting in the major presidential elections, the act of voting is fraught for many of them. While our respondents predominantly assert that their faith promotes participation, we noticed several instances in which they described a faith-based disincentive to participate. Typically a withdrawal from politics is justified by a perceived incompatibility between worldly political institutions and Islamic religious structures. Our focus group participant Eliza, in Washington, DC, captures this tension perfectly:

> A lot of Muslims argue that because this is not a Muslim country . . . our way of governing as Muslims is too different . . . and we should not involve ourselves at all in the political area of this country. And then you have the other side that says if we want things as Muslims, if we want to be respected, if we want our holidays . . . if we want the laws passed that women who wear covers can't be discriminated against at work, then you have to become part of the political arena. So, it's a double-edged sword type of thing.[11]

While Eliza reports voting in 2012, Lydia in Norfolk, Virginia, describes how her attitude toward voting changed after she converted to Islam, partially because of a lack of electoral options—she voted in 2008 before her conversion but did not vote in 2012. Lydia explains,

> The theory is that when you vote, if you believe your vote counts, that means that you were voting for . . . all the decisions that [the government] makes that affect the lives of Muslims in other places. . . . So that means that then you are responsible, you have a part in this, if you believe your vote counts. That was something that really got me. . . . [The reason] I did not vote [was] because I could not decide what was worse to vote for.[12]

Both Lydia and Eliza highlight the internal tension that commonly exists among religious people who participate in secular political institutions: If you strive to live your life according to your religion, how can you justify

---

11. Eliza is a fifty-year-old black covered native-born American living in the District of Columbia.
12. Lydia is a twenty-eight-year-old South Asian covered native-born American living in Virginia.

being part of a system that is at best indifferent to your values and at worst, violates them? Nonetheless, while many of our participants acknowledge this paradox, they generally conclude that political inaction does greater harm than engaging in activism. The most commonly reported reason for voting was a sense of civic duty, and there was consensus that it was the best way to promote the interests and demonstrate the relevance of Muslim Americans within the American political system.

Political Party Membership

Over the past decade, Muslim Americans have shifted their allegiance from Republican to Democratic candidates, particularly after the 2000 presidential elections. In 2000, 40 percent of Muslim Americans supported Republican candidate George W. Bush for president. By 2004, that number had dramatically shifted to only 7 percent of Muslims, while 86 percent supported Democratic presidential candidate John Kerry (Ayers 2007, 191; Read 2007, 1075).[13] In 2008 Barack Obama won 90 percent of the Muslim vote and 85 percent in 2012 (Ghazali 2016; S. Khan 2010).[14] These election results are at odds with Muslims' historical preference for more conservative policies.[15] Saba Ahmed, the female founder and president of the Republican Muslim Coalition, summarized those historical preferences succinctly in a 2016 interview with *Al Jazeera America*: "The appeal to American Muslims is that Republicans have values—such as pro-life, traditional marriage, business, trade, etc., that align with Islamic beliefs. Democrats espouse liberal values which are incompatible with Islam. I couldn't support their pro-choice, pro-LGBT, pro-taxes approach" (Younes 2016).

Many scholars have attributed this party shift to the political marginalization of Muslims by the Republican Party after September eleventh (Ayers 2007; Djupe and Green 2007). Several of our focus group participants recognized anti-Islamic othering as part of a deliberate political strategy by the Republican Party, either to attract votes or to provide a scapegoat for modern social problems. While discussing the tendency among Muslims to identify as Democrats in recent years, Abeera, a covered focus group participant from Virginia, argues that Muslims recognize the Democratic Party as being

13. CAIR's 2016 Muslim Voter Survey found that three-quarters of Muslim respondents supported a Democratic presidential candidate, while 13 percent supported a Republican candidate (11% declined to answer). See Naeem 2016.

14. Ninety percent of our focus group participants also reported voting for the Democratic Party candidate.

15. See Baretto and Bozonelos (2009); Cho, Gimpel, and Wu (2006); Djupe and Green (2007); Pew Research Center (2007); Zogby (2004).

more supportive of their civil liberties, especially freedom of religion, while "Republican is just Christian."[16]

Religiosity has different effects on political party identification for Muslims than it does for American Christians (Barreto and Bozonelos 2009)—namely, Muslim political identity is currently associated with increased disaffection from the major parties, while Christian religiosity has been associated with the Republican Party. This is attributable to the fact that both Democratic and Republican parties actively encourage Christian religiosity, while they are largely either silent on or even opposed to Muslim religiosity.

Still, many Muslims identify religious reasons to support a political party. Jessica from Detroit suggests that Muslims are attracted to the Democratic Party because of its support for social welfare, but she simultaneously recognizes the appeal of the morally conservative Right.[17] She describes how the Republican Party alienates Muslims from a party that might fit their social and religious preferences: "If I was going to vote based on religion only and my religious beliefs, I would probably lean more towards the Republican Party before the Tea Party came along. . . . I think that the Tea Party drives people away . . . people like *me* away from the Republican Party. If the Republican Party were the Republican Party of the Reagan years and before 9/11, your result might have even been a little different."

The shift in Muslim-American party preferences does not, however, imply that Muslim Americans feel sufficiently represented by the Democratic Party. For example, a *Washington Post* article covering Muslim voter preferences in the 2016 presidential elections found that many Muslims perceived the binary choice between candidates as no choice at all. The voters expressed disappointment with the Obama administration and concerns over Democratic candidate Hillary Clinton's hawkishness, particularly relating to her views on Middle East foreign policy (Hauslohner 2016).

Consequently, many Muslims opt not to identify with any party (Barreto and Bozonelos 2009), and the Muslim women in our surveys and focus groups, especially those who covered, affirm this trend.[18] Dinah from Virginia describes

---

16. Abeera is a sixty-four-year-old black covered native-born American living in Virginia.

17. Jessica is a forty-year-old Arab covered native-born American living in Michigan.

18. The sentiment that the two main political parties do not adequately represent the public is not limited to the Muslim population and reveals that the interests of covered Muslim-American women may not be that different from those of their non-Muslim counterparts. Gallup (2012) has reported an increasing number of Americans identifying themselves as politically independent over the last two decades, culminating in a record high of 40 percent in 2011. There is also growing nonpartisanship within the American political system (Hajnal and Lee 2011). Similar to our Muslim respondents, they find minority voters are alienated from the main political parties because of a perceived lack of options that represent diverse interests.

her perception of the constant othering within the American political system: "Whenever [politicians] do talk about Islam in politics, it is always 'the other' or 'those people over there' . . . it's not always in a negative way. It's not always saying 'violent people' or whatever, but it's always 'other people' . . . talking about [Islam] like it doesn't have a place right now in America."[19] Similarly, Hawa', whose words open this chapter, remarks, "We are not one of the focus or target groups for these campaigns. We are still considered the other—the invisible—until there is [sic] more numbers, unfortunately."[20] Kalima from Boston notes the absence of Muslim representation in government: "I have yet to look for a politician that I could be like "oh, yeah, he's Muslim. . . . I think that's kind of sad."[21]

There are some signs that the tide may be turning. Two Muslims, Minnesota's Keith Ellison and Indiana's Andre Carson, have been elected to the House of Representatives (Ellison in 2006 and Carson in 2008), and there have been a number of Muslim state legislators and local representatives elected in recent years.[22] Ellison's profile rose in 2016 as he emerged as a candidate in an ultimately failed bid for the chair of the Democratic National Committee.[23]

During the 2016 election cycle, much media attention was generated by the electoral win of Ilhan Omar in the Minnesota House of Representatives. Omar, a hijab-wearing Somali woman, defeated forty-four-year incumbent Phyllis Kahn to become the first female Muslim legislator in US history. Even more attention was generated during Omar's first official visit to Washington, DC, when after leaving a policy training at the White House, Omar described an interaction with her cab driver in which he called her "ISIS" and threatened to forcibly remove her hijab (Shechet 2016).

These electoral successes aside, the 2016 presidential election cycle did not appear to provide much hope for Muslim Americans seeking increased representation of their interests through the executive branch. While not Muslim himself, the former Maryland governor and 2016 Democratic presidential candidate Martin O'Malley became the first and only presidential candidate to visit a mosque during election season (Wagner 2015). He remained active with the Muslim-American community even after dropping out of

---

19. Dinah lives in Virginia. Other demographic data were not reported.

20. Hawa' is a thirty-four-year-old South Asian covered native-born American living in Illinois.

21. Kalima is a thirty-two-year-old white covered native-born American living in Massachusetts.

22. Compiling a list of all the Muslim legislators and representatives is difficult because of the number of offices and because the holders of public office are not required to declare their religion. Determining a politician's faith requires examining his or her personal statements and speeches.

23. Though many high-profile Democratic legislators supported Ellison, objections quickly emerged, among them his former links to the Nation of Islam, which we discussed briefly in chapter 2.

the primary race. In 2017, after President Trump enacted a ban on immigration from seven Muslim-majority countries, O'Malley again emphasized the importance of Muslim Americans in the electoral and democratic processes in the United States. Speaking outside "Mother" Mosque in Cedar Rapids, Iowa, North America's longest-standing mosque, he said, "In any nation's journey there is both light and shadow. . . . The sense and the feeling in the air was that we are all in this together. . . . Maybe it took this sort of detour to remind us all that the future is something we all make" (Rynard 2017).

One 2016 Republican candidate, Dr. Ben Carson, called Muslims who support democracy "schizophrenic" (Gass 2016), and Trump as president proposed several policies in his first thirty days that would explicitly discriminate against Muslims. At the same time, while Clinton used inclusive rhetoric and appointed Farooq Mitha to work on Muslim outreach (Graham 2016), many Muslims felt stigmatized by her campaign statements about radical jihadists and resented comments on Palestinian terrorism in Israel (Hauslohner 2016). The law professor Khaled Beydoun (2016) summarized Muslim Americans' concern with Clinton as a candidate: "Clinton's hawkish foreign policy inclinations in the Muslim-majority nations, her unwavering alignment with Israel; and on the domestic front, support of the US PATRIOT Act and emergent counter-radicalisation policing, which links (Muslim) religiosity to presumed involvement with terrorism, looms heavy in the minds of Muslim American voters." It is unsurprising that in this political context, our focus group participants have doubts about their future inclusion and representation in the American political system and in the political party apparatus in particular.

Mobilizing Muslim Americans

We have demonstrated that Muslims in America register and vote at slightly lower levels than non-Muslims but that their rates of participation are much higher in the United States than in other democratic countries. Muslim-American voting behavior is likely at least partly attributable to their lacking involvement with the main political parties in the United States. The party affiliation of Muslim Americans has shifted in favor of the Democrats since 2001, but in general, American political parties may be more alienating than they are mobilizing for the Muslim-American population. Given the trends in disenfranchisement, we consider what motivates Muslim Americans to become involved in American politics. This section explores other organizational and social factors that play a role in politically mobilizing them, particularly the role of special interest groups, mosques, and social networks.

Many of our focus group participants discuss avenues of political engagement outside of political parties or elections, such as Muslim organizations that channel their individual experiences and even fledgling Muslim political action committees (PACs). The Islamic Society of North America and the Council on American Islamic Relations featured prominently in our interviews.[24] ISNA, founded in 1983, is the oldest and largest federation of Islamic organizations in the United States. Its broad objective is to promote the welfare of the Muslim community, and its major activities are publishing its monthly magazine, *Islamic Horizon*, and holding an annual convention (Cesari 2004). ISNA has historically maintained an apolitical position in an attempt to remain as inclusive as possible but it has in recent years started to encourage political participation (Haddad, Smith, and Moore 2006).

CAIR, founded in 1994, is the largest overtly political Muslim special interest group. It defines itself as a grassroots civil rights and advocacy group and America's largest Muslim civil liberties organization. Its objective is to counteract the demonization of Islam in the public sphere, to promote a positive image of Islam in America, and to politically empower the Muslim-American community (Cesari 2004). According to their website, their activities include lobbying, monitoring instances of bias, reviewing legislation, media outreach, information transmission, and grassroots mobilization. CAIR has also brought and won numerous lawsuits in defense of Muslims.

In discussing CAIR, Nabila from Chicago suggests that the organization plays an important role in addressing political topics beyond the purview of mosques and Islamic Centers: "Sitting on the steering committee we've had a lot of conversations about how can we, as first generation Muslim Americans, work through programming, have these conversations about these taboo topics that perhaps our mosques don't address when it comes to politics."[25]

The role of special interest groups was especially evident during the 2016 presidential elections, when the US Council of Muslim Organizations, the Islamic Circle of North America, the Arab American Institute, and CAIR collaborated to organize a national bus tour and voter registration drives in order to register a million new voters (Dizard 2015). The drives were organized in response to the increase in anti-Muslim attacks in 2016 during the

---

24. There are many other Muslim organizations that are active in the United States, including the Islamic Circle of North America, U.S. Council of Muslim Organizations, and the Nation of Islam (now the American Muslim Mission). We highlight ISNA and CAIR because of their broad reach but also because together they exemplify the double-pronged approach to engagement through community building and activism.

25. Nabila is an eighteen-year-old Arab covered native-born American living in Illinois.

run-up to the presidential election. As explained by Robert McCaw, the government affairs director at CAIR, "We're not looking to register one million more Muslims. We're looking to work with interfaith partners to register one million more Americans. This is going to be more of an interfaith and community project. When you look at the toxic political climate in the United States, minority community members take the brunt of many political attacks now more than ever. We have to join together so we're heard. The best way is to go to the polls" (Dizard 2015).[26] This effort exemplifies the way Muslim organizations work together (and with non-Muslim religious organizations) to accomplish large goals, as CAIR and ISNA previously did when collaborating on the US Mosque Study in 2010 (Council on American-Islamic Relations 2015).

The activities of the special interest groups are not immune to criticism. Erina, a New Yorker, criticizes CAIR and similar Muslim organizations for their exclusive focus on political mobilization rather than the promotion and facilitation of other forms of active community engagement: "I get pissed because that's the reactionary voice coming out. . . . You don't hear the e-mails coming around saying simply let's be involved in community service more. Let's . . . you know, we're going to do more food pantries, we're gonna do more cleaning the beach, let's do all of these things. . . . You don't hear things like that from these major groups."[27]

Erina is reacting to CAIR's fundamental objective of confronting Islamophobia in American society, a mission that can be seen as reactionary and may continue to highlight difference and discord rather than inclusion. Erina's comments reflect the need for a dual-prong approach to inclusion and one that CAIR and ISNA embody together: ISNA organizes the Muslim community through coalition and community building, and CAIR engages in political lobbying and activism.

Though CAIR does lobby governmental institutions and serves as a Muslim advocacy group, the development of a committed and well-funded Muslim-American lobby similar to American Israel Public Affairs Committee (AIPAC) or the Republican Jewish Coalition has been a main objective of the Muslim-American community (Cesari 2004). Lobbying groups like the American Muslim Alliance and the Muslim Public Affairs Council have developed over time in order to promote "the rights of the Muslim community within the

---

26. The campaign and the growing visibility of the Muslim-American population prompted some to suggest that Muslims could provide a crucial swing vote in the 2016 presidential elections (Hauslohner 2016).

27. Erina is a twenty-eight-year-old black covered native-born American living in New York.

terms of American pluralism" (Cesari 2004, 84). However, the nature of the Muslim-American community has presented a challenge for developing a lobbying organization that is generally representative of the Muslim-American population. As we demonstrate in chapter 2, American Muslims are a diverse and geographically dispersed community, two features that regularly present challenges for minority populations seeking political influence. In the words of the political scientist Muqtedar Khan, "The diversity of the Muslim community means they have too many goals and not enough people to make things happen" (Abrams 2015).

The Muslim community is small in comparison with other religious groups (only about 1–2 percent of the American population), which further confounds their ability to raise funds and attract the attention of lawmakers in the same way the Jewish or the Christian communities can (Abrams 2015). Khan observed, "There are very few Muslims who understand what super PACs are. There are very few Muslim bundlers," referring to the relative lack of Muslim fund-raisers who collect contributions from donors on behalf of their campaign. Khan goes on to explain that "rich and influential" Muslims will sometimes have fund-raisers at their homes but that the practice is not mainstream in Muslim-American society. A quick comparison of donations from religious groups reflects this reality: Muslim PACs compare poorly relative to other religious communities, raising only about $100,000 since 2012, while Jewish PACs raised close to $10 million and Christians groups $4 million in the same period (ibid.). Data from 2000 through 2012 reveals that both Arab and Muslim PACs collected only about $700,000 in donations over more than a decade of fund-raising.[28]

While Muslim advocacy groups such as CAIR, the Muslim Public Affairs Council, and EmergeUSA engage in important grassroots mobilization, they do not regularly fund-raise or donate to campaigns or candidates. A few PACs emerged in the aftermath of September eleventh with the initial wave of anti-Muslim bias, but most are now defunct. The Islamophobia of the 2016 presidential campaign has encouraged EmergeUSA's PAC offshoot to become the most active it has been since its origins in 2006, when it was created to fund

---

28. See also http://www.jewishvirtuallibrary.org/pro-arab-arab-american-and-muslim-pacs-campaign-contributions, for a comparison of Jewish and Muslim/Arab PACs donations. The site lists the following organizations and their donations from 2000 through 2012: Arab American Leadership PAC, Iranian American PAC, American Task Force Lebanon Policy, Council on American-Islamic Relations, Arab American PAC, American Muslim Institute, Muslim American PAC, Indiana Muslim PAC, Americans for a Palestinian State, National Association of Arab-Americans, American League of Muslims. Their total contributions for the twelve years were $743,517.

Minnesota Representative Keith Ellison's successful run for congressional office (Chideya 2016).[29]

The anti-Muslim rhetoric of Trump and his treatment of Ghazala Khan also galvanized the creation of the first US Muslim women's PAC in October of 2016: the American Muslim Women PAC founded by the criminal defense attorney Mirriam Seddiq (*Atlantic* 2016; Zarya 2016). Seddiq wanted to offer Muslim women a "platform from which to speak out in support of political candidates and policies that impact their community," and noted, "Our very existence as a political group—not a charity—has changed things for us" (MAKERS Team 2016). Seddiq was mobilized by the political climate surrounding the 2016 presidential election and saw her work as an escalation of the fight for minority representation within the democratic framework of the United States: "It is open season on minorities, women, people of color of all sorts. We can't ever let this happen again and that's what has caused me to do this. I could tweet angrily, or Facebook extensively, or I could see what candidates are speaking in a voice that supports our values and vision for America and give them our money and our endorsements. So, I started a political action committee. Like Americans do" (ibid). Seddiq recognized the challenges the very diverse Muslim community presents for successful political organizing, and she emphasized the need to represent and celebrate all the Muslim women working to promote the community's concerns in the public realm:

> It is important for all Americans to be heard. And, there are lots of American Muslims who are making change. Debby Almontaser who is on our board is active in New York City politics and was a huge part of getting the NYC school district to give kids the Eid holidays off. Linda Sarsour is out there making waves. I want to show that we are not a monolith. Many of us don't wear hijab [Seddiq does not]. We come in all shapes, sizes and we express our faith differently also. I've always had a voice. Now I just have to use it to help others express theirs. (Ibid.)

Despite receiving an onslaught of hate mail in the aftermath of establishing the PAC (Sidahmed 2016), Seddiq has clear-cut goals for the future of the organization—namely, gearing up for the midterm congressional elections in 2018. She affirmed, "I want women to join us in key states and start fundraising and letting us know which races are important and which people

---

29. More recently, in 2012 the PAC successfully fought the reelection bid of Representative Allen West of Florida, a vocally anti-Muslim congressman.

we should support. I want to 'normalize' us so we aren't the token hijabi'd women in photos on the dais. And then I want to be ready for the next Presidential election. American Muslim women will be in full force then" (MAKERS Team 2016).

Despite the passion of women like Seddiq and marked progress in achieving representation in national and local legislatures, Muslim Americans are still developing an organizational presence that could complement or confront the main legislative, executive, and judicial institutions of the United States. These organizations and PACs provide alternative opportunities for engagement, resources, and advocacy for an otherwise marginalized population, though the diverse nature of the community presents a challenge for developing a comprehensive interest group.

Mosques

Even as interest groups struggle to mobilize Muslim Americans, mosques have an opportunity to aid in the creation of a cohesive political community centered on religious identity and practice. As we discussed in chapter 4, our survey and focus group respondents consider community involvement an expression of their faith. This rhetoric is not foreign to other religious groups in the United States, who often see community service as both a religious and a political obligation. Consequently, it is unsurprising that mosques, like churches and temples, are now forums for political education and mobilization in the United States.

Institutionalized religious associational life can serve as a rallying mechanism and effective tool for the political mobilization of Americans as we see with churches and temples (Jones-Correa and Leal 2001; Lien, Conway, and Wong 2004; Verba, Schlozman, and Brady 1995). It also facilitates the social and political integration of religious, ethnic, and racial minorities (Gordon 1964; Wong and Iwamura 2007). Mosques provide a similar service, as mosque leaders engage in community outreach and promoting integration with the larger community. According to the data gathered through the US Mosque Survey 2011, mosque leaders embrace flexible interpretations of religion adapting to modern social circumstances and promote Muslim involvement in American society. A majority of them (56%) reported adopting a flexible approach to interpretations of the Qur'an and sunnah, with only 11 percent following the classical legal schools of thought. The survey findings also showed that mosque leaders almost unanimously support Muslim involvement in American society: 98 percent agreed with institutional involvement, and 91 percent agreed with political involvement of Muslims (Bagby 2012). A 2004 ISPU report on mosques also noted a more activist stance since September eleventh as well as a turn toward more interfaith outreach (ibid., 10).

Mosque involvement among Arab Americans mobilizes political activities such as making contributions to political candidates, attending political rallies, engaging in political agenda setting through writing petitions, and considering oneself an active party member (Jamal 2005a).[30] The Muslim American Public Opinion Surveys from 2007 and 2008 revealed that respondents involved in mosque activities were more likely to write letters to officials, protest, and participate in community meetings (Barreto and Dana 2009). Individuals polled in other surveys who report higher levels of activity in their local mosques are also more likely to participate in other forms civic and youth engagement (Senzai 2012, 6), and religiously devout Muslims are also more likely to support political participation (Dana, Barreto, and Oskooii 2011.[31]

The focus on mosque attendance as a rallying point for women's community engagement or even as a signal of personal piety can be somewhat problematic, considering that there are differing interpretations on whether sex segregation is a central feature of Islam. While the Qur'an makes no explicit mention of gender segregation, many Muslim cultures practice sex segregation in the mosque, or what is known as purdah—the seclusion of women from the male gaze.[32] This can translate into gender-specific mosque attendance and access (Cesari 2014).

According to several recent surveys (Gallup 2011; Pew Research Center 2007; Younis 2011), men attend mosque more often than women in the United States (48% of men attend regularly, while only 30% of women reported attending mosque on a weekly basis).[33] The journalist Nina Weeks explored

---

30. The majority of research focusing on the role of mosques in encouraging Muslim-American political engagement centers on data gathered from the Arab-American population (Read 2007; Jamal 2005a, 2005b).

31. Some research finds that mosque involvement depresses nonvoting political participation as well as active party membership (Djupe and Green 2007) and that the density of mosques in a given location was associated with significantly diminished Arab-American registration for the major political parties between 2001 and 2003 (Cho, Gimpel, and Wu 2006). It could be that the mobilizing effect of Muslim associational life may be contingent on the kinds of people within the congregation and the types of relationships built there.

32. The notion of *purdah* comes from the Persian word for "curtain" and is a common reference for the practice of secluding women in Muslim communities within South Asia and throughout the Islamic world.

33. Within Islam attending mosque is often presumed to be the province of men. However, according to Pew (2007) and Gallup (2011), women reported praying more often than men do (48% of women but only 34% of men stated that they prayed five times a day). This aligns with a 2016 report issued by Pew (Pew Research Center 2016b) in which women across all religions report praying more often than men do. In contrast to Muslim women's lower mosque attendance, a 2010 Gallup poll showed that 47 percent of Christian women but only 38 percent of Christian men reported attending church on a daily basis.

Muslim-American women's mosque attendance for *Al Jazeera America* and noted, "The relegation of Muslim women to basements, balconies and other less desirable spaces in their houses of worship remains a common practice," perhaps partially explaining why fewer women attend mosque. Some Muslim women who encounter these practices in American mosques have actively agitated against segregation through Friday prayer sit-ins and open protests at Islamic centers across the nation.[34]

The United States has been the site of many mosque-related innovations such as the founding of the first all-female mosque in Los Angeles (Street 2015), as well as the scholar Amina Wadud's leading of a mixed-gender congregation into Friday prayer (Elliot 2005). Furthermore, mosques that are engaged in interfaith activities were much more likely to report hosting women's programs (perhaps to correct for misperceptions regarding gender roles) and in fact have opened up greater space for women to serve as public advocates for Islam.[35]

In our survey, 45 percent of female respondents report attending mosque either "frequently" or "always," which is closer to the findings for men in Pew and Gallup surveys, and our focus group participants highlight the importance of mosques as a tool for political education. In the words of Nabila, "Depending on the ethnic race of who is attending and who is running the mosque, it [the mosque] definitely plays a role when election season comes around, who is running, which workshops and where they are being held. The mosque is definitely a type of [political] institution and it does a very good job of collecting people at times."

As we discuss in chapter 2, mosques and Islamic centers across the United States are known for being very socioculturally diverse communities (Bagby et al. 2001; Barreto and Dana 2009; Lotfi 2001). Mosques therefore serve a political learning function for the community through religious socialization but also through the exposure of members to the diverse ethnic groups, races, and denominations of their fellow congregants (Leighley 1990; McClurg 2003; Scheufele, Hardy et al. 2006; Scheufele, Nisbet et al. 2004). Our focus group participants affirm the importance of their religious communities as a source of political socialization and generally perceive a religious obligation

---

34. This culminated in a series of protests at the Islamic Center of Washington, DC, in 2010. For more information see Nomani 2010 and National Public Radio 2010.

35. Mosques hosting interfaith activities usually also organize women's programs as well as host women's groups. Seventy-six percent of interfaith mosques had women's programs, while only 49 percent of non-interfaith mosques had women's programming. Thirty-five percent of interfaith mosques hosted women's groups, but only 20 percent of non-interfaith mosques hosted them (Sayeed, Al-Adawiya, and Bagby 2013).

to participate in politics. This socializing function of the mosque was affirmed by Rizwan Jaka, chairman of the board of trustees at the All Dulles Area Muslim Society Mosque, in an interview with National Public Radio host Tom Ashbrook on December 9, 2015: "ISIL recruiters are telling their potential targets to stay away from the mosque, because they know that the mosque is an immunization to radicalization. The mosque is the first line of defense. ISIL recruiters are saying 'your mosque is a sellout'" (WBUR 2015).[36] Jaka highlighted the role the mosque plays in discouraging radicalization through encouraging outreach and community integration (Kirby 2007). Religious leaders condemn political violence in public sermons and private conversations, and community members adopt self-policing practices like confronting those who express radical ideologies and communicating concerns about radicalization to law enforcement officials (Schanzer, Kurzman, and Moosa 2010). Mosques in America are generally sites of civic inclusion rather than isolation. While our focus group participants do not often explicitly link their political attitudes to their experiences in a mosque, they do highlight the connection they see between their beliefs and political action. For example, Jasmin of Boston states, "As Muslims we are not supposed to live as monks. We are supposed to be involved and informed. It is all about balance."[37]

Muslim Social Networks

Mosques help mobilize their constituents through community outreach and engagement, but they may also have an indirect effect on political participation through helping Muslim Americans meet and befriend each other. Extensive research has shown how the density and specificity of social networks affects political participation (Huckfeldt and La Due Lake 1998; Kwak, Shah, and Holbert 2004; Leighley 1990; McClurg 2003; Mutz 2002; Scheufele, Hardy et al. 2006; Scheufele, Nisbet et al. 2004). Possessing a diverse social network—where members' views are not consistent with one's own political beliefs—can increase political participation (Leighley 1990; Scheufele, Hardy et al. 2006; Scheufele, Nisbet et al. 2004). Two mechanisms undergird this mobilizing effect: first, diverse social networks expose individuals to a variety of opinions, forcing group members to engage with and compromise across conflicting ideas. Second, diverse networks motivate a deeper, individual

36. ISIL is the acronym for the Islamic State of Iraq and the Levant, also known as ISIS or the Islamic State.

37. Jasmin is a nineteen-year-old Arab covered native-born dual citizen living in Massachusetts.

inquiry into relevant political issues, resulting in personal exposure to a plurality of views and ideologies that allegedly motivate participation.

Robert Putnam (2000) describes social networks formed between diverse groups as providing "bridging" social capital. Formal networks, such as those created through associational memberships and religious institutions, play an important role in promoting bridging social capital. They can ease political involvement through the transfer of civic skills and procedural knowledge, as well as other forms of socialization and information exchange (Brown and Brown 2003; Jamal 2005a; Jones-Correa and Leal 2001; Putnam 1993; Verba, Schlozman,and Brady 1995). The influence of social networks on political participation is particularly significant when the networks "revolved around the exchange of political information" (McClurg 2003, 454), which results in an important political learning function (Inglehart 1979; McLeod, Scheufele, and Moy 1999; Neuman 1986).[38]

The social networks of Muslim Americans do not tend to be as politically charged as those of other religious groups, and they also tend to have higher proportions of women and family members than do the social networks of other religious practitioners (Djupe and Calfano 2012).[39] Putnam (2000) identifies these kinds of intimate friend and family-centered social networks as building bonding social capital. Bonding ties are socially valuable, particularly for oppressed and marginalized members of society, because they allow them to come together in groups and support collective needs. Further, bonding social capital can provide safety nets in hostile environments or provide a cushion during hard times. However, these kinds of networks could result in withdrawal from public institutions because the community fulfills all that an individual might want. In extreme situations, individual communities can become so insular that the broader public sphere becomes dominated by competing special interest groups, which presents a threat to the overall societal cohesion in a healthy democracy (Fukuyama 2002).

This implies that if Muslim social networks are more homogenous and exclusive than social networks in other religious communities, they could disincentivize political engagement. From the social network data reported in chapter 1 (in figure 1.3), we know that our survey respondents have religiously

---

38. Early work by Allport (1954) noted that increased interaction or contact with diverse people in one's social network normally reduced prejudice. Recent evidence reveals that even vicarious contact with members of an out-group through mass media or third-hand interactions seems to reduce prejudice over time (Pettigrew 1998; Pettigrew and Tropp 2006; Pettigrew et al. 2011).

39. They also tend to exhibit lower levels of political knowledge and public discourse, which could ultimately have an effect on levels of political engagement overall (Djupe and Calfano 2012).

homogenous friend groups: an overwhelming 81 percent of our respondents report a friend network in which at least some of their closest friends cover, and 44 percent report that nearly all or all of their friends are Muslim. These results are startling, considering that the Muslim population is estimated to comprise approximately 1–2 percent of the total American population. While we cannot assert that the composition of these social networks is representative of the general Muslim population in the United States, the social network patterns among our respondents raise the question of why their networks tend to be less religiously diverse, how these networks inform the political lives of our respondents, and how the practice of head covering among our respondents influences their social networks.

The Role of the Head Covering

As we discuss in the introduction to this book, forms of head covering have not been legally proscribed and politicized in the United States in the same way as they have been in many other countries. That said, in the current social and political climate in the United States, the head covering is still a powerful symbolic boundary marker with highly politicized meanings. Chapter 3 explained the way in which covered Muslim women are often subjected to societal othering.[40] Such experiences are consequential because they potentially situate the head covering as a political boundary in two ways: (1) in identifying Muslim women as a target for discrimination by non-Muslims and (2) as a rallying point for Muslim group identity and political mobilization in the face of discrimination. Women who cover may be more likely to gravitate toward exclusively Muslim friend groups in the face of this growing Islamophobia. Furthermore, Muslim women may also be particularly sensitive to antireligious acts, which could motivate specific political responses from the Muslim community more broadly (Djupe and Calfano 2012). Thus, the headscarf catalyzes very distinct social interactions between Muslims and non-Muslims and can build community within and across religious lines.

Even independent of the Islamophobic environment in the United States, the practice of head covering can associate our respondents with more exclusive and homogenous networks that ultimately affect their willingness to participate in politics. As discussed in chapter 1, head covering is understood

---

40. Of our covered survey respondents, about 70 percent report that non-Muslims have behaved "differently" around them because of the headscarf: 32 percent have experienced condescension from non-Muslims, 27 percent report hostile staring, approximately 15 percent have experienced verbal abuse, while 14 percent fear for their safety when wearing the headscarf (3% reported violent attacks).

primarily as an indicator of personal piety and religiosity, which may directly affect individual political attitudes (Cole and Ahmadi 2003; Westfall et al. 2016). It is also a visible marker of religious group identity and group commitment, externally expressing a set of social values and attitudes, which can translate into distinct social networks and group-oriented political behaviors (Endelstein and Ryan 2013, 254).[41] Figure 5.1 illustrates that there is a difference in levels of party affiliation and voting across our covered and noncovered survey and focus group participants. There is an approximately 10 percent gap in voter turnout between our participants who cover and those who do not in both the 2008 and 2012 presidential elections, with a larger percentage of our noncovered respondents voting than our covered respondents. Furthermore, there is about a 12 percent gap in terms of reported party affiliation. While the voting rates of our survey participants are higher than those of the general electorate, the gap between covered and uncovered women is notable.

We expect that the headscarf (1) signals a level of religiosity that should result in more frequent mosque attendance and (2) influences the way social networks are formed and the diversity of these networks. According to our understanding of the role of the mosque and informal social networks in

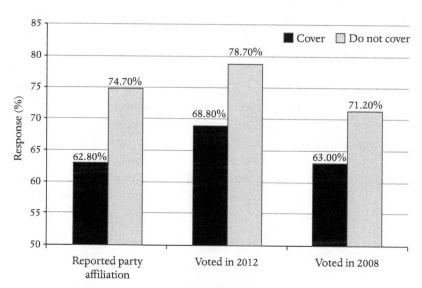

FIGURE 5.1. Head covering and formal political participation

41. There is little evidence that women are explicitly embracing the headscarf as a symbol of political Islam within the United States, as they have in other countries.

conditioning voter turnout and party affiliation, those networks should influence our respondents' political participation. As we discuss above, the headscarf can signal the degree of a particular type of piety and religious socialization to other Muslims, a relevant attribute when one is forming and choosing friends and other parts of one's informal social networks. We therefore expect wearing the head covering to lead to predominantly Muslim social networks that will build bonding—more exclusive and homogenous—social capital.

Exploring the Link between Head Covering and Participation

We use our survey data and a statistical model to verify the relationship between head covering, mosque attendance, informal social networks, and political participation. Because head covering both influences and is influenced by the sociopolitical context, we model the indirect relationship between covering and our respondent's formal political participation with a simultaneous equation model. The simultaneous equation model examines two equations at the same time, one predicting the formation of Muslim bonding networks and one predicting formal political participation. The description of the model and the variables included in it can be found in appendix F. This type of model captures the simultaneous interdependence between the bonding ties created by our participants' religious friend networks, the headscarf conditioning their inclusion into such networks, and, ultimately, how the networks impact their formal political participation—especially voting and party membership.

The diversity of a given social network should increase political participation through the political learning function, and the inverse should also be true: less diverse social networks should decrease political participation because of more limited exposure to a variety of political opinions and information. Thus, the more our survey respondents' informal friend networks are homogenous, the less exposure they have to alternative political ideas. This leads to political disengagement, which in our model is captured through reduced voting and party membership.

Formal social networks like those built through religious associational life in the mosque may affect political participation through their creation of bridging or more socially diverse social capital. The degree and regularity of church attendance is well known to increase political engagement and party affiliation among African Americans (Brown and Brown 2003; Harris 1994), Hispanics (Jones-Correa and Leal 2001), and Asian Americans (Lien, Conway, and Wong 2004) in the United States. As we discuss above, recent polling

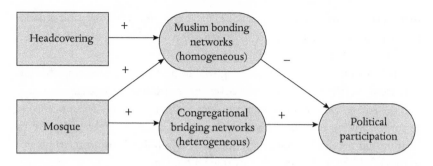

FIGURE 5.2. Flow chart of expected relationships between head covering, the mosque, and political participation

by ISPU (Bagby 2012; Senzai 2012) also finds this pattern for Muslim Americans who attend mosque, and we expect the same for our survey participants. However, the mosque can also be a place where one meets friends and family to build bonding, or more insular, forms of social capital. Therefore, depending on its social composition, the mosque could contribute to social networks that either stimulate or suppress broader political participation based on congregant exposure to diverse groups. Figure 5.2. illustrates the flow of the expected theoretical relationships.

The results from our statistical model confirm that wearing the headscarf increases the likelihood that our respondents will form more informal bonding (insular) networks within the Muslim community. These same networks reduce the likelihood that our survey respondents identify with any political party and vote in both presidential elections (see the statistical results in appendix G).[42] In other words, the act of head covering may connect our subjects to a more exclusively religious social life in the Muslim community, which can diminish levels of engagement with formal political processes. The headscarf may represent a crucial individual step in conditioning the direction of collective social behavior. This finding affirms previous research demonstrating

42. We can confidently assert that the relationships are directional and not endogenous through the simultaneous equation model, as the instrumented endogenous political participation variables do not share a significant relationship with Muslim networks in any of the models. Furthermore, additional robustness tests incorporating the head covering in the second equation yielded no significant relationship with any of our indicators of formal political participation. Interestingly, the relationship between head covering and Muslim networks has the highest magnitude of all the variables included in the model and is independent of individual religiosity and mosque attendance. Married status and mosque attendance also predicted exclusively Muslim bonding social networks, while higher levels of education and employment were associated with a more diverse social network.

that social networks lacking diversity may deter political learning and broader political participation (Leighley 1990; Scheufele, Hardy et al. 2006; Scheufele, Nisbet et al. 2004).

The mosque has a very interesting role to play in the formation of informal social networks. Those who cover are more likely to attend mosque, and the survey respondents who regularly attended mosque are more likely to form bonding ties with other Muslims, as demonstrated by a significant relationship between mosque attendance and bonding Muslim relationships in two of the models. However, mosque attendance *also* increases the likelihood of identifying with a political party and voting in 2012.[43] The mosque tends to be the locus of diverse groups of Muslims across ethnic, racial, and even denominational lines, which engenders important forms of political learning. This suggests that while the mosque facilitates exclusively Muslim friend networks, it can also serve as a venue for political learning and increasing exposure to networks outside the Muslim community or even to more ethnically and culturally diverse members of the Muslim community itself. This exposure seems to translate into increased political engagement with the American political system.

Thus, our model reveals that the bridging networks emerging from mosque attendance increase political participation, while informal and less diverse social networks (bonding networks) result in political withdrawal. The independent effect of mosque attendance on political participation is not distinctly different from what we find with other religious institutions and within other religious communities in the United States (Brown and Brown 2003; Harris 1994; Jones-Correa and Leal 2001; Lien, Conway, and Wong 2004).

Aside from insights relating to head covering and the mosque, our models reveal several other interesting findings about the formation of bonding networks among our respondents. Religiosity (measured with variables capturing the frequency of prayer, practicing Ramadan, and abstaining from pork and alcohol) is associated with the formation of Muslim bonding social networks. This intuitive finding speaks to the likelihood that even outside the mosque, people will select into networks that affirm and support their belief systems and life choices. Similarly, if a respondent is married, she is more likely to select into Muslim bonding networks. This relationship likely reflects the propensity of women in our sample to marry Muslim men: 96

---

43. Our findings also confirm Senzai's (2012) research showing that mosques are increasingly driving the Muslim vote as a means of combating Islamophobia.

percent of our married respondents report that their spouse is also a Muslim. When one's intimate family relationships are bounded by a mutual religion, the extended friend networks that are formed through the spouse are likely to be with Muslim friends. Conversely, respondents who are more likely to encounter non-Muslims in their daily life—through educational institutions and employment—are less likely to have exclusively Muslim friend networks and therefore tend to form bridging social networks with non-Muslims. Religiosity, marriage, and employment are all ultimately indirect determinants of formal political participation.

In the second equation, Muslim bonding networks are found to suppress party identification and voting behaviors. The only other variables aside from Muslim bonding networks (which shares a negative relationship with political participation) and mosque attendance (sharing a positive relationship with political participation) that directly influence political participation are age and education. Older women are more likely to politically participate than younger women, and more educated women are more likely to vote (the relationship between education and party identification is insignificant). Both of these results affirm prior research on political participation within the general American public (Verba, Schlozman, and Brady 1995).

Taken together, the results of all three models demonstrate how the political engagement of our respondents is largely determined by their personal and social characteristics. The relationships between the personal characteristics of the women in our sample and political participation tend to mirror those found in the general population of the United States. However, the indirect relationships revealed through their social networks are unique to the Muslim community. Where the women are institutionally incentivized to interact with non-Muslims, through school and work, they are less likely to form exclusively Muslim social networks, which should increase their propensity for political engagement. Yet the women with the highest levels of religiosity (as represented by head covering and mosque attendance) are more likely to form social networks that are largely composed of Muslims. This insularity is negatively associated with formal political participation.

Despite its contribution to the creation of exclusively Muslim bonding networks, mosque attendance appears to mitigate some of these effects through its direct and positive effect on women's political participation. It is striking that mosques would have the same effect on the Muslim women in our sample when mainstream political candidates and parties focus less on mobilizing this specific religious community. Such a finding is important in light of conflicting research about the role of mosques in promoting Muslim engagement with the American political system.[44] Consequently, our findings hint at the complex, nuanced, and unexpected impact religious associational life may have on political participation but also at how marginalization and in-group exclusivity can lead to a withdrawal from mainstream politics even among a fairly mobilized cohort of Muslim women. In this case, the headscarf plays an intriguing role in informally bonding Muslims.

Considering the broader patterns of Muslim political engagement in the United States, the introductory quote to this chapter by our Chicago focus group participant, Hawa', sounds especially true: "I'm an American. I vote. I participate in everything that every other American does. I don't see myself as being different." We find that the political behaviors of the Muslim-American women in our sample mirror those of the general American public. Both their voting rates and their party affiliation suggest a population willing to participate in the formal political system, but there are patterns of political disengagement and discontent that are distinct from those in the general population. Intriguingly, these patterns are partially linked to the practice of head covering for Muslim-American women.

While each individual is composed of many identities that can be invoked in a variety of situations, the headscarf is an external identifier prioritizing a woman's Muslim identity to external viewers, whether she chooses to prioritize it in such a way or not. The act of donning the headscarf immediately identifies a woman to other like-minded people, but it also identifies her as part of a broader community that has been politically targeted and discriminated against and therefore makes that woman more likely to experience discrimination. These experiences can shape political preferences and may motivate more insular bonding networks within the Muslim community, resulting in increased dissatisfaction and disengagement with a nonresponsive political system. Furthermore, the arbiters of formalized politics in the United States—political parties—make limited overtures to Muslims as electoral participants, resulting in the anomaly that Muslim Americans are the

---

44. For example, Jamal (2005a) finds mosque participation is directly related to higher levels of civic engagement among Muslim Americans, while Cho, Gimpel, and Wu (2006) argue that the density of mosques in Arab-American neighborhoods has had a negative impact on voter registration post–September eleventh. These differences in findings are partly attributable to different measures of informal versus formal participation, and Cho, Gimpel, and Wu (2006) primarily focus on mosques with congregations composed of a specific ethnic group. Our findings help make sense of these contradictory findings by focusing exclusively on formal participation and considering the composition of informal social networks alongside the influence of the mosque.

only religious group where religiosity has been associated with *lower* political participation (Ayers and Hofstetter 2008).

Reduced party identification and voting behavior among covered women relative to uncovered women does not mean that covered women completely reject participating in the American political system. In fact, the political lives of the more religious participants in our sample are informed by the strength of the Muslim community and the priority of collective over personal identity as discussed in chapter 4. Many of our focus group participants note that their religious values and conservatism would naturally ally them with the Republican Party, yet most of them opted to vote for the Democratic Party because they felt it was more inclusive and representative of minorities in the system. Essentially, they vote with an eye toward the broader community and perhaps with a collective identity—the American ummah—in mind. This is not solely the purview of the Muslim-American community but is also common in other marginalized groups when it comes to voting patterns among citizens with both partisan and nonpartisan affiliations. For example, Hispanic, African-American, and Asian-American independents all vote with reportedly similar collective identities and ideas of broader social welfare in mind (Hajnal and Lee 2011).

Ultimately, our findings reveal that, in fact, the covered Muslim women in our sample are *not that different* from other Americans when it comes to both their participation rates and their political disassociation from the formal political system. However, the group identities and experiences of Muslim Americans determine the substance of their participation and influence the degree to which Muslim-American women see themselves as incorporated citizens of the United States. Relatedly, we explore issues of substantive citizenship in chapter 6.

❧ Chapter 6

Citizenship without Representation

Muslim-American women act as full-fledged citizens of the United States despite facing widespread social discrimination. The discrimination is not without its consequences: it influences the way they see themselves in society, and it sets boundaries around their inclusion as equal citizens into American society. This chapter examines how Muslim-American women define American citizenship and the ways they negotiate the symbolic boundaries created by their hybrid identities as Muslims and Americans.

A central feature of American identity is its fluidity and its ability to bridge symbolic boundaries while simultaneously preserving and celebrating diversity. For example, in 2014, the *New York Times* correspondents Damien Cave and Todd Heisler documented the way American identity is changing along the I-35 corridor from Laredo, Texas, to Duluth, Minnesota, "from a city that's 96% Hispanic and struggling to integrate new immigrants, to one that is 90% white and longing for the energy young foreigners bring." Along the way, they asked, "What does it mean to be American?" The answers were as varied as the respondents, but themes of opportunity, community, freedom, and especially diversity emerged. To be American is to live in a country that was constructed by citizens of other countries, and as President Obama argued in his 2014 speech relaying his immigration plan, "Our tradition of welcoming immigrants from around the world has given us a tremendous advantage over other nations" (Obama 2014).

This dominant culture of diversity made then-candidate Donald Trump's anti-Islamic and discriminatory remarks on the 2016 campaign trail particularly shocking to many Americans. In responding to Trump's platform, David Harris of the American Jewish Committee called the statements "un-American" and argued that "in the United States, there is no place for this kind of divisive, hateful rhetoric." Harris alludes to American values born out of the past, when revolutionaries aspired to create a "good society" around an ideology emphasizing liberty, egalitarianism, individualism, populism, and laissez-faire principles (Lipset 1997, 31). The American Revolution used these values to deliberately move away from the more hierarchical, organically rooted communities in old Europe toward a vision of society that fit better with the diverse backgrounds of the colonists. To bridge the rigid social boundaries of the past and bring a diverse people together, the nation had to be set in the bedrock of civil society, with membership determined through participation and citizenship and not through bloodlines or common history. As Michael Walzer argues, "The parts [of the United States] are individual men and women. The United States is an association of citizens. . . . It never happened that a group of people called Americans came together to form a political society called America. The people are Americans only by virtue of having come together" (1990, 636). He goes on to eloquently describe the Great Seal as a prominent symbol of coming together in the United States:

> The Great Seal of the United States carries the motto E pluribus unum, "From many, one," which seems to suggest that manyness must be left behind for the sake of oneness. Once there were many, now the many have been merged, or in Israel Zangwell's classic image, been melted down into one. But the Great Seal presents a different image: The "American" eagle holds a sheaf of arrows. Here there is no merger or fusion but only a fastening, a putting together: many in one. Perhaps the adjective "American" describes this kind of oneness. We might say, tentatively, that it points to the citizenship, not the nativity or nationality, of the men and women it designates. It is a political adjective, and its politics are liberal in the strict sense: generous, tolerant, ample, accommodating—it allows for the survival, even the enhancement and flourishing of manyness. (635)

The fastening that binds the diverse arrows of the American community is political socialization. It is explicitly intended to create unity out of a fundamentally diverse population, embodying multiple symbolic boundaries. American public life is "full of quasi-religious ceremonies and rituals meant to celebrate the country's democratic political institutions: flag-raising ceremonies, the naturalization oath, Thanksgiving, and the Fourth of July" (Lipset 1997, 18). Walzer suggests that this "competition to demonstrate their patriotism" is a product of the missing "fatherland" for Americans: "The kind of natural or organic loyalty that we (rightly or wrongly) recognize in families doesn't seem to be a feature of our politics" (1990, 634). Americans perform their nationalism because the performance brings them together by bridging symbolic boundaries. Integration into American identity requires only adhering to the "Americanist" ideology and participating in the performance and is therefore (theoretically) possible for anyone, including those of different ethnicities, races, religions, and nationalities.

At the same time, mainstream pundits in the West have raised questions about the ability of Muslims to integrate into democratic societies, and they debate whether the participation of Muslim citizens and noncitizens in civic life is possible and/or desirable. Public concern over the compatibility between Islam and American democracy became clear in the wake of the September eleventh terrorist attacks and reached a fever pitch during the 2016 presidential campaign. Muslim Americans are now navigating a tense environment in which their "Americanness" is constantly questioned.

Because they are the most visible adherents of Islam, covered Muslim women are frequently targets of hostility and discrimination, as discussed in chapter 3. Their continued vulnerability highlights a disconnect between discriminatory public sentiment and the rhetoric of civil liberties. This disconnect between liberal civic values and the mistreatment of Muslims raises concerns about the viability of the United States as a pluralistic democratic state, which should theoretically protect and embrace an emergent minority. Social acceptance of Muslims and the ability of covered women to function as citizens in the United States are both predicated on common understandings of American identity, civic values, and whether Muslims are able to participate in identity construction and access their rights of citizenship.

Our focus group participants see citizenship as a contractual arrangement in which citizens participate in a number of ways, and in return, they expect access to the benefits of citizenship, such as the protection of civil rights and freedoms and opportunities for representation. However, while our participants believe they are fulfilling their side of the contract, they feel that their participation is not translating into all the benefits to which they are entitled. In particular, the Muslim-American women we spoke with felt neglected by the formal political system. The perceived disconnect between the duties and benefits of citizenship for Muslim women has serious implications for Muslim Americans and for the preservation and sustenance of democratic ideals in the United States. We explore all these issues in this chapter, including our research participants' understanding of their hyphenated identities and how they translate into a substantive exercise of citizenship rights and responsibilities.

The Hyphenated American

Despite the universal and liberal precepts informing American political ideology, immigrant groups tell narratives of exclusion, discrimination, and experiences inconsistent with American liberalism. Many minority groups respond to alienation by developing their own cohesive and at times exclusive communities within the United States—often through the use of bonding social networks (see chapter 5). The maintenance of distinct cultural groups leads to a proliferation of hyphenated identities in which American citizens might simultaneously be American and something else. There is a multidimensionality created by hyphenation, which highlights the way the ethnic (or in the case of Muslims, religious) identity compounds American identity: "It is not the case that Irish Americans, say, are culturally Irish and politically American, as the pluralists [theorists] claim. . . . Rather they are culturally Irish American and politically Irish American. Their culture has been significantly influenced by American culture. . . . With them and with every ethnic and religious group except the American-Americans, hyphenation is doubled" (Walzer 1990, 651).

In the case of Muslim Americans, hyphenation is doubled in both religious and political spheres, where Muslim Americans create new and altered forms of religious and political practice.[1] The power of multiple identities is flexibility: individuals can conceivably select the identity they wish to draw on in any particular social interaction (Sen 2007). However, that identity can be limited by external circumstances. The context of post–September eleventh America has restricted the focus of Muslim Americans to their religious and national identities, perhaps because the two identities are perceived to be in

---

1. Our findings in chapter 4 affirm the idea of iterated identities in which the religious lives of Muslim Americans are influenced by American cultural and political values, and their political participation is informed by their religious convictions. Though our empirical results affirm the synergy between the two elements of a hyphenated identity—religion and nationality—focusing on only two dimensions of an individual's identity can be limiting. In every individual, there are multitudes of possible personal identities involving class, gender, profession, language, literature, science, music, morals, or politics, all of which influence a person's character and development.

conflict.[2] President Obama addressed these intersectional identities during his first presidential visit to a mosque:

> In our lives, we all have many identities. We are sons and daughters, and brothers and sisters. We're classmates; Cub Scout troop members. We're followers of our faith. We're citizens of our country. And today, there are voices in this world, particularly over the Internet, who are constantly claiming that you have to choose between your identities—as a Muslim, for example, or an American. Do not believe them. If you're ever wondering whether you fit in here, let me say it as clearly as I can, as President of the United States: You fit in here—right here. You're right where you belong. You're part of America, too. You're not Muslim or American. You're Muslim and American. (Obama 2016)

Obama's words implied that an individual is constantly and equally both American and Muslim. However, hyphenated identities are more flexible than he implies, allowing the identified to vary the weight and attention given to one part of the identity over the other: "One can be an *Irish*-American, and *Irish-American*, or an Irish-*American*. Each of those italicized variations represents a difference in the relative emotional weight given to those two central elements of a hyphenated identity. The placement of the italicized portion of the hyphenated identity would seem, at least in theory, to be consistent with a framing of the American identity acquisition process as a progression, albeit probably one with some back and forth movement" (Renshon 2011).

Some of our participants dismiss the hyphenated description of identity. For example, Xara observes, "I understand American Muslim to mean 'Muslim people of faith who live in America.'"[3] Others explicitly discuss where the emphasis falls in their own hyphenated identity.[4] Elmira emphasizes the Muslim component of her identity: "I think Muslim is my identity, it is the noun part. America is just where I happen to live. While I am attached, and I do feel myself American, and I know that I am very culturally different than, say, a Syrian Muslim or a Pakistani Muslim, to me the Muslim is the defining part."[5] Even while emphasizing the Muslim component of her identity,

---

2. We elaborate on the perception and consequences of conflict in chapter 2, though it is worth revisiting the results of the 2015 American Values Survey administered by the Public Religion Research Institute (Cooper et al. 2015), which found that a majority (56%) of American respondents believe that Islam contradicts American values and way of life. This percentage grew since the administration of the 2011 survey, in which 47 percent held this opinion.

3. Xara is a thirty-seven-year-old covered black native-born American living in Illinois.

4. When asking about identity in the focus group interviews, we typically used the phrase "Muslim American," simply because it is the most commonly used descriptor in the literature.

5. Elmira is a thirty-two-year-old covered South Asian foreign-born American living in Texas.

Elmira nonetheless recognizes her sense of belonging to America and her American-ness, perhaps mostly as a cultural component of her hybrid identity. She seems to define herself primarily in terms of her religious identity and secondarily in terms of her American cultural identity.

Conversely, Tamira, who is working on her master's degree, prefers to highlight the American identifier because she believes it spotlights a unique and meaningful context for Muslims:

> I have been struggling with this in my own work, what terms to use, American Muslim or Muslim American. . . . I thought, "Wow, what does Muslim American mean and why is it that I'm not American Muslim?" To me it means two different things. Yes, I am an American who is Muslim, but I'm also a Muslim who is an American. It depends to me on what ways I am using that term. I like the term "American Muslim" when I am doing my own [academic] work. . . . I want to differentiate in the literature a Muslim from another country and a Muslim who lives in America because our experiences are very different here in the American context. We are American Muslims if we are just differentiating from other Muslims.
>
> Now, "Muslim American," how much do I like that term? I don't know, because I don't think that I need to qualify my American-ness. It somehow means to me that America must be a "Christian America," and now I am part of that "Muslim America." I don't believe that. So, I don't know. I've really grappled with these terms. In many ways, I really do like the term "American Muslim." We are still very much American. So, I think I am leaning towards a preference of American Muslim as a term as opposed to Muslim American.[6]

Through her own reflections, Tamira describes how emphasizing one of her identities over the other changes her social interactions and implies different symbolic boundaries. She rejects the term "Muslim American" because she believes the adjective "Muslim" qualifies the noun "American," yet she felt she should not need to qualify her "American-ness." Her refusal to qualify her American-ness reflects that her religious identity should not constitute a symbolic boundary setting her apart from other Americans. At the same time, both Elmira and Tamira see the American component of their identities as something that distinguishes them from Muslims elsewhere in the world.

The following exchange between four covered women in their twenties (Faaiza, Erina, Farah, and Haarisa) in one of our New York focus groups helps unpack the complexity of Muslim-American identity in the United States in

---

6. Tamira is a thirty-seven-year-old covered black native-born American living in Illinois.

a particularly evocative way.[7] In this exchange, these women discuss the relative weight of their identities, the value judgments made within and between identity categories, the fluidity and performative nature of identity, and the individualism inherent in identity formation. Furthermore, their discussion reveals how new hyphenated identities are emerging with generational shifts across Muslim immigrants and the increase in American converts. While nearly all of our focus group participants discuss their understanding of Muslim-American identity, this exchange is the broadest in scope, while capturing the ideas expressed in every one of our interviews. Faaiza maintains,

> I love identifying myself as that, as a Muslim American, especially in that order, too, because this is my country and my religion is the most important to me. But after that, like . . . this is where I was born, this is where I was raised and I was born with these values, American values of tolerating freedom of expression and freedom of religion and freedom of the press, and I think that's one reason why our country is so successful is because we're tolerating so much diversity and therefore people from all over the world can come and bring their talents into our country. So, I take a lot of pride in that phrase, Muslim American.

Despite preferring the "Muslim" descriptor to the "American" noun, Faaiza's initial description of her hyphenated identity does not engage her religious life at all and places emphasis on the "American" noun. She discusses the institutions and qualities of the political culture that allow her, as a member of a religious minority, to participate in American life. Her focus on how diversity flourishes in American society implies an appreciation of how American political values and institutions bridge symbolic boundaries and transform difference into richness. Erina picks up the discussion, but changes the order of her self-ascribed identities:

> It's different whether you're Muslim American or American Muslim and it has different connotations depending on where you come from. I feel like my first identity tends to be American Muslim, because I was born and raised here. I feel like that's always what I lead with, "Oh I'm American." And then people are like "Oh no, no, but what are you?" I know what people are generally getting at, so it's kind of trying to

---

7. Faaiza is a twenty-five-year-old covered South Asian native-born American; Erina is a twenty-eight-year-old covered black native-born American; Farah is a twenty-five-year-old covered South Asian foreign-born American; and Haarisa is a twenty-six-year-old covered South Asian foreign-born American. All four of them live in New York.

divert from that initial, "I'm Muslim, I'm American." And that opens up the conversation in someone's mind before I even say "I'm Muslim" that there are American Muslims here. So I feel like in that way, that's kind of how I identify myself . . . being American Muslim allows me to freely practice.

Even though Erina changes the order to make "Muslim" the noun and "American" the descriptor, she clearly intends to emphasize the American descriptor by placing it first. Similar to Tamira, who rejects the idea of differentiating Americans according to their religious identities, Erina would rather emphasize her similarities with non-Muslims. And similar to Faaiza, Erina emphasizes the importance of the political institutions that allow her to embrace her hyphenated identity.

Farah elaborates on this last point:

I think [the term "Muslim American"] makes me think of a blessing because I think of America as my home so even if there is a better place for Muslims to live, I can't imagine it, because I'm used to here. I like the diversity here and I like the opportunity of being around non-Muslims and just not being isolated . . . being able to interact with other people, other faiths. And what Faaiza said about nothing being imposed on me, or the religious freedom that guarantees me the right to practice, but still protects other people who don't want to practice. I just like having the freedom.

Like Faaiza and Erina, Farah reaffirms American political values, but she adamantly focuses on celebrating the diversity, and in particular religious diversity, of the American context. She ends her statement with another reference to the First Amendment right to freedom of religion but then extends these rights beyond her own religious practice to embrace people who do not practice a religion. Perhaps Farah's perspective is influenced by her personal experiences: though she is a citizen of the United States, she was not born here, and this comparative perspective may give her a unique appreciation of tolerance and religious diversity.

Continuing the conversation, Haarisa's reaction to American Muslim identity is very different from the opinions expressed by Faaiza, Erina, and Farah. Haarisa is a citizen of the United States, though she also maintains the citizenship of her birth country.

I don't know. I think because I wasn't born here and I immigrated here . . . even though I was very young, and I have the passport now, it's not something I choose to identify with. If I need to check off that box or someone

keeps asking me . . . yeah, I'm American. For me, civic identity or nationality, I have the privilege of it being very fluid. I can be British Indian, British
Asian, American, it really doesn't matter to me. That's not something that's
fixed in my identity. And I think that's a real huge privilege to have. Not all
of you have that. But, Muslim . . . I identify as Muslim, yes, but that is also
something I constantly think about as well . . . why am I Muslim? Why do I
believe in God and that Mohammed is the last messenger of God? It's something I really constantly think about, especially in the last year and half. For
me, put the two together, I never really do that honestly, unless I'm doing a
survey or something. But, I don't really say I'm a Muslim American unless
I think about the kind of work I'm doing and I think, "OK, I'm part of the
Muslim American community and I want to tell our stories."

Haarisa is speaking directly to the idea discussed earlier that people can and
do select different aspects of their identity to negotiate particular social situations and symbolic boundaries. She embraces this flexibility with the national
identifier, which she sees more as an administrative or political tool. However, in her mind the Muslim identifier is less flexible: she deliberately and
thoughtfully engages with the beliefs that underlie the identity, making it fundamental to her daily life. For Haarisa, the emphasis is exclusively on Muslim
identity: the hyphenated identity is not useful to her personally, though she
does see its utility in wider society.

Faaiza builds upon Haarisa's introduction of flexible national identities to
introduce the idea of a new "blended" identity:

I feel like there's a new culture starting in America and that's like the
Muslim-American culture because in the past generation, in the sev-
enties and eighties, so many immigrants came from India, Pakistan,
Bangladesh, and Egypt and other Muslim countries around the world.
And then they had children and now these children, they can't really
relate so much to their parents' culture and there's a generation gap. I
experienced that, and my parents were born in Guyana, South America,
which is a British colony. . . . But, even I can't relate to my parents and
my aunt and my uncle. . . . Where do I belong? So I feel like there's a
new up-and-coming Muslim-American culture where there are converts
to Islam, and then there are people born in America who are Muslim,
and they are coming together and they're forming this new American-
Muslim identity, and I feel like it's new, upcoming, and I'm a part of that.

With these remarks, Faaiza is affirming "double hyphenation." Muslim Americans are "Muslim-American" individuals both culturally and religiously and
"Muslim-American" citizens politically. "Double hyphenation" effectively

connects people differentiated by multiple symbolic boundaries, bringing them together under a new collective identity. The new identity is unique and perhaps the purview of a new generation.

Erina celebrates this new identity and suggests its formation comes with new responsibilities:

> I think that by just the phrase Muslim American, American Muslim whatever it is, that comes with the ticket of active engagement. Even if you don't mean to be sort of an activist, or you don't mean to be sort of that person in the limelight of whatever have you—just by identifying as an American Muslim puts you in the limelight. . . . Being here it's not primarily Muslims, so that really forces you to not take it for granted, that you are Muslim. But to really study and to really practice, and to really find out what it is and what does it mean to you as an individual. Not just for your people, not just for your culture, not just for whatever, but for you as an individual. What does it mean to be a Muslim? . . . and you constantly question and constantly reevaluate and you're constantly changing that as you get knowledge, information, school, and education or whatever it is.

In this statement, Erina emphasizes both an external and internal role in identity formation. She argues that identifying with a minority group connotes a political statement that needs to be paired with self-examination. Essentially, the inner lives of Muslims will be influenced by their social lives in a context where they are the minority and vice versa. This iterative process means that change and negotiation across symbolic boundaries is continual. Perhaps the change involves shifting the emphasis to a different part of the hyphenated identity or the eventual formation of a completely new identity.

However, not everyone responds favorably to the notion of hyphenated identity. Lydia, a convert to Islam, feels very frustrated by the way the figurative hyphen separates Americans and Muslims, while it also unnecessarily creates boundaries within the Muslim community:

> They don't say "Christian Americans." The media has such a big role in it. They want to create lines. They want to create issues that aren't there. When we come here we don't say, "What kind of Muslim are you? Are you a Muslim American? Are you a Muslim Palestinian?" If you are a Muslim, you are a Muslim. I don't really care where you are from.[8]

---

8. Lydia is a twenty-eight-year-old covered South Asian native-born American living in Virginia.

Like Tamira, Lydia is focusing on the Muslim community and is frustrated by the boundaries the hyphen represents and creates. Lydia follows up this statement with a discussion of how the media use the Muslim identifier only in reference to negative and antisocial acts in the United States. From her perspective, hyphenated identities are invoked in a disparaging way by non-Muslims.

For better or worse, hyphenated identity allows Muslim Americans to "remember who they [are] and to insist, also, on *what else they are*" (Walzer 1990, 636). For some of our respondents, the "what else they are" is divisive and burdensome, while for others, it is something to be celebrated and emphasized. Ultimately, Muslim-American identity is complex and controversial. In blending elements of religious and political identity and connecting and cutting across multiple symbolic boundaries, it includes aspects of gender and generational norms, ethnicity, migration experiences, and culture. This multitude of identities speaks to the multidimensional lives of Muslim Americans and also gives them access to many different facets of American society.

From Identity to Citizenship

While participation in the creation and maintenance of American and/or hyphenated identities can be a personal and social activity, it also serves an important institutional purpose by enabling full participation in a democratic political system. Norms define expectations about citizens' roles in politics, and these expectations shape behavior. In the United States, citizenship norms include those of political participation, personal autonomy, a commitment to social order, and solidarity (Dalton 2008, 78–79).

However, the broader American public often perceives citizenship in simpler terms capturing the notions of duties and engagement. Citizenship duties involve behaviors such as voting, obeying the law, and serving in the military or on a jury; engagement encompasses more liberal or communitarian goals reflecting autonomy in opinion formation, a commitment to addressing social needs, and participation in civil society. Most Americans perceive both as important aspects of citizenship, though the relative importance of the duty dimension is less controversial and more highly valued, largely because the duties are more concrete and less charged with ideological politics (Dalton 2008).

Discussing duties and engagement as the two norms of citizenship tells only part of the story. Citizenship is inherently reciprocal, resembling a contract that relates citizens to the government through mutually enforceable claims: "[Citizenship is] variable in range, never completely specifiable, always depending on unstated assumptions about context, modified by practice, constrained by collective memory, yet ineluctably involving rights and obligations sufficiently defined that either party is likely to express indignation and take corrective action when the other fails to meet expectations built into the relationship" (Tilly 1997, 600). In this contractual sense, citizenship defines a relationship between the individual and the state that can be traced back to Lockean notions of consent and contract. Modern liberal notions of citizenship are rooted in John Locke's idea of a social contract that is justified by the consent of the governed. The viability of this contract depends on the mutual performance of the rights and duties between the government and the governed. Effectively, while citizens may have a responsibility to fulfill the duties of citizenship and engage with the political system, a legitimate liberal and democratic government also has a responsibility to secure the rights of its citizens. The strength of the citizenship bond and a sense of belonging to the polity both depend on the performance of this inherently reciprocal relationship. Institutional arrangements and social interactions over time and space give citizenship its multilayered and flexible character (Tilly 1997). In this broader perspective, citizenship defines a complex and evolving contractual relationship between the individual and the state that encompasses dimensions of rights, duties, participation, and identity (Delanty 1997). Muslim-American women's sense of being accepted as full-fledged citizens of the United States depends on their feelings of belonging, fostered along all these dimensions of citizenship.

As a religious minority composed of individuals from diverse racial, ethnic, and cultural backgrounds, Muslims in America have long been carving a space for themselves in the political fabric of American society at both the individual and the organizational levels (Ghanea-Bassiri 2010; Spellberg 2013). At the individual level, our respondents noted the contractual nature of citizenship, recognizing their civic responsibilities to the government but clearly also expecting a reciprocal relationship with the United States government. For example, while discussing her two children, Hafeeza explains that as full Americans, her children, "have rights from this country, but they also have rights to this country."[9] The rest of this chapter examines how our focus group participants' faith and the practice of head covering have reinforced their concepts of citizenship, particularly the way they perceive the benefits of citizenship and the reciprocal responsibilities to the government.

---

9. Hafeeza is a thirty-one-year-old covered white native-born American living in Massachusetts.

Contractual Citizenship: Benefits from the Government

In negotiating their contractual relationship with the government, our focus group participants collectively defined the common good as the protection of individual rights, personal freedoms, and democratic representation. Our discussions with them about individual freedoms largely related to their religious practice, while their prioritization of democratic representation came out of a more general narrative about being a minority group in America. Overall, we found that our respondents have three primary expectations from government: respect for civil liberties (inalienable freedoms protected in the Bill of Rights), recognition of individual freedoms (these arise from the primacy of the individual), and the application of civil rights (the right to participate in civil and political life free from discrimination and repression). We develop these three benefits of citizenship below with reference to head covering.

Civil Liberties

The most direct association between American democracy and the Islamic faith is in the First Amendment, particularly the Establishment Clause and the Free Exercise Clause. The former prevents government interference in religious affairs, while the latter blocks the government from interfering in individual religious practice. Our focus group participants automatically and regularly make the connection between their religious lives and American civil liberties, as Faaiza and Erina do in their conversation on Muslim-American identity earlier in this chapter. Elmira elaborated on the compatibility of American and Islamic identities: "I don't see why I can't follow American laws and my own laws. There is nothing in America that keeps me from praying or from fasting or from doing any of the other religious requirements whatsoever. So, as an identity, to me it is fairly seamless." In this statement, Elmira distinguishes between political and religious laws while simultaneously acknowledging her personal obligation to follow both. At the same time, she highlights the American law that protects her religious practice.

In chapter 4 we discussed the ways Muslim women will reinterpret the head covering through the lens of the First Amendment in order to justify or explain the practice to non-Muslims. Our respondents also quickly invoke the First Amendment as an explanation for why head covering is an appropriate and protected behavior in the United States. Gudia, a woman from Washington, DC, who wears the niqab (the face veil) ventures, "Living here I find [wearing a niqab] very easy. I like it because we can practice our religion freely."[10] Similarly, when asked what message was sent through wearing a head covering, Hafeeza in Boston replies, "You are practicing your faith . . . you have that right. . . . Just like anything else, the right to vote, the right to do anything. It is my right." Perhaps Gudia and Hafeeza are exhibiting sentiments like those noted by Michael Fine and Selcuk Sirin, who observed in their study of Muslim-American youth that "for many of the young women, the US offers a questionable but desirous freedom, a deep sense of power and the opportunity for young women to engage Islam without fear of repercussion" (2008, 159).

Hafeeza goes on to explain the importance of the First Amendment for affirming Muslims' faith in and identification with the American political system by describing a university paper she wrote on the United States and the Revolutionary War:

> It really helped me to understand that the values of this country were based on religious freedom. So, I feel very, very confident in myself in living here as American because I know that a lot people came here escaping religious persecution. I know my country protects people's rights, which I think is so beautiful. People have more rights here being a Muslim than they do in some Muslim countries. I am so grateful I live here and I would never want to live anywhere else. I love my country just as much as any other American out there.

For Hafeeza, her First Amendment right to freedom of religion affirms her American identity and her patriotism as a citizen of a country where her beliefs are respected. Many of our other participants mention appreciation for and expectation of protected religious practice in the United States and the freedom to wear a head covering (or not to wear one) in whatever form. Often these observations are made within a larger conversation about the geopolitics of the headscarf and disputes surrounding covering in Turkey and Iran. The comparisons are always used to highlight the relative freedoms in the United States and to express satisfaction with the legal system.

The right to practice Islam does not protect Muslim citizens from experiencing social criticism or discrimination. When encountering opposition, some of our participants explicitly invoke civil liberties and the First Amendment as a legal defense and justification for the visible manifestations of their Islamic faith. Lydia in Norfolk, Virginia, references recent opposition to the

---

10. Gudia is a covered native-born American woman living in Virginia. She did not fill out any additional details in our demographics survey.

construction of a mosque and argues, "The law is on [the Muslims'] side. Because there is a law that says they can practice their religion, they can build a mosque." Farah in New York mentions the First Amendment as a personal defense from discrimination in the workplace and identifies governmental authority in antidiscrimination law: "I work in a government building. . . . If it's a government building then I'm protected by law against anyone mistreating me. My religious rights are protected and no one is ever going to question my dress code." For Lydia and Farah, the First Amendment provides them with more than legal permission to practice. It provides them with a legal defense against discrimination.

In general, our participants affirm their access to civil rights and frame civil rights as both a justification of difference and a protection from discrimination. The protection and enforcement of these rights is perhaps the strongest and most consistently worded expectation of citizenship provided by our respondents. However, many of them extended the discussion into more general individual freedoms that preserve the quality of life of American citizens, which we discuss in the following section.

Individual Freedoms

Our focus group participants refer to many of the political assumptions, or norms, that regulate conduct in the United States, particularly respect for freedom, privacy, and autonomy. They indicate that they are abiding by and reflecting American values and express a desire to be recognized as participants in both the architecture and the construction of American norms of behavior. This desire manifests itself clearly in exchanges about the meaning of the head covering. For example, In Detroit, Jessica and her daughter Amy invoke personal autonomy as emblematic of head-covering practices:

> Jessica: Wearing hijab is not an oppressive thing. A lot of times people have the misconception that it takes away your freedom, but I don't equate freedom with modesty. I still go to the mall. I still go to school. I work. I hang with my friends. We go out to eat. I still do everything the average American would do. We just wear a little bit more than you do.
>
> Amy: I would, just to piggyback on that, I would want people to know that we are not oppressed. . . . Some women are, but here in America we practice our religion in the way it should be, and it doesn't mean that women are not allowed the same things that men are. We just tend to be more modest.

> Jessica: Sometimes people confuse culture with religion. Sometimes the oppressive component comes in with the culture. Sometimes people seem to misinterpret that and think that Islam oppresses women. . . . Living here in the United States, most of us are pretty much free and not oppressed at all.[11]

For Amy and Jessica, wearing the head covering is an expression of their American value system and their faith in its ability to guarantee freedom and autonomy. All our covered focus group participants affirm this perspective. They believe their faith in general and the headscarf in particular are the products and expression of free choice, made in a context where choice should and can be celebrated.

Similarly, Erina explains how freedom and privacy within the United States allow her to practice Islam privately and publicly, as she chooses. She maintains, "Being an American Muslim, it allows me to freely practice. . . . It's the idea that's attached to that side of choice. So I have a choice to practice, I have a choice to fast." In this statement, Erina references other contexts where practicing Islam in a certain way might be legally mandated or socially enforced. In the United States, she feels the freedom to practice in whatever way she wants, and that freedom allows her faith to be more genuine. It also allows her to individualize her religious practice, a choice that complements the emphasis on individualism in American political culture.

All our respondents stress the importance of personal autonomy within the United States and argue that the way they practice Islam is an exercise in individualism and individual freedoms, which are rooted in and protected by civil liberties. In asserting their freedom, our respondents also express an expectation that their free choices will be respected as one of the benefits of belonging to the American community and of citizenship.

Civil Rights

A large part of the social experience of Muslim-American women is distorted by discrimination, othering, and negative stereotyping from non-Muslims. In reaction, many women relate their current struggles to those from the civil rights era. Unsurprisingly, the tendency to connect the Muslim-American experience to that of the civil rights struggle is strongest among our

---

11. Jessica is a forty-year-old covered Arab native-born American, and Amy is a twenty-one-year-old covered Arab native-born American. Both live in Michigan.

African-American participants, many of whom grew up during the civil rights movement.

Kadijah is an African-American woman in Boston, Massachusetts, who tells us her story of finding Islam through involvement with the civil rights and black power movements of the 1970s.[12] She mentions, "Since that time I have never taken off my scarf. I've never had reservations about it. I think part of it is because being in this country and being a black woman and having the experiences of being a black woman in this country has made me stronger in terms of who I am." Kadijah is referencing a particular type of political socialization achieved through being a targeted racial minority living in the American South, where she learned how to navigate difference and discrimination.

Xara also discusses the intersection of her racial and religious experience:

> I identify myself as an African-American Muslim Woman. There was an issue with another white sister who had been harassed in California. She was wearing a headscarf, so she wrote about it on her blog. I sent her a message. I normally don't do this. "Well it's good that you can take off your headscarf and get treated like a human being. I can't take off my skin and be treated like a human being. . . . Probably because of my background, first I will say [I identify as] African American. . . . African-American Muslim Woman, that is the way I identify myself. Because whether I wear headscarf or not, I've had the experience because I wasn't wearing the headscarf my entire life that I'll get certain kinds of treatment, maybe added a little bit to it, but not much.

Xara describes being socialized into learning to handle discriminatory treatment, though she simultaneously demonstrates a lack of empathy for those less well equipped to negotiate othering from non-Muslims. She perceives discriminatory acts as targeting either her religion or her race, but attributes the bulk of her past mistreatment to racial bias. This is perhaps because, as she observes, her race is visible and unchangeable and therefore inflexible. This inflexibility and constant vulnerability may require racial minorities to expect different responsibilities from the government in shaping and enforcing civil liberties (see Fineman 2008).

Earlier in the same focus group in Chicago, Tamira, another African-American woman, recounts a similar story:

> Even my friend who is a Muslim convert and is white, we've had this conversation about her and hijab, and I keep telling her, we

---

12. Kadijah is a twenty-year-old covered Arab native-born American living in Massachusetts.

go round and round, and I said, "Your issue is you don't want to give up white privilege." This idea of being recognized and not being harmed, you don't want to move through the world being an "other." When she does she is incredibly uncomfortable. She says, "I don't want to be the flag-bearer." "Guess what? Welcome to being a minority."

Kadijah, Xara, and Tamira express greater ease with the headscarf as an identifier because they grew up in a climate where their visible minority status was inflexible and constantly enforced. In some respects, they had already developed strategies to deal with an ascribed hyphenated identity, sometimes through their participation in politics as activists in the civil rights movement.

While African-American women experience particular patterns of political socialization that enable them to effectively confront discrimination, they are also well positioned to invoke civil rights in defense of themselves and other minorities. The same Chicago focus group illustrates this skill when Lara describes the African-American Muslim population: "I would literally say many of the women who became Muslim were from the black power movement. They were from the civil rights movement. They had already gotten over some things to be leaders in that movement and were in no way going to the back of anybody's bus, however it is that you conceive a bus."[13] In this comment, Lara speaks of the pervasive influence of the civil rights movement in determining both race relations and gender equality within and outside the Muslim community. The civil rights movement developed the political identity of African Americans, and that identity transferred into the lives of Muslim African Americans.

While civil rights are available to all American citizens, our participants do not invoke civil rights in the same way, and most do not mention them at all. The discussion of civil rights organically emerges especially in conversations with African-American participants. Perhaps because they are part of another socially targeted group, these respondents tend to be more cynical regarding how much they can rely on the government to ensure civil rights to the same extent as it protects civil liberties or individual freedoms. Nevertheless, civil rights are a galvanizing force for many Muslim Americans, and citizens at least theoretically expect them to be upheld by the American government.

---

13. Lara is a fifty-year-old covered black native-born American woman living in Illinois.

Contractual Citizenship: Responsibilities to the Government

Our focus group participants recognize the reciprocal nature of democratic citizenship and understand that citizens have obligations to the state. They argue that participation in the formal politics of the state and general civic engagement fulfill a citizenship requirement. Though our participants debate the nature of this link and how it relates to their religious life (see chapter 4), the general consensus is that they have an obligation to participate, and that this participation entitles them to the full range of citizenship benefits. Hafeeza, the mother who previously identified her children's "rights to" and "rights from" this government, also poignantly argues that the rights to the government include fulfilling civic duties and participating in civil society. We develop these two themes below.

Participation

Our research population participates in politics at levels exceeding those for the average American population.[14] When they discuss political participation, our participants frame it as "something Americans do" and see themselves as indistinguishable from non-Muslim Americans. Malika in Boston argues for a more functional approach to politics, which should equally serve all members of American society.[15] She claims, "When you vote for someone . . . you vote for them because of their values and what they believe in. You look at them at face value. Do they have the policy I like? If they do, I'm going to vote for them. If they do not, then I'll vote for somebody that is able to represent me." Malika sees room for inclusion around universal issues that do not necessarily relate to one belief system. Khalifa, also from Boston, remarks, "As an American citizen I feel like we're completely represented," and she builds on this theme with explicit references to secularism:

> We live in a secular government for a reason so I don't think religion should ever be brought up in any form of government. . . . It's just the

---

14. Of our covered focus group participants, 57 percent regularly vote for a political party (exclusively the Democratic Party), compared with 63 percent of our survey respondents. Sixty-four percent of our focus group participants report voting in the 2012 presidential elections, compared with 69 percent of our covered survey respondents. Forty-seven percent of our focus group respondents report voting in 2008, compared with 63 percent of the survey respondents. Of our uncovered focus group participants, 80 percent of them report voting in both 2008 and 2012. Ninety percent regularly vote for the Democratic Party. See chapter 5 for further discussion.

15. Malika is an eighteen-year-old covered black native-born American living in Massachusetts.

American political system, not the Muslim political system. So, I vote on internal affairs and foreign affairs based on what I believe is right. There's not really any Christian values or Jewish values or Muslim values. . . . At the end of the day, we're all American, we're in a democracy, we're able to vote for what we want. . . . I get to vote for what I want and it may not be carried out but my voice was heard. And just having the right to vote even though I come from a religion that's not as popular as other religions in America, I feel like that in itself is like I'm being represented.[16]

For Khalifa, secularism creates opportunities for representation within formal institutions centered on the common interests that all Americans share.

The majority of our participants are full American citizens who believe in a citizen's obligation to participate in the American political system. Though their personal and political values are influenced by their religious beliefs, when it comes to formal participation, our respondents express confidence in the democratic political process and support for secular politics. The merging of religious and political life is most obvious in the civic engagement of our focus group participants as hinted at in chapter 4.

Civic Engagement

At his 2016 mosque visit, President Obama implored Muslim Americans, "Understand your power to bring about change. Stay engaged in your community. Help move our country forward—your country forward" (Obama 2016). This statement recognizes the many different ways Muslim Americans can provoke change through informal politics and civic engagement. There is evidence that they are participating in politics both informal and formal in different ways than they did a couple of generations ago. Some recent research on American citizenship (e.g., Putnam 2000) focuses on the perceived deterioration of the norms of citizenship duty, highlighting generational differences in voting behavior, trust in government, obedience to authority, and civic engagement. However, "Generational patterns also indicate that the erosion of duty-based citizenship is counterbalanced by an increase in engaged citizenship, especially among the young and better educated" (Dalton 2008, 83). The contractual nature of citizenship in the United States may not be failing, just changing.

---

16. Khalifa is an eighteen-year-old covered Arab native-born American living in Massachusetts.

Our respondents personify this trend toward emphasizing civic engagement, and many of them blend civic engagement with their religious obligations. Martha in Boston connects religious law with a broad definition of public service: "But when it just comes to the city council or just public work, parks, roads, investment in public infrastructure, I feel like it's fair and it's very Islamic. I mean, that's what you should be doing. That's what Shari'a is . . . you establish a welfare system. . . . There are a bunch of things you do for the town, there are a bunch of things you do for the country."[17] Many of our participants echo these ideas and connect Islam to broader social values and community service.

Even though our participants connect their faith to their community service, they do not necessarily restrict their activities to those within the Muslim community. They see their responsibility to help more broadly. For example, Emily explains the communal activities of her local mosque:

> Dearborn [mosques are] very active in community service and giving back to the community. From both sects [Sunni and Shi'a]. At our local mosque, we are always having Kids against Hunger. It is not a Muslim organization, but we do bring it. We pack food for the poor. We are always running drives for poor people, homeless shelters in Detroit. Giving them free clothing. Muslims are very active with that. Giving, even if they are not Muslim. If someone is in need, we do give.[18]

Jessica, also in Detroit but in another focus group, connects her civic engagement to religiously affirmed concerns about equality and "embracing the community as a whole and making sure the less fortunate are taken care of. Making sure that you have a government and that you have people representing you and that care about the less fortunate and that care about other people as well. That you are not only about the rich and famous and the upper class; that you are there for everybody."

However, some of our participants in Boston reject the idea of religiously mandated participation and connect the idea of political engagement back to obligations of living in a community, perhaps closer to the concept of contractual citizenship. A conversation between Kadijah and Jasmin captures this:

> Kadijah: I think someone may think just by virtue of doing community service you're doing it because you're Muslim and you want to fulfill that religious aspect of it and so you might go into it with that kind of

---

17. Martha is a twenty-four-year-old covered South Asian noncitizen living in Massachusetts.
18. Emily is a twenty-year-old covered Arab native-born American living in Michigan.

mind-set. But, in my opinion, I don't even think about that kind of stuff. Community service is just community service.

Jasmin: Ideally that is what the religion teaches is to be involved, active, thinking in general. It's not like you necessarily do everything because I'm a Muslim. I mean, people they do it because they want to help.[19]

Kadijah and Jasmin imply here that linking community service to religious command weakens the civic power of the service. This raises interesting ideas about whether the primary motivation for civic engagement matters for contractual citizenship and whether participation has to be performed with citizenship in mind. In a way, moving beyond religious teachings to participating in community service links engagement more directly with universal citizenship responsibilities and represents a distinct political socialization process. If citizenship is inherently reciprocal, living in a political community involves giving back to the community as well as benefiting from it. However, perhaps community engagement performed with nonreligious motivations may reflect stronger bonds of citizenship in a secular state.

In general, our participants are concerned with the welfare of their communities and regularly participate in civic engagement, often through their religious organizations. They connect the extent and nature of this involvement to their religious values but also recognize a social obligation to Muslims and non-Muslims alike. Ultimately, in both political participation and community service, women are active, visible American citizens.

The Citizen-Government Disconnect

The majority of our focus group participants recognize a responsibility to fulfill the obligations of citizenship, though they may disagree over the form their participation takes. Many participants view the ability to participate in the democratic process as the most crucial component of democratic representation, and they recognize an effort on the part of the majority group to fulfill the obligations of citizenship by deliberately including Muslim citizens in the political process, though they suggest outreach is rare.[20]

---

19. Jasmin is a nineteen-year-old covered Arab foreign-born American living in Massachusetts.

20. Our interviews took place during 2013 and therefore don't capture the more explicit efforts to reach out to Muslims on the part of the 2016 Hillary Clinton campaign. The campaign hired Farooq Mitha to work on Muslim outreach and hosted numerous meetings and roundtables with Islamic groups around the country (Graham 2016).

Despite voices of optimism and general satisfaction with American political values, many of our participants feel that their contractual citizenship
is being violated. This is in part a feature of the way multiple dimensions
of citizenship interact to produce inclusion and exclusion. While rights and
duties define citizenship mainly as a legal status that is universal and equal, the
promise of formal equality reflected in this conventional notion falls short of
forging a potentially stronger bond of citizenship—this stronger bond would
be grounded on political and civic participation and emotional attachment
to a common source of identity (Bloemraad, Korteweg, and Yurdakul 2008;
Carens 2000; Leydet 2011). Individuals may have different feelings of belonging to the polity along these multiple dimensions of citizenship (Carens 2000,
162). Because the institutional arrangements that regulate citizenship define
membership in the polity, citizenship necessarily entails a tension between
inclusion and exclusion that operates through its legal, participatory, and identity dimensions. Particularly in the case of immigrants and minorities, feelings of belonging fostered along these dimensions may sometimes conflict.
Inclusion along legal dimensions may not align with potentially exclusionary
aspects of citizenship operating along participatory and identity dimensions
(Bloemraad, Korteweg, and Yurdakul 2008). The political and civic engagement of citizens, as well as their identities as members of the polity, is largely
shaped by social and symbolic boundaries stemming from differences of race,
ethnicity, gender, class, culture, and religion (ibid.). Their legal status, on the
other hand, is defined by rights and obligations, which constitute a "constitutionally based relationship between the individual and the state" (Delanty
1997, 285). Thus, citizenship's promise of substantive equality among the
members of the polity crucially depends on how social and symbolic boundaries in the polity affect the engagement and identity of its members. When
the social and symbolic boundaries of citizenship do not align commensura-
bly with those that are defined constitutionally, citizens may feel that the state
is falling short of providing the benefits of communal membership equally
to all its citizens.

Our participants recognize several areas in which the symbolic boundaries
between the notions of being Muslim and being American restrict their full
inclusion into the American polity and in which the lived experiences of Muslims in America do not measure up to the standard of equal and fair treatment
expected by American citizens more generally. Our respondents recognize
the use of anti-Islamic othering as part of the political strategy adopted by
political parties. They feel, and often are, politically neglected because of the
relatively small population of Muslims and their geographic dispersion across
the United States. Perhaps more seriously, a vast majority of our participants

report experiencing active discrimination from governmental and other official institutions.

State-sanctioned forms of othering are distinguished from social othering. State-sanctioned othering, or profiling, involves the use of someone's physical appearance to predict his or her capabilities or propensity to engage in misconduct. Within the last decade, the appropriateness of profiling as a cost-saving measure has been discussed with reference to people of Middle Eastern descent in airports, to Hispanic people amid concerns about illegal immigration, and to African Americans (Legomsky 2005). Typically, these instances result in some form of search or arrest predicated on no evidence except an individual's appearance, which supposedly links him or her to a problematic population. Legal scholars report that while American society had begun to reach consensus about the inappropriateness of racial profiling in 2001 (see Gross and Livingston 2002), this consensus was significantly disrupted by the events of September eleventh. After the attack public opinion shifted to favor targeted searches for potential terrorists: In the fall of 1999, 81 percent of respondents in a national poll said they disapproved of "racial profiling," which was defined as the practice by some police officers of stopping "motorists of certain racial or ethnic groups because the officers believe that these groups are more likely than others to commit certain types of crimes." Two years later, 58 percent said they favored "requiring Arabs, including those who are US citizens, to undergo special, more intensive security checks before boarding airplanes in the US" (ibid., 1413).

In a special issue of the journal *Political Psychology* that investigates the aftermath of September eleventh, Schildkraut (2002) reports data from a survey in which she explores a similar effect: 66 percent of Americans polled suggested that it would be acceptable for law enforcement to stop and search anyone who looked Middle Eastern in order to prevent another attack, while only 21 percent supported profiling motorists on the basis of their race or ethnicity. In a later study, she investigates this comparison with a split-sample study comparing attitudes about profiling targeting black motorists and profiling with a counterterrorism objective. She finds that support for counterterrorism profiling (66%) is higher than support for profiling black motorists (23%) and that people are more permissive when the profiling targets immigrants than when it targets American citizens (Schildkraut 2009). She explains her results with reference to popular notions of American identity: defining American identity with Caucasian, Christian attributes is the strongest predictor of support for profiling, and support for profiling is only marginally offset by a liberal understanding of being an American.

In the experiences of our participants, state-sanctioned discrimination was most obvious at airports, and all our focus group interviews include a discussion of headscarf profiling in security-rich contexts. When profiling suspected terrorists in airports, security personnel have historically and controversially used country of origin as a selection mechanism. People of Arab descent were among those "increasingly caught in the net of the screenings" but this selection was administratively difficult because Arab Americans are generally classified as "white" by formal institutions (Gabbidon, Higgins, and Nelson 2012, 2). Religious identifiers are therefore perhaps a more specific selection mechanism for those seeking to profile Islamic terrorists in airport or other contexts. For men, common signifiers may include a beard and for women, the head covering.[21] When former president George W. Bush introduced racial-profiling rules in 2003 in an effort to ban the use of race or ethnicity in federal investigations, the prohibition of profiling extended only to race and not to other visible identifiers (Lichtblau 2003). When the Obama administration introduced new restrictions on racial profiling by federal offices in 2014, it encountered such serious opposition from the Department of Homeland Security that the agency was exempted from the provision. This means that the Transportation Security Administration, Immigration and Customs Enforcement, and Customs and Border Protection will continue to use profiling when conducting their searches (Horowitz and Markon 2014).

Our focus group participants mentioned airport profiling in every single interview. The expectation of airport screening is so pervasive that many of our respondents downplay it, like Mariam in Chicago, who sarcastically remarks "airports are special." At other times our participants felt indignant about their experiences.[22] For example, Malika, an African-American citizen who was eighteen years old at the time of the interview, mentions discriminatory treatment toward her mother and herself in airport security: "I wore the scarf even though it wasn't like a permanent thing for me yet. Like I just felt like wearing it that day, and I did get checked. Like me and my mom, may her soul rest in peace, I did get checked and it was strange that it was just me and

---

21. Specific examples of profiling practices in airports appear to be less supported by the public than more general policing profiling practices directed at Arab Americans. Gabbidon et al. (2009) analyzed national Gallup poll data to show that while 60 percent of the respondents believed profiling was widespread at airports, only 25 percent supported the practice. Similarly, data from a random sample of Pennsylvanians in 2011 revealed that most Pennsylvanians believe profiling is occurring at airports (77%) but do not support it (40% report supporting this form of profiling) (Gabbidon, Higgins, and Nelson 2012).

22. Mariam is a twenty-year-old covered South Asian foreign-born American living in Illinois.

my mom who got checked and none of my other siblings or my dad. And I have two younger sisters and they weren't wearing the scarf."[23]

Malika is frustrated by the apparent inconsistencies in security practices. She understands that they are profiling Muslims but is struck by the unfairness of the selection mechanism. In this instance, the headscarf alone constitutes a reason for being separated from other family members, showing that the security personnel target the headscarf rather than (or in addition to) race, nationality, or some other visible marker.

Many other respondents discuss what Erina calls the "not really random" security checks at airports. Khalifa, a United States citizen of Arab ethnicity, reports having "mixed feelings" about her experience of being "picked out" and "searched because [she is] wearing the scarf." For her, the airport security personnel are "just doing their job" to guarantee everyone's security, but nonetheless she adds, "There's definitely a heightened sense of security ... for Muslims." Zia from Detroit feels that the profiling goes beyond the selections for a search and senses that the searches performed on her were "deeper" or more exhaustive than the searches performed on non-Muslims.[24]

For the most part, our respondents report that the head covering plays a role in security searches primarily as a selection mechanism. On occasion, however, the treatment of covered individuals during the search process can create tension in a security-rich environment. For example, Haarisa recounts an incident in which she was asked to remove her scarf:

> But when it comes to officials, it's always like being patted down, being separated. A couple of times they've asked me to take my hijab off. They're like, "Can you please remove your scarf?" In front of everyone, and I was in shock and said no. And they just kept asking me, again and again, and I didn't have the patience to explain that this is part of my religion. I just got really frustrated and just kept saying no. And then this other woman came and said, "It's OK, just let her go."[25]

Haarisa believes that she and other covered women are deliberately selected for additional screening on the basis of their appearance, but the anecdote about being asked to remove her scarf is not necessarily an example of othering or profiling. Instead, it may reflect a failure to accommodate diversity in that the security guard expected Haarisa to behave like anyone else wearing a hat. The failure to understand the significance of the headscarf might reflect

---

23. Malika is an eighteen-year-old covered black native-born American living in Massachusetts.
24. Zia is a forty-seven-year-old covered Arab foreign-born American living in Michigan.
25. Haarisa is a twenty-six-year-old covered South Asian foreign-born American living in New York.

institutional ignorance rather than profiling. The ignorance paired with pro-filing proves especially frustrating for many of our participants.

Airports are so notorious for negative and discriminatory experiences among Muslim women that Martha decided to take her experience at the airport as a litmus test to help decide whether to cover:

> Because the airport security is so famous for mistreating Muslims, I was like, if I pass that, then maybe it is a litmus test and I could [cover] even back in college. I was scared because I was part of the student government and I ran for elections just before leaving for the summer and now when I come back and I'm wearing a headscarf it will be so different. But I decided to keep it on, especially because the experience at the airport was so nice.

Perhaps because Martha's expectations were so low, the fact that she was not explicitly mistreated qualified her treatment as "nice" in her eyes. Alternatively, it is highly likely that the experience of profiling is not universal or constant over time for every Muslim. However, as with all forms of othering, a single experience of profiling at one airport might be enough to root the perception that the system is biased.

Sometimes our participants recall instances of discrimination in interactions with law enforcement or within the legal system. Sarah, a covered focus group participant from Boston, reports feeling "extremely uncomfortable" in an American courtroom,[26] and Hawa', another covered participant and lawyer in Chicago, observes, "I feel like we have these laws to protect us, I was ready to fight for our rights and do all these things; but then I see this system, the American system of law that I have so much faith in, collapsing on itself and not functioning in the way it is supposed to function. . . . There are divides in how a Muslim and a non-Muslim going through that system are treated."[27]

Many of our respondents also mention the more general double standard applied to Muslims, under which they are often unfairly singled out by and for prejudicial treatment. Several women bemoan the fact that religion is the main descriptor of Islamic terrorism but not other forms of terrorism and that the freedom of speech of those who slander Muslims is protected but these protections are not afforded to Muslims if they respond in kind. As Hafeeza explains, "It's really backwards because your rights are supposed to be protected as an American, but as a Muslim they are not." In this statement,

---

26. Sarah is a forty-two-year-old covered black native-born American living in Massachusetts.

27. Hawa' is a thirty-four-year-old covered South Asian native-born American living in Illinois.

she is referencing her own experiences, when people generalized about Muslims after the September eleventh attack and directly threatened her and her children:

> You are telling me that my kids should be killed because they are Muslims. They are little kids and they should die. This is what this crazy guy said. He did not lose his job, nothing happened. There were no ramifications. But if I as a Muslim woman said the things back, I would have [been sent] jail, would have a fine. . . . To me it comes out like a backward society. This does not make sense.

Hafeeza feels that though she is entitled to equal treatment as a citizen of the United States, she is neither protected from abuse nor confident that the system would uphold her rights were she to defend herself.

These anecdotes suggest that our focus group participants perceive profiling and unequal treatment in official government institutions. Even if these experiences are rare, the mere perception of profiling may be more important than the frequency of it. While targets of social othering can dismiss the actions of "stupid" and "ignorant" individuals who might treat Muslims as the "other," when the othering extends to the political institutions, the scale and institutionalization of such marginalization suggests that the bias is systemic and affirmed by society at large. If left unchecked, the perceived scale of the othering could create almost insurmountable barriers to social cohesion, provoking feelings of being excluded that may undermine the bond of citizenship.

Citizenship is a multifaceted set of institutional arrangements and interactions in the political sphere that define a relationship between individuals and their government based on reciprocal expectations. Narrow understandings of citizenship define it as a legal status establishing a formal membership in the polity determined by a constitutionally defined bundle of rights, duties, and freedoms. However, a broader notion of citizenship acknowledges its inherently reciprocal and evolving nature along the participatory and identity dimensions. Muslim-American women's understandings of their identity as Muslim Americans and their participation within the American political system reflect this broader and dynamic notion of citizenship. For them citizenship is a formal tie that guarantees their political equality and also a contractual relationship whereby they expect practical recognition, respect, and protection in return for their investment in the political system. Their investment in the political system through formal and informal participation results in strong expectations of inclusion in the American polity through representation but also through sociopolitical acceptance.

However, their expectations are not always met. While our participants celebrate the legal institutions protecting civil liberties, individual freedoms, and civil rights, they simultaneously feel that neither the American political system nor the larger society meets them halfway in their struggle for inclusion and representation. From this perspective, the experiences of covered Muslim-American women constitute a test case for American citizenship's capacity to evolve and bridge symbolic boundaries, which otherwise may restrict their full inclusion into the polity.

Conclusions and Implications

In June 2013 we conducted a focus group interview in New York City. It was a beautiful Saturday morning. The weather was sunny and warm but not uncomfortable. The focus group was composed of five young women, all in their mid- to late twenties. They were wearing bright colors, the latest fashions, and represented the racial, ethnic, and sartorial diversity for which New York City is justifiably famous. Four of the five women wore headscarves. In fact, we were not a particularly conspicuous group that morning at Bryant Park. We sat around a table in the shade under a large tree, surrounded by runners and joggers, dog walkers, young couples enjoying their coffee, families playfully chasing their children, and the other typical noises and distractions weekend crowds bring forth.

About fifteen minutes into the focus group, a prescient moment occurred. Fadia, the uncovered participant, began discussing how in her experience the head covering was a symbol of strength.[1] As she saw it, many people were closed-minded and associated covered women with inaccessible and foreign communities. Wearing the head covering was a bold statement in such an environment, she contended. Then she trailed off warily and observed, "People are looking over at this table . . ."

---

1. Fadia is a thirty-year-old uncovered black native-born American woman living in New York.

Suddenly a middle-aged African-American man walked past our table and angrily said, "You need to remember where you're at!" These women didn't belong here, at least according to him, and they felt it acutely.

The women stopped and looked at each other. And then one of the other participants, Erina, picked up the conversation without missing a beat:

> Being Muslim we are taught that the hijab is going to be a constant struggle. So I think that with the hijab you have your days where you do feel weaker, you know in your practice, as with anything . . . you have to find that confidence. So I think that when it comes to strength, which I think is a good word for it, that when you decide even at your weakest point . . . to put on that hijab and walk out the door and . . . knowing that you may find confrontation from someone. . . . I think knowing that the hijab, the cloth, or whatever you want to call it, is a disrupter, in a good way. . . . I feel like when you have this sort of disruption and the cycle of how people perceive life . . . that's at the point when they begin to learn something new. So, I think from that . . . it is a sign of strength.[2]

In the ensuing conversation, the women spoke of how the headscarf was a statement by the wearer, that it implied she was strong enough to withstand the hassle, the harassment, and the exclusion of everyday life that her choice often entailed in American society. In their view, the head covering was a disrupter but also a prompt for new possibilities in the free exchange of ideas, in the dialogue across religions, and in the opportunity to enhance and expand community.

Muslim Americans face a difficult challenge post–September eleventh. As minorities, they are often pitted against the majority. It is a majority whose vision for the country regularly does not seem to include them, especially following the election of President Donald Trump. In this milieu, Islam is perceived as perhaps the greatest threat to the United States, further entrenching differences of the American "us" versus the Muslim "them." In fact, many Americans consider Islam a political ideology as well as a particularly menacing type of political threat.[3] Those who hold these attitudes see a potential terrorist threat in every practicing Muslim in the United States, with serious implications for Muslim Americans' civil rights and their sense of belonging.

Our book is a testimony to how one group—Muslim-American women—embodies and negotiates everyday life in this context. Their lived experiences

---

2. Erina is a twenty-eight-year-old covered black native-born American woman living in New York.

3. Several Republican lawmakers have explicitly stated that Islam is a political system and not a religion. President Trump's first national security adviser (General Michael Flynn) stated, "Islam is a political ideology" that "hides behind the notion of it being a religion" (Schulson 2017).

represent a litmus test for the promise of inclusion and the promise of American democratic pluralism. These women have been part of the changing demographics of the United States over the past half century, and their self-described hyphenated identities are clearly representative of an America that includes forms of identity that are compatible with full citizenship. The women self-identify as both Muslims and Americans, and they understand and explain their practice of head covering as an endorsement of the American values of individualism and freedom with the intent of enriching their communities.

Almost universally, our research participants articulated a strong sense of choice in their head-covering practices. Enacting this choice creates a symbolic boundary between Muslim women and everyone else, and it dictates terms for Muslims' social and political engagement. A Muslim woman's head-covering practice impacts her social environment, which in turn conditions the way she participates in politics and engages political institutions. In theory, American political institutions are neutral when it comes to religion, which gives the system the ability to adapt and change as the demographics of the country change. Such flexibility has limits and is contingent on societal mores that eventually imprint on institutions.

The experiences of othering by women who wear the headscarf warn us that open political institutions and guaranteed protections for minorities may disappear if American society does not insist on their substantive inclusion into the social and political sphere. Americans must advocate for inclusive institutions for minorities as part of the democratic process. A true democracy is only possible through participation and mindful pluralism from everyone. Emphasizing the importance of an active political culture in his farewell speech, former president Barack Obama (2017) noted, "Our constitution is a remarkable, beautiful gift. But it's really just a piece of parchment. It has no power on its own. We, the people, give it power—with our participation, and the choices we make. Whether or not we stand up for our freedoms. Whether or not we respect and enforce rule of law." The future of American democracy requires popular vigilance in demanding responsive and accessible political institutions for all Americans.

American Exceptionalism?

America's relative strength has long been its evolving acceptance of diversity. Fareed Zakaria (2016) argued in an op-ed that "[the United States] was a country founded not on race, ethnicity or religion, but on ideas. And, crucially, those ideas were open to all. This openness to people, ideas, cultures and religions resulted in the creation of a new person—the American." It is important to remember, however, that the history of the inclusion of immigrants and minorities into American society has in fact regularly fallen short of the ideal country Zakaria describes.

Nonetheless, this imperfect history matters for understanding the challenges faced by American Muslim women in their sociopolitical lives today. American citizenship has always been fraught with questions of race, gender, and religion. In the Constitution, the founding fathers recognized landowning white men as the only full citizens. By the mid-nineteenth century religion had become a decisive category for citizenship as Protestants fought the inclusion of Irish Catholic immigrants. Ethnicity, too, became a salient category as Chinese immigrants were excluded from citizenship (Kramer and Lee 2017), as were the Jews and the Italians. The European immigrants were more easily able to perform an Anglo-Saxon variant of whiteness to obtain and enjoy citizenship. Likewise, Muslim Americans were also expected to perform whiteness. Indeed, the history of immigrant integration reveals that Muslims are merely the latest group experiencing the flawed integration processes other ethnicities and religions have also undergone.

America's inclusionary ideal is largely a by-product of recent immigrants and their descendants. As Kramer and Lee (2017) wrote, "More than anyone else, it was immigrant-descended intellectuals . . . who rebuilt the Statue of Liberty into a sign of greeting and protection." While immigrants may have been behind America's ideal as the refuge for "your tired, your poor, your huddled masses yearning to breathe free," it also caught the wider public imagination and fed into an understanding of American national identity.

Despite such lofty ideals, American society continues to endorse the ideal American as an individual of European heritage who adheres to Christian beliefs and values. This continues to create barriers to inclusion along lines of race or ethnicity and religion. Moreover, in the contemporary context the white Christian ideal is often defended with reference to national security and by invoking popular political sentiment.[4]

Muslim Americans find themselves particularly disadvantaged in this context. On the one hand, there are still significant racial and religious qualifiers

---

4. For example, those who might defend exempting Muslims from civil liberties might use arguments that Muslim terrorists are a threat to the United States (national security) or that the majority of people support this action (popular political sentiment). Whether or not these claims are true, to the average American listener, they resonate with previously held beliefs and assumptions. Furthermore, these norms can be used alongside and sometimes in the same sentence with stereotypes or blatantly racist or anti-immigrant justifications, which can confuse the issue.

for full inclusion into the American mainstream. On the other, concerns about the so-called terrorist threat and a public that often treats Islam as a dangerous political ideology deprive American Muslims of an opportunity that many other immigrant groups have had in the past. While other groups were able to use their ethnic and religious institutions to facilitate their inclusion into American society (Irish Catholics, for example) and protect their rights to practice their religion, the religious involvement of Muslim Americans is increasingly marking them as outsiders and threats to the American mainstream. This means that Muslims are not allowed to join American society without renouncing their religious involvement, and that same religious involvement is often used as an excuse for denying them their democratic rights. "Once you look at Islam as a political ideology, especially one that is threatening, you can ignore or neglect all kinds of civil procedures or protection of religious freedoms that go with the state of being religious in this country" (Schulson 2017).

As Dalia Mogahed, the director for research as the Institute for Social Policy Understanding, reminds us, "We have to decide as a country: What does it mean to be an American? Is it a set of ideas and values or is it a cultural, ethnic background and specific religion. . . . Muslims will never be insiders if the cost of membership is to be white, Anglo-Saxon Protestant" (Aleaziz 2016). As the most visible and easily identifiable members of their religious communities, covered Muslim-American women are carrying the burden of the societal politicization of their religious identities more than other members of their communities.

Throughout this book, we demonstrate that American Muslims were no strangers to these deep questions and troubling issues in the past. In particular, covered Muslim-American women have felt socially targeted and increasingly endangered in public settings. Since 2015 alone there has been a 78 percent rise in the number of reported Islamophobic attacks in the United States (Lichtblau 2016). This raises legitimate uncertainties as to how the country and its institutions will guarantee the civil liberties and personal security afforded under democracy to everyone in American society, especially to groups and citizens who are particularly vulnerable.

We highlight these concerns and inconsistencies to urge American society to do better. To reduce American identity to white Protestant Christianity is to dangerously reinvent purity narratives directed at the exclusion of American Muslims but also other communities as well. However, striving toward an evolving, inclusive, and dynamic definition of America based on shared ideas and values will give the United States a chance to be truly exceptional.

Safeguarding American Pluralism

In American society, immigrant and marginalized communities have been met by political institutions that are open to their participation but do not specifically encourage it. Theoretically, this open access should provide equal opportunity for participation and representation of all social groups. However, as our respondents indicated time and again, Muslims are frequently not accommodated. Furthermore, participation is impeded because the community has been widely portrayed as threatening and/or un-American—consequently, women who choose to cover become distinctly and very publicly vulnerable.

The legal and the social environments of Muslim-American women convey contradictory attitudes toward the practice of head covering. On the one hand, the legal mandates are clear that head covering is a protected right. Yet, on the other hand, our respondents commented frequently that to exercise such a right makes one a target of Islamophobic threats, particularly after high-profile terrorist attacks. As is discussed in chapter 3, there was a spike in anti-Muslim hate crimes in 2001, followed by a consistently elevated rate of Islamophobic hate crimes, and then there were subsequent spikes correlated to other high-profile terrorist attacks. Many of our respondents indicated that they are increasingly frightened to cover in public. Such a social environment effectively bars these women from full access to public space and political institutions, and restricts their ability to meaningfully engage the public realm on their own terms. Furthermore, constant vigilance by Muslims who must be ever ready to defend themselves against accusations of terrorism diverts energy from the important tasks of community building and societal inclusion. In order to improve the prospects for a healthy and diverse democratic nation, mainstream society must make deliberate efforts to include Muslim Americans and to represent them as valuable members of society.

Building Communities

When covered Muslim women opt out of the public sphere, there is less political engagement overall. Citizenship then becomes less meaningful, and American democracy—especially in its liberal and pluralistic forms—is poorer as a result (Putnam 2007). Building communities is necessary to foster inclusive norms in the public sphere. New and integrated communities become possible through the development of social capital bridging differences between and across diverse groups. Bridging social capital effectively creates a connection between different communities who might not otherwise interact with each other, with a view toward fostering sustainable cooperative and collaborative relationships between them. As the head of the Islamic Center at New York University, Khalid Latif, noted, "In Social Justice 101, the fundamental concept is you don't put struggles in competition with each other. You are able to come together and collaborate and build solidarity to take on inequity in all of its forms" (Demick 2017). Bridging social capital thus becomes a necessary part of nation and identity building, encouraging collective action across diverse communities (Putnam 2000).

One of the greatest strengths of the American Muslim community is the diversity exemplified within its mosques. This diversity, which is also visually represented through the many types of head-covering practices (see figure I.1 in the introduction), makes the mosque a forum for community building, bringing people of different classes, ethnicities, races, and even levels of religiosity together. This is an important part of how the American mosque helps to counter religious radicalization, and it also explains why mosque attendance is associated with increased political participation among our respondents.

Outside the mosque, the Muslim-American community has actively built bridges between faith communities through organizing interfaith conferences and activities. Strong mutual outreach and support between the Jewish and Muslim communities, alongside the recent increase in anti-Semitism and Islamophobia, provides an example of this outreach. These interfaith efforts create bonds between communities that might otherwise be seen to have irreconcilable differences. In this case, they overcome their differences by highlighting shared experiences of discrimination and marginalization, as well as strategies to overcome them.

It is important that community building not be limited to the religious sphere. Focusing exclusively on religious identities can risk creating new fault lines leading to unproductive social differentiation and conflict across communities. It "also downgrades the civic initiative people who happen to be Muslim by religion can and do undertake (along with others) to deal with what are essentially political and social problems" (Sen 2007, 78). Furthermore, outreach through exclusively religious means risks heightening a single dimension of identity. Muslims and non-Muslims alike have layered identities, which create the necessary depth of connections that makes bridging communities possible.

Likewise, the work of building communities through bridging social capital should not fall solely on the shoulders of Muslim Americans. Many of the women we interviewed were engaged in community building, and they often felt particularly frustrated by the myriad ways they had to teach, train, and educate non-Muslims about Islam. It is unfair to expect Muslim women to play this role perpetually. In the words of the award-winning novelist and activist, Chimamanda Ngozi Adichie (2016), "The responsibility to forge unity belongs not to the denigrated but to the denigrators. The premise for empathy has to be equal humanity; it is an injustice to demand that the maligned identify with those who question their humanity." Such a task is difficult but necessary for the collective reimagining, expansion, and reforging of a common American identity through community building. As Robert Putnam eloquently explains, "The task of becoming comfortable with diversity will not be easy or quick, but it will be speeded by our collective efforts and in the end well worth the effort. One great achievement of human civilization is our ability to redraw more inclusive lines of social identity. The motto on the Great Seal of the United States (and on our dollar bill) and the title of this essay—*e pluribus unum*—reflects precisely that objective—namely to create a novel 'one' out of a diverse 'many'" (2007, 165).

Ideally, these efforts would emerge naturally from well-intentioned and passionate members of their respective communities. However, governmental intervention and assistance may be required where there is structural discrimination through social boundaries. Public policy can encourage the development of bridging social capital by supporting organizations that seek to bring people together with opposing views or identities.[5] In particular, the education system plays a critical role in promoting diversity through exposing students to difference across religion, race, gender, and other categories of differentiation early and often, socializing the students to see diversity as a normal and desirable social commodity.

Mainstreaming Muslims through the Media

In order for community building efforts to work, they must be reinforced in other areas of society. The media play a very important role in mainstreaming Muslim identity and confronting stereotypes, which can be vital precursors to community building. As the September eleventh attacks pushed American Muslims to the forefront of national discourse, media coverage of Muslims and potential terrorist threats dramatically increased (Nacos and Torres-Reyna 2007). The media as well as many key policymakers no longer portrayed Islam as a faith but as a dangerous political ideology (Gotanda 2011).

---

5. Dialogue groups, witness activities, education and training to teach people how to work with others from different communities, conflict management and mediation, community service, and work in economic development are a few proven methods and can be encouraged by incentive or mandate. See Nelson, Kaboolian, and Carver 2003.

This contributed to the public perception that any practicing Muslim was a potential terrorist. In fact, many of our covered research participants have either been called a terrorist or known someone who had been called one.

News media are powerful actors that define normality and shape perceptions about cultural and religious differences (Fleras 2011). The media can shift public opinion with negative or positive representations of the Muslim community. Representations of Muslims as terrorists or depictions of Islam as a political threat or as un-American can turn public opinion against Muslims and constrain possibilities for community building. The news media have the power to accommodate religious difference and to counter negative targeting of Muslim Americans.

We do not mean to suggest that the media refrain from or temper reporting on criminal events involving Muslims. However, they must be mindful of the ways in which they report similar events involving perpetrators of different faiths or ethnicities and the descriptors they use. The news media should exercise caution in reporting unverified assumptions during breaking news. Even further, they must make an effort to depict Muslims as regular members of American society in everyday settings. Mainstreaming Muslim-American identity and covered Muslim women through media would have an iterative and lasting impact on the normalization of their religious difference.

Mainstreaming media engagement with Muslims from different walks of life is already happening through recent commercials and coverage featuring covered Muslim women. During the 2016 December holiday season, Amazon and a number of other advertisers promoted interfaith commercials, and many major American brands (including Coca Cola, Honey Maid, Microsoft, YouTube, Chevrolet, and Covergirl) have highlighted Muslims in their advertisements (Maheshwari 2017). Mona Haydar—a covered Muslim activist featured in a Microsoft commercial—told the *New York Times* in an interview, "For me as a Muslim woman, I represent something right now in the country that for some people incites fear. . . . This [ad] normalizes the narrative that we are just human beings." She continued, "In 10 years, this commercial might have lived on in the heart of some young kid who saw a Muslim woman in a commercial and didn't see the boogeyman in my face, and instead saw a normal human being. . . . Then if somebody says something about Muslims that's kind of crazy maybe that kid can say, 'I saw this commercial, and she actually just seemed kind of normal.' You don't know what the reverberations look like" (ibid.).

Muslim women are becoming more visible in roles beyond corporate advertising. In the last decade, the United States has hosted Muslim beauty contestants; a hijabi medalist was on the 2016 summer Olympics fencing team; there are newscasters in head coverings; and the virtual world is filled with an infinite variety of covered fashion bloggers as well as activists and academics.

As our book demonstrates, the politicization of Muslim identity is happening mainly in the social rather than the institutional sphere; thus, the role of the media gains even greater import. This book shows time and again that Muslim-American women are enacting and negotiating their Americanness through the headscarf and their religious social and political involvement. Their hyphenated-American identities can provide a point of convergence for the non-Muslim and Muslim communities through shared ideals. Still, the risk is that symbolic differences enacted in social forums may entrench inequalities and influence formal political institutions. Community building and mainstreaming representations of Muslims in the media can prevent structural inequalities from becoming permanent.

The American Muslim Woman

Ultimately, the women in this book are like other American women. Their identities exist in layers, and one of those layers happens to be religious. These women believe fiercely in the American values of individual freedom and equality, especially when it comes to social justice and community engagement. American Muslim women reflect a wide range of aspirations and opinions, forming and maintaining their own understandings of what it means to be a Muslim woman living in a largely secular and non-Muslim environment. They respond to widespread othering through community outreach and engagement with issues of social justice. They participate in formal politics in the same ways that other Americans do, despite feeling alienated and left out by the major political parties. Most important, they perceive themselves as participating citizens and serving members of the American society, and demand equal voice and representation in the political system.

Their religious practice and identity gravitate toward the very same ideas and norms that have shaped American identity historically. Furthermore, Muslim-American women understand their head-covering practice as a personal choice made on the basis of a constitutionally protected commitment to live as pious individuals expressing their personal identities within a democratic society that values religious freedom. Like other Americans, Muslim women desire to pursue their own happiness within the larger American community.

According to our respondents, that happiness is linked to their ability to behave as autonomous women. Autonomy extends to the practice of head covering, which allows Muslim women the opportunity to choose whether and how to cover; they expect the flexibility and individuality of their practice to be protected and respected by both Muslims and non-Muslims. The headscarf is a reflection of multiple identities, and while religious conviction may be the main driver behind the practice, it is far from their only consideration. The diversity of covering practices and the societal reaction to them make the politics of the headscarf a microcosm of the politics of diversity and identity within the United States. The headscarf debate will not lose its salience as long as questions of American identity dominate the political landscape, and thus the power of the headscarf as a political symbol will grow.

Muslim-American women are a vibrant thread in the tapestry of American life, a thread that traces deep into the history of the United States. The imprint of Islam on our national story is illustrated through the evocative history of the Statue of Liberty, the ultimate symbol of idealized American values. In its original conception, the statue was modeled on a veiled Muslim woman (Blakemore 2015). American Muslim women are effectively yet another testament to the strength of democratic values within American society. As covered women are recognized and included as full members of American social and political life, they will be the sign of the health of our democracy and of our nation.

✒ APPENDIX A

Survey and Variable Descriptions

VARIABLE	CODING	N	MEAN
Age—In what year were you born?	Respondent selected year from 1900 to 1995 Converted to age in 2012	1,733	34.07
Education—What is the highest level of education you have completed?	No schooling completed	0	7.77
	Nursery school to eighth grade	1	
	Ninth, tenth, or eleventh grade	9	
	Twelfth grade, no diploma	9	
	High school graduate or equivalent	66	
	Some college credit, less than one year	63	
	One year or more of college, no degree	306	
	Associate degree	155	
	Bachelor's degree	562	
	Master's degree	372	
	Professional degree	143	
	Doctorate degree	91	
Foreign-born—Where were you born?	*Open-ended, coded* 0 = Born in United States 1 = Born outside the United States	1,495	0.49
US citizen—What is your citizenship?	*Open-ended, coded* 0 = Non-US citizen 1 = US citizen	1,730	0.88
Youth—Where did you live between the ages of six and eighteen?	*Open-ended, coded* 0 = Didn't spend youth in Muslim-majority country 1=Spent youth in a Muslim-majority country	1,454	0.26
Race—Are you white, black or African American, American Indian or Alaskan Native, Asian, Native Hawaiian or other Pacific islander, or some other race?	*Recoded into two potential variables* Nonwhite 0 = White 1 = Nonwhite (all other responses) Black 0 = All nonblack responses 1 = Black	1,486 1,486	0.64 0.08
Married—What is your relationship status?	0 = Unmarried 1 = Married	1,768	0.61
Muslim significant other—If you are in a relationship, is your significant other a Muslim?	0 = No 1 = Yes	1,232	0.92

(Continued)

(Continued)

VARIABLE	CODING	N	MEAN
Employed—Which of the following categories best describes your employment status? (Select all that apply.)	*Categorical variable, each recoded into dummy variables with 0 indicating other responses were selected and 1 indicating the selected response.*		
	Options:		
	Employed part-time	1,489	0.30
	Employed full-time	1,489	0.32
	Not employed, looking for work	1,489	0.10
	Not employed, not looking for work	1,489	0.24
	Retired	1,489	0.02
	Disabled, not able to work	1,489	0.01
	Student	1,489	0.24
	Recoded		
Party—Which political party do you most often vote for?	0 = Does not belong to a political party 1 = Belongs to a political party	1,396	0.65
Vote 2008—Did you vote in the 2008 presidential election or not?	0 = Did not vote 1 = Voted	1,484	0.58
Vote 2010—Did you vote in the 2010 midterm election or not?	0 = Did not vote 1 = Voted	1,427	0.31
Vote 2012—Did you vote in the 2012 presidential election or not?	0 = Did not vote 1 = Voted	1,320	0.71
Cover mandatory—Agree or disagree: Covering one's head is mandatory according to the terms of Islam.	0 = Disagree 1 = Agree	1,748	0.79
Cover protect—Agree or disagree: Wearing a head covering protects a woman from unwanted sexual attention.	0 = Disagree 1 = Agree	1,754	0.75
Cover pious—Agree or disagree: Wearing a head covering makes a woman more pious.	0 = Disagree 1 = Agree	1,731	0.43
Cover opinion—Agree or disagree: Covering one's head makes one's ideas and opinions count more than one's sexuality.	0 = Disagree 1 = Agree	1,721	0.68
Cover discriminate—Agree or disagree: Policies banning Muslim head coverings are discriminatory.	0 = Disagree 1 = Agree	1,753	0.99
Cover fashion—Agree or disagree: Wearing a head covering is fashionable.	0 = Disagree 1 = Agree	1,713	0.51
Cover opportunity—Agree or disagree: Wearing a head covering creates positive opportunities.	0 = Disagree 1 = Agree	1,685	0.55
Cover plain—Agree or disagree: Muslim head coverings should be plain and unadorned.	0 = Disagree 1 = Agree	1,470	0.32
Cover movement—Agree or disagree: Wearing or not wearing a head covering represents belonging to a political movement.	0 = Disagree 1 = Agree	1,372	0.04
Cover politics—Agree or disagree: Wearing or not wearing a head covering expresses my political opinions and beliefs.	0 = Disagree 1 = Agree	1.375	0.11

VARIABLE	CODING	N	MEAN
Wears Muslim head covering—Do you wear a head covering?	0 = Does not regularly wear Muslim head covering 1 = Regularly wears Muslim head covering	1,761	0.77
If they respond affirmatively to "Wears Muslim head covering"			
Why cover—Why did you decide to wear a Muslim head covering? (Select top two.)	*Categorical variable, each recoded into dummy variables with 0 indicating other responses were selected, and 1 indicating the selected response.*		
	Options:		
	Personal piety	1,361	0.82
	Protection from sexual harassment	1,359	0.12
	Expression of personal identity	1,362	0.45
	To spread the word about Islam	1,359	0.25
	Political protest	1,359	0.02
	Family expectations	1,360	0.08
	Individual freedom of movement	1,360	0.18
	Social expectations	1,359	0.04
	Other	1,359	0.05
Age cover—How old were you when you started to wear your head covering?	*Open-ended, age given in years*	1,307	20.7
Behave differently—Do people behave differently toward you when you wear your head covering?	0 = No 1 = Yes	1,302	0.70
If they respond affirmatively to "Behave differently"			
Othering—How do people behave differently when you wear your head covering? (Please describe or provide an example.)	*Open-ended, responses coded as one of the following:* Positive othering: 0 = Response does not indicate the perception that people see her more positively 1 = Response indicates the perception that people see her more positively	914	0.49
	Negative othering: 0 = Response does not indicate the perception that people see her more negatively 1 = Response indicates the perception that people see her more negatively	921	0.68
	Categorical variable, each recoded into dummy variables with 0 indicating the perception of different behavior that does not include this behavior, and 1 indicating the selected response.		
	Options:		
	Violence	908	0.03
	Verbal abuse	911	0.15
	Stare	914	0.27
	Condescension	913	0.33
	Fear	911	0.14
	Respect	914	0.39
	Ask questions	910	0.22

(Continued)

(Continued)

VARIABLE	CODING	N	MEAN
If they respond negatively to "Wears Muslim head covering"			
Ever worn—Have you ever worn a type of Muslim head covering before?	0 = No 1 = Yes	399	0.68
If they respond affirmatively to "Ever worn"			
When worn—When have you worn a Muslim head covering?	*Open-ended, simple count of those who mention one of the following:*		
	To the mosque	143	
	During prayer	119	
	When traveling abroad	91	
	Periodically	131	
Why stop—Why did you stop wearing a Muslim head covering?	*Open-ended, simple count of those who mention one of the following:*		
	Stopped because of religious insight	90	
	Stopped because of negative attention	92	
If they respond negatively to "Ever worn"			
Why never—If you have never worn a Muslim head covering, why not?	*Open ended, simple count of those who mention one of the following:*		
	Don't believe it's required	64	
	Don't have the courage	37	
	Don't feel ready	41	
Family cover—Does anyone in your family wear a Muslim head covering? (Select all that apply.)	*Categorical variable, each recoded into dummy variables with 0 indicating other responses were selected, and 1 indicating the selected response.*		
	Mother		
	Mother-in-law	1,847	0.46
	Sister	1,847	0.28
	Daughter	1,847	0.37
	Maternal grandmother	1,847	0.16
	Paternal grandmother	1,847	0.27
	Cousin	1,847	0.25
	Aunt	1,847	0.44
Friend cover—How many of your closest friends wear Muslim head coverings?	0 = None 1 = Very few 2 = Some 3 = Nearly all 4 = All	1,709	2.24
Friend Muslim—How many of your closest friends are Muslims?	0 = None 1 = Very few 2 = Some 3 = Nearly all 4 = All	1,713	3.44

VARIABLE	CODING	N	MEAN
Islamic sect—Which elements of Islam do you identify with (check all that apply)?	*Simple count of those who mention one of the following:*		
	Sunni	861	
	Shiite	43	
	Salafi	33	
	Sufi	92	
	Ismaili	1	
	12er Shiism	15	
	Hanafi	183	
	Malaki	52	
	Shafii	98	
	Hanbali	28	
	Jafari	8	
	TOTAL	1,084	
Convert—If you converted to Islam, when did you convert?	*Open-ended, recoded into two variables:* Convert 0 = No 1 = Yes	1,592	0.26
	Age at conversion	410	27.26
Pork—Do you eat pork?	4 = Always 3 = Frequently 2 = Sometimes 1 = Infrequently 0 = Never	1,694	0.02
Alcohol—Do you drink alcohol?	4 = Always 3 = Frequently 2 = Sometimes 1 = Infrequently 0 = Never	1,691	0.09
Pray—Do you perform daily prayers?	4 = Always 3 = Frequently 2 = Sometimes 1 = Infrequently 0 = Never	1,692	3.37
Ramadan—Do you fast during Ramadan?	4 = Always 3 = Frequently 2 = Sometimes 1 = Infrequently 0 = Never	1,691	3.76
Mosque—Do you go to the mosque?	4 = Always 3 = Frequently 2 = Sometimes 1 = Infrequently 0 = Never	1,701	2.34

❧ Appendix B

Comparison of Survey Respondent Characteristics with Those from Pew Surveys

Though neither representative of the Muslim population generally nor conducted with a probability sample, our survey demographics compare favorably with the large-scale Pew surveys of Muslim Americans conducted in 2007 and 2011, which provide a validity check for our survey sample, collected in 2012. In 2007 and 2011, the Pew Research Center conducted interviews with, respectively, 1,050 and 1,033 Muslim-American adults eighteen or older from a probability sample consisting of two sampling frames. Interviews were conducted by phone, and interview subjects were identified through random digit dialing (the list contained landlines for the 2007 survey and landlines and cellular phones for 2011) and by recontacting self-identified Muslim households from previous Pew studies. The Pew surveys set appropriate demographic benchmarks because the Pew research design was careful to yield a probability sample, meaning that each adult in the United States had a known probability of being included in the sample, allowing for important statistical adjustments to make the sample representative. Pew estimates the sampling error of its interviews as plus or minus 5 percent. We are able to isolate the female population for both studies. The 2007 study included 495 women out of 1,050 American Muslim respondents. When the 2011 data set was released, we were able to compare demographics of 495 American Muslim women in 2007 with 461 women in 2011. In order to check the validity of our sample, the table below compares basic demographic information (age, education, employment, citizenship, marital status, and race) of our survey participants with information available to date of the nationally recognized 2007 and 2011 Pew Muslim-American studies surveys.

Generally, the participants in our own survey from 2012 are slightly younger, more educated, more likely to be employed in part-time labor, and more likely to be US citizens than the female participants of the previous studies conducted by Pew. African-American Muslims are significantly underrepresented in our survey, constituting only 8 percent of the sample, which is not reflective of their size in the general population or the sample in the Pew or Gallup surveys of Muslims. Conversely, the size of the white and Asian populations in our sample is overrepresented, compared with the Pew samples. Gallup maintains that the most numerous ethnic group among Muslim Americans is African Americans (35%), while according to Pew, the plurality (over 30%) of their respondents identified themselves as white in both 2009 and 2011 (Hodges 2009; Keeter and Smith 2009). Ultimately, there is no clear consensus on the exact size of the specific ethnic groups underlying the Muslim-American population even between Pew and Gallup.

The differences in the demographic profile can be explained by several factors, the most important of which are likely attributable to the online survey method, which may not be equally accessible across all socioeconomic and generational strata in the Muslim-American survey population. Online survey distribution requires potential participants to have access to a computer and the Internet. According to the 2010 US Census, populations under the age of forty-four have wide access to the Internet, and Internet usage rises with both age and school enrollments as well as household incomes (US Census Bureau 2012). This makes our relatively young survey respondents likely to have accessed our survey through their educational networks and/or their socioeconomic positioning. For example, Muslim student associations provided frequent assistance in distributing our survey, leading to the overrepresentation of college-age survey participants.

There are some interesting demographic differences in the head-covering behaviors observed across the two samples. In both our survey and the Pew survey, African-American Muslims tend to cover at higher rates than Muslims of other races. Conversely, Asian Muslims are less likely to cover than their white and black counterparts. Lower rates of covering may correlate with immigrant status—a substantial proportion of our general sample was born abroad and may still face the pressures of being first-generation immigrants. The African-American community, on the other hand, feels marginalized by both American mainstream culture and the immigrant Muslim community and surprisingly enacts this difference by covering with more zeal than immigrants.[1] Perhaps embracing the headscarf is a way to further set themselves apart and elevate what is essentially a Muslim identity marker to an emblem of African-American Muslim identity.[2]

We also see some striking socioeconomic differences. Whereas the majority of Muslim women working full-time in the 2011 Pew sample did not

---

1. See Elliot 2007; Karim 2009; McCloud 1995.
2. See Wong, Lien, and Conway 2005, 557, and chapter 5 of this book.

Table B.1 Comparison of survey participant demographics with those in Pew surveys from 2007 to 2011

DEMOGRAPHIC	OUR SURVEY	PEW 2007 WOMEN	PEW 2007	PEW 2011 WOMEN	PEW 2011
Age					
18–29	37%	24%	21%	26%	25%
30–39	29%	25%	24%	26%	23%
40–54	22%	35%	37%	30%	31%
55+	12%	16%	18%	18%	21%
Education					
Graduate study	34%	20%	24%	18%	23%
College degree	32%	27%	27%	30%	28%
Some college	30%	23%	21%	20%	20%
HS graduate[a]	4%	21%	19%	33%	29%
Not HS graduate	1%	9%	8%		
Employment					
Employed full-time	20%	36%	51%	32%	48%
Employed part-time	32%	21%	17%	16%	15%
Not working	39%	42%	31%	51%	38%
Family life					
Married	61%	66%	67%	65%	65%
Committed[b]	6%			2%	2%
Divorced	4%	10%	7%	6%	6%
Separated	1%	3%	3%	2%	1%
Widowed	1%	4%	2%	5%	3%
Single[c]	25%	18%	21%	20%	23%
Race					
White	47%	36%	34%	32%	27%
Black	8%	18%	21%	16%	20%
Asian	39%	29%	30%	29%	31%
Other	7%	16%	16%	23%	23%
Citizenship					
US	88%	68%	71%	77%	77%
Foreign-born	48%	69%	73%	68%	72%

Note: Percentages may not add up to 100 because of rounding, a refusal to answer, or a "don't know" response.

[a] The 2011 Pew survey combines the high school graduate and less than high school educational levels into "High school or less."

[b] In our survey, this response option is labeled "Engaged" or "In a committed relationship," while in the Pew 2011 survey, this category is labeled "Living with partner."

[c] In the Pew surveys, this category is labeled "Never married."

cover, our survey exhibited the opposite trend. Both our survey and Pew found a substantial majority of unemployed women covering—most likely women who stay at home and tend to the family. While covered women in our survey tend to be more highly educated, women with no formal schooling are more likely to cover both in our survey and in the Pew survey.

Finally, in terms of political and ideological sentiment, both surveys find similar patterns overall. The minority of women identify with the Republican Party; however, covered women are more likely to be "very conservative," while uncovered women are slightly more likely to be "liberal" on the ideological spectrum. The plurality of both covered and uncovered participants described themselves as "moderate" in the Pew survey.

Certainly, global perceptions of the headscarf are inflected by multiple understandings of Islam in general and gendered piety in particular. The Muslim community is not uniform in its practice and embrace of head covering, which may signal cultural, generational, and/or immigrant identities. It could also hint at the specific use of the headscarf as a distinguishing religious marker specific to Muslims living in Western societies.

Appendix C

Primary Open-Ended Interview Questions for Focus Groups

We asked the following questions of our participants in each focus group. The order of the questions was not predetermined, and we let the participants determine the amount of time dedicated to each question.

- What are the top five considerations that come into play when you consider covering or not covering?
- What does being a Muslim American mean to you?
- How do you react when you hear someone make a negative comment about Muslims?
- In what ways are your interests represented in the American political system?
- Follow-up question: How are you involved in your community?
- What is the relationship between Islam and political participation?
- What solutions can you offer to improve relations between Muslims and non-Muslims?

✿ Appendix D

Focus Group Demographics

VARIABLE	VARIABLE CATEGORY	NUMBER OF PARTICIPANTS	PERCENTAGE
Focus group location, $N=72$			
	DC 1	5	7%
	DC 2	3	4%
	DC 3	10	14%
	Houston 1	4	6%
	Houston 2	2	3%
	NYC	5	7%
	Boston 1	2	3%
	Boston 2	10	14%
	Boston 3	2	3%
	Chicago 1	3	4%
	Chicago 2	6	8%
	Chicago 3	5	7%
	Detroit 1	2	3%
	Detroit 2	2	3%
	Virginia Beach/Norfolk 1	3	4%
	Virginia Beach/Norfolk 2	5	7%
	Virginia Beach/Norfolk 3	2	3%
Education, $N=67$			
	Elementary	2	3%
	High school	6	9%
	Some college	16	24%
	A.A.	4	6%
	B.A.	19	28%
	M.A.	14	21%
	Professional degree	1	1%
	Ph.D.	5	7%

(*Continued*)

(Continued)

VARIABLE	VARIABLE CATEGORY	NUMBER OF PARTICIPANTS	PERCENTAGE
Age, $N=68$			
	18–29	35	51%
	30–49	27	40%
	50–69	5	7%
	70+	1	1%
Foreign-born, $N=69$		27	39%
Youth outside United States, $N=69$		21	30%
Citizenship, $N=70$			
	USA	50	71%
	Foreign	15	21%
	Dual	5	7%
Race, $N=70$			
	White	18	26%
	Black	16	23%
	Arab	14	20%
	South/Central Asian	17	24%
	SE Asian	3	4%
	Hispanic	2	3%
Employment, $N=68$			
	Not working	10	14%
	Unemployed	5	22%
	Part-time	17	47%
	Full-time	16	24%
	Retired	1	1%
	Student	19	28%
Political party most frequently voted for, $N=58$			
	Democrat	41	71%
	Republican	0	0%
	Other	7	12%
	Inconsistent	10	17%
Voted in 2012, $N=63$		45	71%
Voted in 2010, $N=61$		20	33%
Voted in 2008, $N=62$		35	56%
Regularly wears a head covering, $N=69$		59	86%

Note: Percentages may not add up to 100 because of rounding, a refusal to answer, or a "don't know" response.

❧ APPENDIX E

Logistic Regression Predicting the Probability of Experiences with Othering among Covered Respondents

	MODEL 1	MODEL 2	MODEL 3	MODEL 4
Dependent variable	Behave differently	Negative behavior	Positive behavior	Behave differently
Nonwhite	−0.212(0.165)	−0.241(0.194)	0.142(0.182)	−0.197(0.166)
Foreign-born	−0.210(0.173)	−0.214(0.202)	0.005(0.192)	−0.174(0.174)
Convert	0.454(0.218)*	0.038(0.243)	0.432(0.227)*	0.443(0.219)*
Education	0.272(0.082)*	0.039(0.103)	0.103(0.097)	0.270(0.082)*
Employed	0.058(0.152)	0.011(0.179)	0.175(0.169)	0.021(0.153)
Age	−0.027(0.007)*	0.006(0.009)	0.011(0.008)	−0.027(0.007)*
Head covering is mandatory				−0.639(0.293)*
Constant	1.054(0.355)*	0.668(0.424)	−1.099(0.404)*	1.624(0.448)*
N	876	613	608	870
Pseudo R^2	0.029	0.007	0.014	0.033

* p=<0.05.

✍ APPENDIX F

Description of Simultaneous Equation Model and Variables

In order to model the predicted relationships illustrated in figure 5.1, we use a simultaneous equation model. This model is less likely to result in the imposition of our biases on the data because the models allow the data to reveal whether two dependent variables might simultaneously determine each other—the dependent variables from one equation are included as an independent variable in the other equation, allowing for simultaneous causation, rather than a unidirectional model with one exclusively dependent variable. Many scholars have suggested that social networks influence political behaviors, as we hypothesize, but it is also theoretically possible that political behaviors determine the strength of Muslim social networks. The simultaneous equations allow us to examine both of these possibilities. Our model contains two equations: the first predicting the bonding religious ties within our respondents' friend networks and the second predicting their formal political participation. We believe the head covering mediates our respondents' inclusion into specific friend networks, making the formation of bonding social networks more likely, and that it therefore indirectly impacts political participation. The endogenous variables are the friend networks and our indicators of formalized political participation, while the exogenous variables are composed of whether our respondents' cover, our respondents' reported mosque attendance, whether the respondent is a convert, and an array of control variables.[1]

(1) y_1 (Muslim Bonding Networks) $= \gamma_1 y_2 + \beta_1$ (Predicted values for formal political participation) $+ \beta_2$ (head covering) $+ \beta_3$ (mosque attendance) $+ \beta_4$ (religiosity index) $+ \beta_5$ (convert) $+ \beta_6$ (education) $+ \beta_7$ (employed) $+ \beta_8$ (foreign-born) $+ \beta_9$ (married) $+ e$

---

1. In the interest of satisfying the minimum requirement for exclusion criteria common to SIM models, we have exogenous variables in both equations (head covering, convert, pray, married in the first equation and age and African American in the second equation).

(2) y_2 (formal political participation) $= \gamma_2 y_1 + \beta_1$ (predicted values for Muslim bonding networks) $+ \beta_2$ (mosque attendance) $+ \beta_3$ (education) $+ \beta_4$ (African American) $+ \beta_5$ (age) $+ \beta_6$ (employed) $+ \beta_7$ (foreign-born) $+ e$

In the first equation, the Muslim bonding networks are measured with an additive index combining our respondents' estimation of the proportion of their closest friend group that is Muslim and the proportion of their closest friend group that wears a head covering. Each variable is ranked on a five-point scale, resulting in an index with scores ranging from zero to eight, then standardized to range from 0 to 1.[2] While this measurement of bonding ties is not ideal because the networks are anonymous, the inclusion of the phrase "closest friends" in the survey question allows the respondent to determine her own bonding network and then designate the proportion that is Muslim and/or wearing a head covering.

A facilitator of social networks is approximated with the frequency of mosque attendance. As indicated in figure 5.1, mosque attendance can expose individuals to both bridging and bonding networks within the religious community. Mosque attendance can facilitate the creation and maintenance of bonding networks as a person forms intimate friendships with people from the mosque community, and bridging networks are generated from acquaintance relationships within the mosque and through the mosque's potential role as a social agent, connecting congregants to the wider community through service work, interfaith events, or community resources. We model the bonding networks as mediated through our Muslim bonding network variable and trust that the effect of bridging networks would manifest in a more direct relationship between mosque attendance and political participation. Therefore, we include it in both equations as a predictor of Muslim bonding networks and political participation. Like the measurement of Muslim bonding networks, the mosque measurement is imprecise.

Our primary independent variable in the first equation measures whether our individual respondents wear an Islamic head covering.[3] We expect head covering to be positively associated with the religious homogeneity of our respondents' friend networks (bonding networks) because of its role as a group identi-

---

2. The Cronbach's Alpha or inter-item correlation statistic for the two variables is 0.57. While this is lower than the conventionally accepted level of 0.7, we believe that the low value is a product of the low number of items (two), rather than poor correlation between the variables. The variables are moderately correlated with a Pearson's R statistic of 0.4, and combining them into an index provides us with a more theoretically valuable measure of network homogeneity than that which the individual indicators could provide.

3. Seventy-seven percent of survey participants (1,416) indicate that they wear a head covering.

fier and simultaneous marker of religious values. The equation also includes controls for whether the respondent is a convert because converts to Islam should have less direct or immediate access to the familial or ethnic networks (bonding networks) that connect an individual to Muslim social networks. Finally, we control for individualized religiosity using an indexed variable composed of indicators reflecting whether our respondents eat pork, drink alcohol, perform daily prayers, and fast during Ramadan on a five-point scale from "never" to "always." The inclusion of the index allows us to tease out whether head covering proxies for religiosity or is capturing some other phenomenon.

In the second equation of our model, political participation is captured through a series of binary variables reflecting whether our respondents voted in the 2008 and 2012 presidential elections and whether they identified with any political party.[4] Sixty-five percent of our respondents reported voting in the 2008 presidential elections, while 72.7 percent voted in the 2012 presidential election. This is similar to general voting trends in the US population, where 62.2 percent of the population voted in the 2008 presidential election and 58.6 percent voted in the presidential election of 2012 (McDonald 2016).[5]

For our third measure of political participation, we measure whether our respondents identify with any political party rather than measuring party identity through membership in the Democratic or Republican Party, because our subjects who identify with a political party are almost universally Democrats. Previous research affirms that this party bias is not merely a feature of our data.[6]

---

4. Because voting and party membership privileges are limited to citizens of the United States, our sample is necessarily restricted to those respondents self-reporting US citizenship (88% of our sample). While there are other ways to measure political engagement that capture political activity more broadly such as attending rallies or campaigning for office (see Jamal 2005a), we chose to focus on electoral turnout and party identification, as they have been operationalized in previous studies of Muslim-American political engagement (see Barreto and Bozonelos 2009; Cho, Gimpel, and Wu 2006). Furthermore, our primary interest is to capture participant exposure to and engagement in the primary political institutions of the United States. When estimating voting patterns and running models predicting turnout in 2008, we restrict our sample to individuals over twenty-one so as to include only those who could legally vote in 2008.

5. Though the self-reported turnout in our sample in 2008 is very close to general turnout, our respondents report much higher turnout than the general population in 2012. Our data also report an increase in turnout between 2008 and 2012, while the general turnout declined over the same period. This could be a feature of the self-reported data in our survey, with our respondents being more likely to report participation, especially since the data were collected shortly after the presidential elections in 2012.

6. The 2011 survey of Muslim Americans also shows overwhelming support for the Democratic Party. Here is the party membership breakdown of Pew's female respondents (461 total): 21 Republicans (4.56%); 240 Democrats (52.06%); 141 independents (30.59%); 32 declined any party membership (6.94%); and 20 did not know which party they wanted to join (5.86%).

Structural Parameter Estimates of Simultaneous Equation Models (SIMs)

EQUATION 1

DEPENDENT VARIABLE	MODEL 1: MUSLIM BONDING NETWORKS	MODEL 2: MUSLIM BONDING NETWORKS	MODEL 3: MUSLIM BONDING NETWORKS
Political participation DV	−0.011(0.035)	−0.015/(0.025)	0.008/(0.021)
Wears Islamic head covering	0.081(0.022)*	0.073/(0.020)*	0.092/(0.017)*
Mosque attendance	0.015(0.009)	0.017/(0.008)*	0.015/(0.007)*
Religiosity index	0.098(0.016)*	0.091/(0.016)*	0.089/(0.016)*
Convert	−0.011(0.015)	−0.018/(0.014)	−0.010/(0.014)
Education	−0.010/(0.004)*	−0.010/(0.005)*	−0.012/(0.005)*
Employed	−0.052/(0.013)*	−0.045/(0.013)*	−0.049/(0.012)*
Foreign-born	−0.017/(0.015)	−0.006/(0.014)	−0.008/(0.016)
Married	0.044/(0.013)*	0.044/(0.013)*	0.043/(0.013)*
Constant	0.219/(0.064)*	0.249/(0.065)*	0.244/(0.062)*

EQUATION 2

DEPENDENT VARIABLE: POLITICAL PARTICIPATION	MODEL 1: PARTY AFFILIATION	MODEL 2: VOTED 2012	MODEL 3: VOTED 2008
Muslim bonding networks	−2.257/(0.759)*	−2.338/(0.901)*	−1.659/(0.788)*
Mosque attendance	0.180/(0.059)*	0.216/(0.068)*	0.083/(0.060)
Education	0.049/(0.031)	0.124/(0.037)*	0.106/(0.032)*
African American	−0.161/(0.166)	−0.043/(0.213)	0.233/(0.191)
Age	0.013/(0.004)*	0.019/(0.005)*	0.025/(0.005)*
Employed	0.001/(0.114)	0.001/(0.129)	0.045/(0.113)
Foreign-born	−0.158/(0.100)	−0.105/(0.115)	−0.499/(0.101)*
Constant	0.719/(0.571)	0.202/(0.668)	−0.083/(0.584)
N	868	796	900
R^2 Equation 1	0.21	0.20	0.20
R^2 Equation 2	0.03	0.07	0.08

* $p = <0.05$.

✒ GLOSSARY OF FOREIGN WORDS

abaya—Long, black, loose-fitting cloak often worn in Middle Eastern countries of the Levant and Persian Gulf.

al-amira—A type of hijab that typically covers the head but not the neck or face.

balto—Colloquial name for a jelbab specifically in Yemen.

burqa—Long, blue, full-body covering with mesh covering over the eyes often worn in Afghanistan; colloquially often used interchangeably with the niqab.

chador—Long, black, loose-fitting cloak often worn in Iran.

da'wa—Arabic, lit., "to call"; the call to proselytize and convert new adherents to Islam.

din—Arabic term for "religion."

dupatta—Long piece of material worn as a head covering often in South Asia.

feredza—The colloquial term for the hijab in Bosnia-Herzegovina.

hadith (pl. ahadith)—Islamic traditions and sayings attributed to the Prophet Mohammed.

hijab—The most generalized term for the Islamic women's head covering; it typically covers the head and neck but not the face; also the general practice of head covering.

jilbab—A long and loose-fitting coat.

khimar—A covering for the head, face, shoulders, and torso.

madhhab—School of law in Islamic jurisprudence.

masjid—Arabic term for "mosque."

maslaha—The concept of public interest in Islamic jurisprudence

niqab—A face veil that reveals only the eyes.

paranja—A long cloak that shrouds the body and head typically worn with the chachvon, or horsehair face veil, in Central Asia.

purdah—The practice of screening off women from the male gaze through seclusion or by garments.

Qur'an—The holy book of Islam.

Shari'a—Islamic law, as composed of the Qur'an, sunnah, and the hadith.

shayla—A scarf that covers the head and a part of the neck, often in a loose wrap.

sheikh—A religious scholar.

shura—Arabic term for the practice of consultation.

sunnah—The normative example of the Prophet Mohammed's teaching and personal conduct.

surah—A chapter in the Qur'an.

ummah—The whole, supranational community of Muslims.

za'im—Arabic term for "leader."

❧ References

Abrams, Abigail. 2015. "Muslims Want to Influence US Elections, but without Big Donors, Can They Make a Difference?" *International Business Times*, December 8. http://www.ibtimes.com/muslims-want-influence-us-elections-without-big-donors-can-they-make-difference-2214422.

ACLU Women's Rights Project. 2008. "Discrimination against Muslim Women—Fact Sheet." American Civil Liberties Union. November. https://www.aclu.org/other/discrimination-against-muslim-women-fact-sheet.

Adichie, Chimamanda Ngozi. 2016. "Now Is the Time to Talk about What We Are Actually Talking About." *New Yorker*, December 2. http://www.newyorker.com/culture/cultural-comment/now-is-the-time-to-talk-about-what-we-are-actually-talking-about.

Ahmed, Leila. 2011. "Veil of Ignorance." *Foreign Policy*, April 25. https://foreignpolicy.com/2011/04/25/veil-of-ignorance-2.

——. 2005. "The Veil Debate—Again." In *On Shifting Ground: Muslim Women in the Gobal Era*, edited by Fereshteh Nouraie-Simone, 153–71. New York: Feminist Press.

——. 2014. "The Veil Debate—Again." In *On Shifting Ground: Muslim Women in the Global Era*, edited by Fereshteh Nouraie-Simone, 2nd ed., 153–71. New York: Feminist Press.

Ajrouch, Kristie J. 2007. "Global Contexts and the Veil: Muslim Integration in the United States and France." *Sociology of Religion* 68 (3): 321–25.

Akom, Antwi A. 2003. "Reexamining Resistance as Oppositional Behavior: The Nation of Islam and the Creation of a Black Achievement Ideology." *Sociology of Education* 76 (4): 305–25.

Aleaziz, Hamed. 2016. "Not Americans? Trump's Charge Astounds Bay Area Muslims." *San Francisco Chronicle*, July 1. http://www.sfchronicle.com/bayarea/article/For-American-Muslims-claims-about-8337416.php.

Ali, Syed. 2005. "Why Here, Why Now? Young Muslim Women Wearing Hijāb." *Muslim World* 95 (4): 515–30.

Allport, Gordon W. 1954. *The Nature of Prejudice*. Reading, MA: Addison-Wesley.

Al-Sheikh, Najwa Faris. 2016. "Implications for Middle Easterners and North Africans in the United States within the 2020 Census." https://ly.smith.edu/ef/etd1606.

Amer, Sahar. 2014. *What Is Veiling?* Chapel Hill: University of North Carolina Press.

Anderson, Curt. 2002. "FBI Reports Jump in Violence against Muslims." November 25. Associated Press.

Atkinson, Rowland, and John Flint. 2001. "Accessing Hidden and Hard-to-Reach Populations: Snowball Research Strategies." *Social Research Update* 33 (1): 1–4.

Atlantic. 2016. "Islamophobia and Donald Trump Motivate American Muslim Women to Speak Out." August 24. https://www.theatlantic.com/politics/archive/2016/08/muslim-women-trump-islamophobia-ghazala-khan/496925.

Austin, Allan D. 1997. *African Muslims in Antebellum America: Transatlantic Stories and Spiritual Struggles*. New York: Routledge.

Ayers, John W. 2007. "Changing Sides: 9/11 and the American Muslim Voter." *Review of Religious Research* 49 (2): 187–98.

Ayers, John W., and C. Richard Hofstetter. 2008. "American Muslim Political Participation Following 9/11: Religious Belief, Political Resources, Social Structures, and Political Awareness." *Politics and Religion* 1 (1): 3–26.

Aziz, Sahar F. 2012. "From the Oppressed to the Terrorist: Muslim-American Women in the Crosshairs of Intersectionality," *Hastings Race & Poverty Law Journal* 191. http://scholarship.law.tamu.edu/facscholar/100.

Bagasra, Anisah. 2010. "Religious Commitment, Acculturation, and Identity Formation among Twenty-First-Century Muslim-Americans." Paper presented at the American Academy of Religion Annual Meeting, Atlanta, October 29–November 1.

Bagby, Ihsan. 2012. "The American Mosque 2011." Council on American-Islamic Relations: US Mosque Study 2011. http://www.icna.org/wp-content/uploads/2012/02/The-American-Mosque-2011-web.pdf.

——. 2004 "A Portrait of Detroit Mosques: Muslim Views, Politics and Religion." http://www.ispu.org/wp-content/uploads/2016/08/385_Detroit-Mosque-Study-Ihsan-Bagby.pdf.

Bagby, Ihsan, Paul M. Perl, Bryan T. Froehle, Carl Dudley, and David Roozen, eds. 2001. *The Mosque in America: A National Portrait: A Report from the Mosque Study Project*. Washington, DC: Council on American-Islamic Relations.

Badr, Hoda. 2004. "Islamic Identity Re-covered: Muslim Women after September 11th." *Culture and Religion* 5 (3): 321–38.

Barreto, Matt A., and Dino N. Bozonelos. 2009. "Democrat, Republican, or None of the Above? The Role of Religiosity in Muslim American Party Identification." *Politics and Religion* 2 (2): 200–229.

Barreto, Matt A., and Karam Dana. 2009. "Religious Identity and Muslim American Political Incorporation: Mosque Involvement and Similarities between Sunni and Shi'a." Paper presented at the annual meeting for the Midwest Political Science Association, Chicago, April 4. http://www.muslimamericansurvey.org/papers/mpsa2009.pdf.

Bartkowski, John P., and Jen'nan Ghazal Read. 2003. "Veiled Submission: Gender, Power, and Identity among Evangelical and Muslim Women in the United States." *Qualitative Sociology* 26 (1): 71–92.

Baumeister, Roy F., Ellen Bratslavsky, Catrin Finkenauer, and Kathleen D. Vohs. 2001. "Bad Is Stronger Than Good." *Review of General Psychology* 5 (4): 323–70.

Bayat, Asef. 2007a. *Making Islam Democratic: Social Movements and the Post-Islamist Turn*. Stanford, CA: Stanford University Press.

——. 2007b. "A Women's Non-Movement: What It Means to Be a Woman Activist in an Islamic State." *Comparative Studies of South Asia, Africa and the Middle East* 27 (1): 160–72.

——. 2013. *Post-Islamism:The Changing Faces of Political Islam*. Oxford: Oxford University Press.

Ba-Yunus, Ilyas, and Kassim Kone. 2004. "Muslim Americans: A Demographic Report." In *Muslims' Place in the American Public Square: Hope, Fears, and Aspirations*, edited by Zahid H. Bukhari, 299–321. Walnut Creek, CA: AltaMira Press.

BBC News. 2014. "Sydney Cafe: Australians Say to Muslims 'I'll Ride with You.'" *BBC Trending* (blog). December 15. http://www.bbc.com/news/blogs-trending-30479306.

Benhabib, Sheyla. 2004. *The Rights of Others: Aliens, Residents, and Citizens*. Cambridge: Cambridge University Press.

Berger, Peter L. 1969. *The Sacred Canopy: Elements of a Sociological Theory of Religion*. Garden City, NY: Anchor Books.

——. 1990. "Social Sources of Secularization." In *Culture and Society: Contemporary Debate*, edited by J. Alexander and S. Seidman, 239–48. New York: Cambridge University Press.

Beydoun, Khaled A. 2013. "Between Muslim and White: The Legal Construction of Arab American Identity." *New York University Annual Survey of American Law* 69 (1): 29–76.

——. 2015. "A Demographic Threat? Proposed Reclassification of Arab Americans on the 2020 Census." *Michigan Law Review* 114 (1): 1–8.

——. 2016. "Muslim Voters between Hillary Clinton and a Hard Place." Al Jazeera. July 25. http://www.aljazeera.com/indepth/opinion/2016/07/muslim-voters-hillary-clinton-hard-place-160725094634857.html.

Bilge, Sirma. 2010. "Beyond Subordination vs. Resistance: An Intersectional Approach to the Agency of Veiled Muslim Women." *Journal of Intercultural Studies* 31 (1): 9–28.

Black Youth Project. 2016. "GenForward September 2016 Toplines." September. http://genforwardsurvey.com/assets/uploads/2016/10/GenForward September2016Toplines.pdf.

Blair, Olivia. 2016. "Noor Tagouri Becomes First Hijab-Wearing Muslim Woman to Feature in Playboy Magazine/The Independent." *Independent*, September. http://www.independent.co.uk/news/people/noor-tagouri-playboy-muslim-woman-hijab-first-magazine-a7339201.html.

Blakemore, Erin. 2015. "The Statue of Liberty Was Originally a Muslim Woman." *Smithsonian*, November 24. http://www.smithsonianmag.com/smart-news/statue-liberty-was-originally-muslim-woman-180957377.

Bloemraad, Irene, Anna Korteweg, and Gökçe Yurdakul. 2008. "Citizenship and Immigration: Multiculturalism, Assimilation, and Challenges to the Nation-State." *Annual Review of Sociology* 34 (1): 153–79.

Bracke, Sarah. 2008. "Conjugating the Modern/ Religious, Conceptualizing Female Religious Agency: Contours of a 'Post-Secular' Conjuncture." *Theory, Culture & Society* 25 (6): 51–67.

Bracke, Sarah, and Nadia Fadil. 2012. "Is the Headscarf Oppressive or Emancipatory?" In *The Postcolonial Low Countries: Literature, Colonialism, and Multiculturalism*, edited by Elleke Boehmer and Sarah de Mul, 73–93. Lanham, MD: Lexington Books.

Breeden, Aurelien, and Lilia Blaise. 2016. "Court Overturns 'Burkini' Ban in French Town." *New York Times*, August 26. https://www.nytimes.com/2016/08/27/world/europe/france-burkini-ban.html.

Bridge Initiative Team. 2015a. "Is the Hijab Becoming a New Normal in Western Media?" The Bridge Initiative: A Research Project on Islamophobia. October 9. http://bridge.georgetown.edu/is-the-hijab-becoming-a-new-normal-in-western-media.

———. 2015b. "The Super Survey: Two Decades of Americans' Views on Islam and Muslims." The Bridge Initiative: A Research Project on Islamophobia. November. http://bridge.georgetown.edu/wp-content/uploads/2015/11/The-Super-Survey.pdf.

Brown, R. Khari, and Ronald E. Brown. 2003. "Faith and Works: Church-Based Social Capital Resources and African American Political Activism." *Social Forces* 82 (2): 617–41.

Brubaker, Rogers. 2001. "The Return of Assimilation? Changing Perspectives on Immigration and Its Sequels in France, Germany, and the United States." *Ethnic and Racial Studies* 24 (4): 531–48.

Business & Human Rights Resource Centre. 2010. "Recent Allegations of Workplace Discrimination against Muslims in USA." https://business-humanrights.org/en/documents/recent-allegations-of-workplace-discrimination-against-muslims-in-usa.

Butler, Judith. 1990. *Gender Trouble and the Subversion of Identity.* London: Routledge.

———. 2011. *Bodies That Matter: On the Discursive Limits of "Sex."* London: Routledge.

Cadge, Wendy, and Lynn Davidman. 2006. "Ascription, Choice, and the Construction of Religious Identities in the Contemporary United States." *Journal for the Scientific Study of Religion* 45 (1): 23–38.

"CAIR Muslim Voter Survey Indicates 86 Percent Turnout, Support for Hillary Clinton." 2016. Common Dreams. October 13. http://www.commondreams.org/newswire/2016/10/13/cair-muslim-voter-survey-indicates-86-percent-turnout-support-hillary-clinton.

CBC News. 2015. "Canadians of All Stripes Oppose Face Coverings at Citizenship Ceremonies: Vote Compass." October 17. http://www.cbc.ca/news/politics/vote-compass-canada-election-2015-issues-canadians-1.3237138.

Carens, Joseph H. 2000. *Culture, Citizenship, and Community: A Contextual Exploration of Justice as Evenhandedness.* New York: Oxford University Press.

Carvalho, Jean-Paul. 2009. "A Theory of the Islamic Revival." Working paper, Department of Economics, University of Oxford. https://www.santafe.edu/~bowles/TheoryIslamicRevival.pdf.

———. 2013. "Veiling." *Quarterly Journal of Economics* 128 (1): 337–70.

Cave, Damien, and Todd Heisler. 2014. "The Way North: On Being American." *New York Times*, May 17. https://www.nytimes.com/interactive/2014/us/the-way-north.html.

Cesari, Jocelyne. 2004. *When Islam and Democracy Meet: Muslims in Europe and in the United States.* New York: Palgrave Macmillan.

———. 2014. "Political Participation among Muslims in Europe and the United States." In *Engaging the Other: Public Policy and Western-Muslim Intersections,* edited by Karim H. Karim and Mahmoud Eid, 173–89. New York: Palgrave Macmillan. http://www.palgrave.com/us/book/9781137403681.

Chan, Sewell. 2016. "EU Legal Opinion Upholds Employer's Ban on Head Scarves." *New York Times*, May 31. https://www.nytimes.com/2016/06/01/world/europe/eu-legal-opinion-upholds-employers-ban-on-head-scarves.html.

Charrad, Mounira. 2011. "Gender in the Middle East: Islam, State, Agency." 2011. *Annual Review of Sociology* 37 (1): 417–37.

Chideya, Farai. 2016. "Muslim Americans Respond to a Caustic Campaign by Raising Money and Mobilizing." *FiveThirtyEight*. October 11. https://fivethirtyeight.com/features/muslim-americans-respond-to-a-caustic-campaign-by-raising-money-and-mobilizing.

Cho, Wendy K. Tam, James G. Gimpel, and Tony Wu. 2006. "Clarifying the Role of SES in Political Participation: Policy Threat and Arab American Mobilization." *Journal of Politics* 68 (4): 977–91.

Clemetson, Lynette. 2004. "Homeland Security Given Data on Arab-Americans." *New York Times,* July 30. http://www.nytimes.com/2004/07/30/us/homeland-security-given-data-on-arab-americans.html?_r=0.

Cole, Darnell, and Shafiqa Ahmadi. 2003. "Perspectives and Experiences of Muslim Women Who Veil on College Campuses." *Journal of College Student Development* 44 (1): 47–66.

Cooper, Betsy, Daniel Cox, Rachel Lienesch, and Robert Jones. 2015. "Anxiety, Nostalgia, and Mistrust: Findings from the 2015 American Values Survey." PRRI. November 17. http://www.prri.org/research/survey-anxiety-nostalgia-and-mistrust-findings-from-the-2015-american-values-survey.

Cornwall, Marie. 1987. "The Social Bases of Religion: A Study of Factors Influencing Religious Belief and Commitment." *Review of Religious Research* 29 (1): 44–57.

Council on American-Islamic Relations. 2015. "CAIR, ISNA Announce Study of U.S. Mosques" Press release. March 11. https://www.cair.com/press-center/press-releases/3511-cair-isna-announce-study-of-u-s-mosques.html.

——. 2016a. "CAIR-FL to Respond to Florida Night Club Shooting, Urge Muslims to Donate Blood for Victims." American Muslim News Briefs. June 12. http://myemail.constantcontact.com/Breaking--CAIR-FL-to-Respond-to-Florida-Night-Club-Shooting--Urge-Muslims-to-Donate-Blood-for-Victims.html?soid=1103010792410&aid=Jiag7_sUDMk.

——. 2016b. " CAIR Releases Results of Muslim Voter Survey Ahead of Primary." Press release. February 9. http://www.cair.com/press-center/press-releases/13365-cair-releases-results-of-muslim-voter-survey-ahead-of-primary-elections.html.

——. 2016c. "CAIR Urges Trump to Reject Proposal for 'Registry' of Muslims, Talk of 'Internment.'" Press release. November 17. https://www.cair.com/press-center/press-releases/13899-cair-urges-trump-to-reject-proposal-for-registry-of-muslims-talk-of-internment.html.

Crosby, Faye. 1984. "The Denial of Personal Discrimination." *American Behavioral Scientist* 27 (3): 371–86.

——. 2004. *Affirmative Action Is Dead: Long Live Affirmative Action.* New Haven, CT: Yale University Press.

Curtis, E. E., IV. 2009. *Muslims in America: A Short History*. New York: Oxford University Press.

Dalton, Russell J. 2008. "Citizenship Norms and the Expansion of Political Participation." *Political Studies* 56 (1): 76–98.

Dana, Karam, Matt A. Barreto, and Kassra A. R. Oskooii. 2011. "Mosques as American Institutions: Mosque Attendance, Religiosity and Integration into the Political System among Muslim Americans." *Religions* 2 (4): 504–24.

Delanty, Gerard. 1997. "Models of Citizenship: Defining European Identity and Citizenship." *Citizenship Studies* 1 (3): 285–303.

Demick, Barbara. 2017. "How Trump's Policies and Rhetoric Are Forging Alliances between U.S. Jews and Muslims." *Los Angeles Times*, February 5. http://www.latimes.com/nation/la-na-jew-muslim-2017-story.html.

Detrow, Scott. 2016. "Keith Ellison's Bid to Lead the DNC Faces Increasing Resistance." NPR.org. December 2. http://www.npr.org/2016/12/02/504166336/keith-ellisons-bid-to-lead-the-dnc-faces-increasing-resistance.

Deutsche Welle. 2016a. "German Interior Ministers Call for Partial Burqa Ban." *DW. COM.* August 19. http://www.dw.com/en/german-interior-ministers-call-for-partial-burqa-ban/a-19487376.

——. 2016b. "Survey: Germans Want a Burqa Ban." *DW.COM.* August 26. http://www.dw.com/en/survey-germans-want-a-burqa-ban/a-19504358.

Diamond Jeremy. 2016. "Silently Protesting Muslim Woman Ejected from Trump Rally." CNN. http://www.cnn.com/2016/01/08/politics/donald-trump-muslim-woman-protesting-ejected.

Diouf, Sylviane A. 2013. *Servants of Allah: African Muslims Enslaved in the Americas.* New York: New York University Press.

Dizard, Wilson. 2015. "Muslim Groups Unite for Voter Drive, Outreach to Confront Islamophobia." Al Jazeera America. December 21. http://america.aljazeera.com/articles/2015/12/21/muslim-vote-drive.html.

Djupe, Paul A., and Brian R. Calfano. 2012. "American Muslim Investment in Civil Society: Political Discussion, Disagreement, and Tolerance." *Political Research Quarterly* 65 (3): 516–28.

Djupe, Paul A., and John C. Green. 2007. "The Politics of American Muslims." In *From Pews to Polling Places: Faith and Politics in the American Religious Mosaic,* edited by J. Matthew Wilson, 213–50. Washington, DC: Georgetown University Press.

Dovidio, John F., Peter Ed Glick, and Laurie A. Rudman. 2005. *On the Nature of Prejudice: Fifty Years after Allport.* Malden, MA: Blackwell.

Donovan, Laura. 2016. "What to Do If You Witness Islamophobia in Public." Attn. com. August 31. http://www.attn.com/stories/11075/tumblr-comic-how-confront-islamophobia.

Droogsma, Rachel Anderson. 2007. "Redefining Hijab: American Muslim Women's Standpoints on Veiling." *Journal of Applied Communication Research* 35 (3): 294–319.

Dukovic, Pari, and Judith Thurman. 2016. "Modest Models." *New Yorker*, January 9. http://www.newyorker.com/magazine/2016/09/19/modest-models.

Durando, Jessica. 2016. "After Orlando Shooting, Muslim Americans Show Support for Victims." *USA TODAY*, June 12. http://www.usatoday.com/story/news/nation/2016/06/12/orlando-nightclub-muslim-reaction/85790320.

Economist. 2014. "Hijab Couture." April 26. http://www.economist.com/news/international/21601249-designers-are-profiting-muslim-womens-desire-look-good-hijab-couture.

Eickelman, Dale F., and James P. Piscatori. 2004. *Muslim Politics*. Princeton, NJ: Princeton University Press.

Elliott, Andrea. 2005. "Woman Leads Muslim Prayer Service in New York." *New York Times*, March 19. http://www.nytimes.com/2005/03/19/nyregion/woman-leads-muslim-prayer-service-in-new-york.html.

——. 2007. "Between Black and Immigrant Muslims, an Uneasy Alliance." *New York Times*, March 11. http://www.nytimes.com/2007/03/11/nyregion/11muslim.html.

Ellison, Keith. 2016. "I Should Have Listened More and Talked Less." Opinion page. *Washington Post*, December 2. https://www.washingtonpost.com/news/acts-of-faith/wp/2016/12/02/rep-keith-ellison-i-should-have-listened-more-and-talked-less.

Endelstein, Lucine, and Louise Ryan. 2013. "Dressing Religious Bodies in Public Spaces: Gender, Clothing and Negotiations of Stigma among Jews in Paris and Muslims in London." *Integrative Psychological and Behavioral Science* 47 (2): 249–64.

Epstein, Cynthia Fuchs. 1992. "Tinkerbells and Pinups: The Construction and Reconstruction of Gender Boundaries at Work." In *Cultivating Differences: Symbolic Boundaries and the Making of Inequality*, edited by Michèle Lamont and Marcel Fournier, 232–569. Chicago: University of Chicago Press.

Esposito, John L., and Dalia Mogahed. 2007. *Who Speaks for Islam? What a Billion Muslims Really Think*. New York: Gallup Press.

Everett, Jim A. C., M. Fabian, H. Schellhaas, Brian D. Earp, Victoria Ando, Jessica Memarzia, Cesare V. Parise, Benjamin Fell, and Miles Hewstone. 2015. "Covered in Stigma? The Impact of Differing Levels of Islamic Head-Covering on Explicit and Implicit Biases toward Muslim Women." *Journal of Applied Social Psychology* 45 (2): 90–104. http://dx.doi.org/10.1111/jasp.12278.

Fadel, Mohammed. 2013 "Re: How the Dialogue on Queer Muslims Is Shifting" (blog comment). March 23. http://www.monotheizm.com/bb/viewtopic.php?t=1946.

Federal Bureau of Investigation. 2016. "2015 Hate Crime Statistics Released." November 14. https://www.fbi.gov/news/stories/2015-hate-crime-statistics-released.

——. 2017. "Hate Crime." https://ucr.fbi.gov/hate-crime.

Fine, Michael, and Selçuk R. Şirin. 2008. *Muslim American Youth: Understanding Hyphenated Identities through Multiple Methods*. New York: New York University Press.

Fineman, Martha Albertson. 2008. "The Vulnerable Subject: Anchoring Equality in the Human Condition." *Yale Journal of Law and Feminism* 20 (1): 1–23.

Fiske, Susan T. 1998. "Stereotyping, Prejudice, and Discrimination." In *The Hand-book of Social Psychology*, edited by Daniel Gilbert, Susan T Fiske, and Gard-ner Lindzey, 357–411. Boston: McGraw-Hill.

Fleras, Aufie. 2011. *The Media Gaze: Representations of Diversities in Canada*. Vancou-ver: UBC Press.

Foran, Clare. 2016. "How American Muslim Women Are Taking on Trump." *Atlan-tic*, August 24. https://www.theatlantic.com/politics/archive/2016/08/muslim-women-trump-islamophobia-ghazala-khan/496925.

Franks, Myfanwy. 2000. "Crossing the Borders of Whiteness? White Muslim Women Who Wear the Hijab in Britain Today." *Ethnic and Racial Studies* 23 (5): 917–29.

Frieden, Terry. 2004. "U.S. to Defend Muslim Girl Wearing Scarf in School." CNN.com. March 31. http://www.cnn.com/2004/LAW/03/30/us.school.headscarves.

Fukuyama, Francis. 2002. "Social Capital and Development: The Coming Agenda." *SAIS Review* 22 (1): 23–37.

———. 2006. "Identity, Immigration, and Liberal Democracy." *Journal of Democracy* 17 (2): 5–20.

Gabbidon, Shaun L., George E. Higgins, and Matthew Nelson. 2012. "Public Sup-port for Racial Profiling in Airports: Results from a Statewide Poll." *Criminal Justice Policy Review* 23 (2): 254–69.

Gabbidon, Shaun L., Everette B. Penn, Kareem L. Jordan, and George E. Higgins. 2009. "The Influence of Race/Ethnicity on the Perceived Prevalence and Support for Racial Profiling at Airports." *Criminal Justice Policy Review* 20 (3): 344–58.

Gallup. 2009. "The Gallup Coexist Index 2009: A Global Study of Interfaith Rela-tions." http://www.euro-islam.info/wp-content/uploads/pdfs/gallup_coexist_2009_interfaith_relations_uk_france_germany.pdf.

———. 2011. "Muslim Americans: Faith, Freedom and the Future." Gallup.com. August 2. http://www.gallup.com/poll/148931/presentation-muslim-americans-faith-freedom-future.aspx.

———. 2012. "Record-High 40% of Americans Identify as Independents in '11." Gallup.com. January 9. http://www.gallup.com/poll/151943/Record-High-Americans-Identify-Independents.aspx.

———. 2017. "Islamophobia: Understanding Anti-Muslim Sentiment in the West." Gallup.com. January. http://www.gallup.com/poll/157082/islamophobia-understanding-anti-muslim-sentiment-west.aspx.

Gaspard, Françoise, and Farhad Khosrokhavar. 1995. *Le foulard et la République*. Paris: Découverte.

Gass, Nick. 2016. "Carson: Muslims Who Embrace American Values Have to Be 'Schizophrenic.'" *Politico*, February 16. http://politi.co/1Xvy9Eg.

Gatens, Moira. 1996. *Imaginary Bodies: Ethics, Power and Corporeality*. London: Routledge.

Gellner, Ernest. 1992. *Postmodernism, Reason and Religion*. London: Psychology Press.

Ghanea-Bassiri, Kambiz. 2010. *A History of Islam in America: From the New World to the New World Order*. Cambridge: Cambridge University Press.

Ghazali, Abdus Sattar. 2016. "American Muslims in Politics." American Muslim Perspective. http://www.amperspective.com/Muslims-in-Politics/muslims-in-politics.html.

Ghumman, Sonia, and Linda Jackson. 2010. "The Downside of Religious Attire: The Muslim Headscarf and Expectations of Obtaining Employment." *Journal of Organizational Behavior* 31 (1): 4–23.

Gibson, Dawn-Marie, and Jamillah Ashira Karim. 2014. *Women of the Nation: Between Black Protest and Sunni Islam.* New York: New York University Press.

Giddens, Anthony. 2004. "Beneath the Hijab: A Woman." *New Perspectives Quarterly* 21 (2): 9–11.

Glick, Peter, and Susan T. Fiske. 1996. "The Ambivalent Sexism Inventory: Differentiating Hostile and Benevolent Sexism." *Journal of Personality and Social Psychology* 70 (3): 491–512.

Golley, Nawar Al-Hassan. 2004. "Is Feminism Relevant to Arab Women?" *Third World Quarterly* 25 (3): 521–36.

Golshan, Tara. 2016. "Trump Claims American Muslims Don't Assimilate. The Data Shows He's Wrong." *Vox.* June 15. http://www.vox.com/2016/6/15/11943160/donald-trump-muslim-assimilation-us.

Gomez, Michael A. 1994. "Muslims in Early America." *Journal of Southern History* 60 (4): 671–710.

Goodman, J. David, and Ron Nixon. 2016. "Obama to Dismantle Visitor Registry before Trump Can Revive It." *New York Times,* December 22. https://www.nytimes.com/2016/12/22/nyregion/obama-to-dismantle-visitor-registry-before-trump-can-revive-it.html.

Goodstein, Laurie. 2016. "Both Feeling Threatened, American Muslims and Jews Join Hands." *New York Times,* December 5. https://www.nytimes.com/2016/12/05/us/muslim-jewish-alliance-after-trump.html.

Gordon, Daniel. 2008. "Why Is There No Headscarf Affair in the United States?" *Historical Reflections/Reflexions Historiques* 34 (3): 37–60.

Gordon, Milton Myron. 1964. *Assimilation in American Life: The Role of Race, Religion, and National Origins.* New York: Oxford University Press.

Gotanda, Neil. 2011. "Beyond Supreme Court Anti-Discrimination: An Essay on Racial Subordinations, Racial Pleasures and Commodified Race." *Columbia Journal of Race and Law* 1 (3): 273–301.

Graham, David A. 2016. "Clinton's Careful Courtship of Muslim Voters." *Atlantic,* October 24. https://wwNacos and Torres-Reyna 2002w.theatlantic.com/politics/archive/2016/10/clinton-muslim-outreach/503915.

Granovetter, Mark S. 1973. "The Strength of Weak Ties." *American Journal of Sociology* 78 (6): 1360–80.

Gray, Doris H. 2015. *Beyond Feminism and Islamism: Gender and Equality in North Africa.* London: I.B. Tauris.

Gross, Samuel, and D. Livingston. 2002. "Racial Profiling under Attack." *Columbia Law Review* 102 (5): 1413–38.

Grosz, Elizabeth A. 1994. *Volatile Bodies: Toward a Corporeal Feminism.* Bloomington: Indiana University Press.

Güngör, Derya, Fenella Fleischmann, and Karen Phalet. 2011. "Religious Identification, Beliefs, and Practices among Turkish Belgian and Moroccan Belgian

Muslims: Intergenerational Continuity and Acculturative Change." *Journal of Cross-Cultural Psychology* 42 (8): 1356–74.

Gunnoe, Marjorie Lindner, and Kristin A. Moore. 2002. "Predictors of Religiosity among Youth Aged 17–22: A Longitudinal Study of the National Survey of Children." *Journal for the Scientific Study of Religion* 41 (4): 613–22.

Gvosdev, Nikolas K. 2010. "Managed Pluralism: The Emerging Church-State Model in the United States?" In *The Oxford Handbook of Church and State in America*, edited by Derek Davis, 226–45. Oxford: Oxford University Press.

Haddad, Yvonne Yazbeck. 2007. "The Post-9/11 Hijab as Icon." *Sociology of Religion* 68 (3): 253–67.

Haddad, Yvonne Yazbeck, and Jane I. Smith, eds. 1994. *Muslim Communities in North America*. New York: SUNY Press.

Haddad, Yvonne Yazbeck, Jane I. Smith, and Kathleen M. Moore. 2006. *Muslim Women in America: The Challenge of Islamic Identity Today*. New York: Oxford University Press. http://public.eblib.com/choice/publicfullrecord. aspx?p=272356.

Hagi, Sarah. 2016. "What Hillary Clinton Still Gets Wrong about Muslim Voters." *Broadly*, October 21. https://broadly.vice.com/en_us/article/what-hillary-clinton-still-gets-wrong-about-muslim-voters.

Hajnal, Zoltan, and Taeku Lee. 2011. *Why Americans Don't Join the Party: Race, Immigration, and the Failure (of Political Parties) to Engage the Electorate*. Princeton, NJ: Princeton University Press.

Harris, Fredrick C. 1994. "Something Within: Religion as a Mobilizer of African American Political Activism." *Journal of Politics* 56 (1): 42–68.

Hauslonher, Abigail. 2016. "Clinton Is Trying to Woo Muslim Voters. They Could Make All the Difference." *Washington Post*, September 8. https://www.washingtonpost.com/national/clinton-is-trying-to-woo-muslim-voters-they-could-make-all-the-difference/2016/09/07/876821f6-6bae-11e6-99bf-f0cf3a6449a6_story.html.

Heyes, Cressida. 2016. "Identity Politics." In *The Stanford Encyclopedia of Philosophy*, edited by Edward N. Zalta. https://plato.stanford.edu/archives/sum2016/entries/identity-politics.

Hirschmann, Nancy J. 1998. "Western Feminism, Eastern Veiling, and the Question of Free Agency." *Constellations* 5 (3): 345–68.

——. 2002. *The Subject of Liberty: Toward a Feminist Theory of Freedom*. Princeton, NJ: Princeton University Press.

Hodges, Sam. 2009. "Gallup: Muslim Americans the Most Diverse U.S. Religious Group." *Dallas News*, March 2. http://www.dallasnews.com/life/faith/2009/03/02/gallup-muslim-americans-the-mo.

Hoodfar, Homa. 1991. "Return to the Veil: Personal Strategy and Public Participation in Egypt." In *Working Women: International Perspectives on Labour and Gender Ideology*, edited by Nanneke Redclift and M. Thea Sinclair, 320–44. London: Routledge.

——. 2001. "The Veil in Their Minds and on Our Heads: Veiling Practices and Muslim Women." In *Women, Gender, Religion: A Reader*, edited by Elizabeth A. Castelli and Rosamond C. Rodman, 420–46. New York: Palgrave Macmillan.

———. 2003. "More Than Clothing: Veiling as an Adaptive Strategy." In *The Muslim Veil in North America.*, edited by Moodfa Alvi, Homa Hoodfar, and Sheila McDonough, 3–40. Toronto: Canadian Scholars' Press and Women's Press. http://public.eblib.com/choice/publicfullrecord.aspx?p=4642100.

Horowitz, Sari, and Jerry Markon. 2014. "Racial Profiling Will Still Be Allowed at Airports, along Border despite New Policy." *Washington Post*, December 5. https://www.washingtonpost.com/politics/racial-profiling-will-still-be-allowed-at-airports-along-border-despite-new-policy/2014/12/05/a4cda2f2-7ccc-11e4-84d4-7c896b90abdc_story.html.

Hu, Chin, Hooshang Pazaki, Kholoud Al-Qubbaj, and Marianne Cutler. 2009. Gender Identity and Religious Practices of First-Generation Muslim Women Immigrants in the US. *Making Connections: Interdisciplinary Approaches to Cultural Diversity* 11 (1): 50–63.

Huckfeldt, Robert, and Ronald La Due Lake. 1998. "Social Networks as Social Capital: Individual and Collective Incentives for Political Participation." *Political Psychology* 19 (3): 567–84.

Huffington Post. 2016. "With Trump as President, Muslim Women Are Scared to Wear the Hijab." November 9. http://www.huffingtonpost.ca/2016/11/09/muslim-women-hijab-donald-trump_n_12880946.html.

Hussain, Murtaza. 2016. "Majority of Americans Now Support Donald Trump's Proposed Muslim Ban, Poll Shows." *The Intercept*, March 30. https://theintercept.com/2016/03/30/majority-of-americans-now-support-trumps-proposed-muslim-ban-poll-shows.

Ibn Ishāq, Muhammed. 1995. *The Life of Muhammad*. Edited by Alfred Guillaume. New York: Oxford University Press.

Inglehart, Ronald. 1979. "Political Action: The Impact of Values, Cognitive Level, and Social Background." In *Political Action: Mass Participation in Five Western Democracies*, edited by Samuel H Barnes and Max Kaase, 343–80. Beverly Hills, CA: Sage Publications.

Islam Project. 2017. http://www.islamproject.org/home.htm.

Jamal, Amaney A., 2005a. "Mosques, Collective Identity, and Gender Differences among Arab American Muslims." *Journal of Middle East Women's Studies* 1 (1): 53–78.

———. 2005b. "The Political Participation and Engagement of Muslim Americans: Mosque Involvement and Group Consciousness." *American Politics Research* 33 (4): 521–44.

———. 2006. "Reassessing Support for Islam and Democracy in the Arab World? Evidence from Egypt and Jordan." *World Affairs* 169 (2): 51–63.

———. 2010. "Democratic Governance and Women's Rights in the Middle East and North Africa (MENA)." https://idl-bnc-idrc.dspacedirect.org/bitstream/handle/10625/43867/130389.pdf?sequence=1.

Jamal, Amaney A., and Nadine Christine Naber, eds. 2008. *Race and Arab Americans before and after 9/11: From Invisible Citizens to Visible Subjects*. Syracuse, NY: Syracuse University Press.

Jamal, Amaney A., and Mark A. Tessler. 2008. "Attitudes in the Arab World." *Journal of Democracy* 19 (1): 97–110.

Johnson, Toni. 2011. "Muslims in the United States." Council on Foreign Relations. September 19. http://www.cfr.org/united-states/muslims-united-states/p25927.

Jones-Correa, Michael A., and David L. Leal. 2001. "Political Participation: Does Religion Matter?" *Political Research Quarterly* 54 (4): 751–70.

Karim, Jamillah. 2005. "Between Immigrant Islam and Black Liberation: Young Muslims Inherit Global Muslim and African American Legacies." *Muslim World* 95 (4): 497–513.

———. 2008. *American Muslim Women: Negotiating Race, Class, and Gender within the Ummah*. New York: New York University Press.

———. 2009. *The American Ummah*. New York: New York University Press.

Keeter, Scott, and Greg Smith. 2009. "Why Surveys of Muslim Americans Differ." Pew Research Center. March 6. http://www.pewresearch.org/2009/03/06/why-surveys-of-muslim-americans-differ.

Kelsay, John. 1990. "Religion, Morality, and the Governance of War: The Case of Classical Islam." *Journal of Religious Ethics* 18 (2): 123–39.

———. 2009. *Arguing the Just War in Islam*. Cambridge, MA: Harvard University Press.

Kepel, Gilles. 2006. *Jihad: The Trail of Political Islam*. London: I.B. Tauris.

Khan, Azmat. 2011. "America and Muslims: by the Numbers." PBS, *Frontline*. September 26. http://www.pbs.org/wgbh/frontline/article/america-and-muslims-by-the-numbers/.

Khan, Suhail. 2010. "America's First Muslim President." *Foreign Policy*, August 23. https://foreignpolicy.com/2010/08/23/americas-first-muslim-president.

Khosrokhavar, Farhad. 1997. *L'Islam des Jeunes*. Paris: Flammarion.

Killian, Caitlin. 2003. "The Other Side of the Veil: North African Women in France Respond to the Headscarf Affair." *Gender and Society* 17 (4): 567–90.

King, Pamela Ebstyne, James L. Furrow, and Natalie Roth. 2002. "The Influence of Families and Peers on Adolescent Religiousness." *Journal of Psychology and Christianity* 21 (2): 109–20.

Kirby, Aidan, 2007. "The London Bombers as 'Self-Starters': A Case Study in Indigenous Radicalization and the Emergence of Autonomous Cliques. *Studies in Conflict & Terrorism*, 30 (5): 415–28.

Kitzinger, Jenny. 1995. "Qualitative Research: Introducing Focus Groups." *BMJ* 311 (7000): 299–302.

Kohut, Andrew, Luis Lugo, and Scott Keeter. 2007. "Muslim Americans: Middle Class and Mostly Mainstream." Pew Research Center. May 22. http://www.pewresearch.org/2007/05/22/muslim-americans-middle-class-and-mostly-mainstream.

Kopp, Hollie. 2002. "Dress and Diversity: Muslim Women and Islamic Dress in an Immigrant/Minority Context." *Muslim World* 92 (1–2): 59–78.

Kramer, Paul A., and Robert Lee. 2017. "Not Who We Are." *Slate*, February 3. http://www.slate.com/articles/news_and_politics/history/2017/02/trump_s_muslim_ban_and_the_long_history_of_american_nativism.html.

Krook, Mona Lena. 2009. *Quotas for Women in Politics: Gender and Candidate Selection Reform Worldwide*. New York: Oxford University Press.

Kühle, Lene. 2012. "In the Faith of Our Fathers: Religious Minority Socialization in Pluralistic Societies." *Nordic Journal of Religion and Society* 25 (2): 113–30.

Kwak, Nojin, Dhavan V. Shah, and R. Lance Holbert. 2004. "Connecting, Trusting, and Participating: The Direct and Interactive Effects of Social Associations." *Political Research Quarterly* 57 (4): 643–52.

Laborde, Cécile. 2006. "Female Autonomy, Education and the Hijab." *Critical Review of International Social and Political Philosophy* 9 (3): 351–77.

Lamont, Michèle, and Virág Molnár. 2002. "The Study of Boundaries in the Social Sciences." *Annual Review of Sociology* 28 (1): 167–95.

Lauter, David. 2015. "Americans Closely Split Over Whether Islam Is Violent." *Los Angeles Times*, December 15. http://www.latimes.com/politics/la-na-islam-violence-polls-20151215-story.html.

Legomsky, Stephen H. 2005. "The Ethnic and Religious Profiling of Noncitizens: National Security and International Human Rights." *Boston College Third World Law Journal* 25: 161.

Leighley, Jan E. 1990. "Social Interaction and Contextual Influences on Political Participation." *American Politics Research* 18 (4): 459-75.

Leming, Laura M. 2007. "Sociological Explorations: What Is Religious Agency?" *Sociological Quarterly* 48 (1): 73–92.

Levine, Brian. 2015. "Hate Crime Data and Reports." https://csbs.csusb.edu/hate-and-extremism-center/data-reports/hate-crime-data-and-reports

Lewis, Reina. 2007. "Veils and Sales: Muslims and the Spaces of Postcolonial Fashion Retail." *Fashion Theory* 11 (4): 423–41.

——, ed. 2013. *Modest Fashion: Styling bodies, Mediating Faith*. London: IB Tauris.

Leydet, Dominique. 2014. "Citizenship." In *The Stanford Encyclopedia of Philosophy*, edited by Edward N. Zalta. https://plato.stanford.edu/archives/spr2014/entries/citizenship.

Lichtblau, Eric. 2003. "Bush Issues Federal Ban on Racial Profiling." *New York Times*, June 17. http://www.nytimes.com/2003/06/17/politics/bush-issues-federal-ban-on-racial-profiling.html.

——. 2015. "Crimes against Muslim Americans and Mosques Rise Sharply." *New York Times*, December 17. https://www.nytimes.com/2015/12/18/us/politics/crimes-against-muslim-americans-and-mosques-rise-sharply.html.

——. 2016. "Hate Crimes against American Muslims Most Since Post-9/11 Era." *New York Times*, September 17. https://www.nytimes.com/2016/09/18/us/politics/hate-crimes-american-muslims-rise.html.

Lien, Pei-te, M. Margaret Conway, and Janelle Wong. 2004. *The Politics of Asian Americans: Diversity and Community*. New York: Routledge.

Lings, Martin. 1983. *Muhammad: His Life Based on the Earliest Sources*. London: Islamic Texts Society and George Allen & Unwin.

Lipset, Seymour Martin.1997. *American Exceptionalism: A Double-Edged Sword*. New York: Norton.

Liptak, Adam. 2015. "Muslim Woman Denied Job over Head Scarf Wins in Supreme Court." *New York Times*, June 1. https://www.nytimes.com/2015/06/02/us/supreme-court-rules-in-samantha-elauf-abercrombie-fitch-case.html.

Lotfi, Abdelhamid. 2001. "Creating Muslim Space in the USA: Masjid and Islamic Centers." *Islam and Christian–Muslim Relations* 12 (2): 235–54.

MacHacek, David W. 2003. "The Problem of Pluralism." *Sociology of Religion* 64 (2): 145–61.

Maheshwari, Sapna. 2017. "In Year of Anti-Muslim Vitriol, Brands Promote Inclusion." *New York Times*, January 1. https://www.nytimes.com/2017/01/01/business/media/anti-muslim-vitriol-brands-promote-inclusion.html.

Mahmood, Saba. 2004. "Women's Agency within Feminist Historiography." *Journal of Religion* 84 (4): 573–79.

——. 2005. "Feminist Theory, Agency, and the Liberatory Subject." In Nouraie-Simone, *On Shifting Ground*, 111–41.

——. 2012. *Politics of Piety: The Islamic Revival and the Feminist Subject*. Princeton, NJ: Princeton University Press.

Mailman, Stanley, Jeralyn E. Merritt, Theresa M. B. Van Vliet, and Stephen Yale-Loehr. 2002. Uniting and Strengthening America by Providing Appropriate Tools Required to Intercept and Obstruct Terrorism (USA PATRIOT ACT) Act of 2001: An Analysis. Newark, NJ: LexisNexis.

MAKERS Team. 2016. "Get to Know Mirriam Seddiq: Founder of the First-Ever American Muslim Women PAC." October 19. http://www.makers.com/blog/mirriam-seddiq-founder-first-ever-american-muslim-women-pac.

Maliepaard, Mieke, and Marcel Lubbers. 2013. "Parental Religious Transmission after Migration: The Case of Dutch Muslims." *Journal of Ethnic and Migration Studies* 39 (3): 425–42.

Mangla, Ismat Sarah. 2015. "Meet the Hijabi Fashionistas of Instagram: Chic Muslim Women Share Their Modest Style on Social Media." *International Business Times*, November 10. http://www.ibtimes.com/meet-hijabi-fashionistas-instagram-chic-muslim-women-share-their-modest-style-social-2178021.

Mann, Michael. 2005. *The Dark Side of Democracy: Explaining Ethnic Cleansing*. New York: Cambridge University Press.

Mannarino, Dan. 2016. "New Yorkers Rally behind Muslim Women Being Harassed on F Train." New York's PIX11/WPIX-TV. June 15. http://pix11.com/2016/06/15/new-yorkers-rally-behind-muslim-women-being-harassed-on-f-train.

March, Andrew F. 2014. "Political Islam: Theory." SSRN Scholarly Paper No. 2467117, Social Science Research Network, Rochester, NY. https://papers.ssrn.com/abstract=2467117.

Markovinovic, Monika. 2016. "American Muslim Women 'Afraid to Wear the Hijab' after Donald Trump Wins Presidency." *Huffington Post Canada*, November 10. http://www.huffingtonpost.ca/2016/11/09/muslim-women-hijab-donald-trump_n_12880946.html.

Marshall, Susan E., and Jen'nan Ghazal Read. 2003. "Identity Politics among Arab-American Women." *Social Science Quarterly* 84 (4): 875–91.

McCaw, Robert S. 2016. "American Muslim Voters and the 2016 Election: A Demographic Profile and Survey of Attitudes." Council on American-Islamic Relations (CAIR). https://www.cair.com/images/pdf/CAIR_2016_Election_Report.pdf.

McCloud, Aminah B. 1995. "American Muslim Women and U. S. Society." *Journal of Law and Religion* 12 (1): 51–59.

McClurg, Scott D. 2003. "Social Networks and Political Participation: The Role of Social Interaction in Explaining Political Participation." *Political Research Quarterly* 56 (4): 449–64.

McDonald, Michael P. 2016. "Voter Turnout Data—United States Elections Project." http://www.electproject.org/home/voter-turnout/voter-turnout-data.

McGinty, Anna Mansson. 2012. "The 'Mainstream Muslim' Opposing Islamophobia: Self-Representations of American Muslims." *Environment and Planning A* 44 (12): 2957–73.

——. 2014. "Emotional Geographies of Veiling: The Meanings of the Hijab for Five Palestinian American Muslim Women." *Gender, Place & Culture* 21 (6): 683–700.

McGinty, Anna Mansson, Kristin Sziarto, and Caroline Seymour-Jorn. 2013. "Researching within and against Islamophobia: A Collaboration Project with Muslim Communities." *Social & Cultural Geography* 14 (1): 1–22.

McGraw, Barbara A. 2003. *Rediscovering America's Sacred Ground: Public Religion and Pursuit of the Good in a Pluralistic America*. Albany: State University of New York Press.

McLeod, Jack M., Dietram A. Scheufele, and Patricia Moy. 1999. "Community, Communication, and Participation: The Role of Mass Media and Interpersonal Discussion in Local Political Participation." *Political Communication* 16 (3): 315–36.

McPhate, Mike. 2016. "Pastors Praise Anti-Gay Massacre in Orlando, Prompting Outrage." *New York Times*, June 27. https://www.nytimes.com/2016/06/28/us/pastors-praise-anti-gay-massacre-in-orlando-prompting-outrage.html.

McPherson, J. Miller, and Lynn Smith-Lovin. 1982. "Women and Weak Ties: Differences by Sex in the Size of Voluntary Organizations." *American Journal of Sociology* 87 (4): 883–904.

Mellor, David, Gai Bynon, Jerome Maller, Felicity Cleary, Alex Hamilton, and Lara Watson. 2001. "The Perception of Racism in Ambiguous Scenarios." *Journal of Ethnic and Migration Studies* 27 (3): 473–88.

Miller, Cassie, and Alexandra Werner-Winslow. 2016. "Ten Days After: Harassment and Intimidation in the Aftermath of the Election." Southern Poverty Law Center. https://www.splcenter.org/20161129/ten-days-after-harassment-and-intimidation-aftermath-election.

Moaddel, Mansoor. 2002. "The Study of Islamic Culture and Politics: An Overview and Assessment." *Annual Review of Sociology* 28: 359–86.

Mohamed, Besheer Mohamed. 2016. "A New Estimate of the U.S. Muslim Population." Pew Research Center. January 6. http://www.pewresearch.org/fact-tank/2016/01/06/a-new-estimate-of-the-u-s-muslim-population.

Moors, Annelies, and Emma Tarlo. 2007. "Introduction." *Fashion Theory* 11 (2–3): 133–41.

Morin, Richard, and Juliana Menasce Horowitz. 2006. "Europeans Debate the Scarf and the Veil." Pew Research Center's Global Attitudes Project. November 20. http://www.pewglobal.org/2006/11/20/europeans-debate-the-scarf-and-the-veil/.

Murray, Rheana. 2016. "Designer's Historic All-Hijab Runway Show Earns Standing Ovation." TODAY.com. September 15. http://www.today.com/style/designer-s-historic-all-hijab-runway-show-gets-standing-ovation-t102877.

Mutz, Diana C. 2002. "Cross-Cutting Social Networks: Testing Democratic Theory in Practice." *American Political Science Review* 96 (1): 111–26.

Myers, Scott M. 1996. "An Interactive Model of Religiosity Inheritance: The Importance of Family Context." *American Sociological Review* 61 (5): 858–66.

Naber, Nadine. 2000. "Ambiguous Insiders: An Investigation of Arab American Invisibility." *Ethnic and Racial Studies* 23 (1): 37–61.

Nacos, Brigitte L., and Oscar Torres-Reyna. 2007. *Fueling Our Fears: Stereotyping, Media Coverage, and Public Opinion of Muslim Americans.* Lanham, MD: Rowman & Littlefield.

Naeem, Nabeelah. 2015. "CAIR-San Diego: Muslim Student Wearing Headscarf Allegedly Attacked on SDSU Campus." Press release. November 20. https://www.cair.com/press-center/press-releases/13265-cair-san-diego-muslim-student-wearing-headscarf-allegedly-attacked-on-sdsu-campus.html.

———. 2016. "CAIR Releases Results of Muslim Voter Survey ahead of Primary Elections." Press release. February 9. http://www.cair.com/press-center/press-releases/13365-cair-releases-results-of-muslim-voter-survey-ahead-of-primary-elections.html.

Nashat, Guity. 1983. *Women and Revolution in Iran.* Boulder, CO: Westview Press.

National Public Radio. 2005. "A History of Black Muslims in America." *News & Notes.* http://www.npr.org/templates/story/story.php?storyId=4811402.

———. 2010. "Muslim Women Debate Gender Segregation in Mosques." *Tell Me More.* http://www.npr.org/templates/story/story.php?storyId=124623737.

Nelson, Barbara J., Linda Kaboolian, and Kathryn A. Carver. 2003. *The Concord Handbook: How to Build Social Capital across Communities.* Concord Project, UCLA School of Public Policy and Research. http://luskin.ucla.edu/sites/default/files/nelson_concord.pdf.

Neuman, W. Russell. 1986. *The Paradox of Mass Politics: Knowledge and Opinion in the American Electorate.* Cambridge, MA: Harvard University Press.

Nomani, Asra Q. 2010. "Let These Women Pray!" *Daily Beast,* February 27. http://www.thedailybeast.com/articles/2010/02/27/let-these-women-pray.html.

Noon, Mike. 2010. "The Shackled Runner: Time to Rethink Positive Discrimination?" *Work, Employment and Society* 24 (4): 728–39.

Nouraie-Simone, Fereshteh. 2005. *On Shifting Ground: Muslim Women in the Global Era.* New York: Feminist Press at the City University of New York.

Nyang, Sulayman S. 1999a. *Islam in the United States of America.* Chicago: ABC International Group, Inc.

———. 1999b. "The Muslim Community in the United States: Some Issues." *Studies in Contemporary Islam* 1 (2): 57–69.

Obama, Barack. 2014. "Transcript: Obama's Immigration Speech." *Washington Post,* November 20. https://www.washingtonpost.com/politics/transcript-obamas-immigration-speech/2014/11/20/14ba8042-7117-11e4-893f-86bd390a3340_story.html.

———. 2016. "Remarks by the President at Islamic Society of Baltimore." https://obamawhitehouse.archives.gov/the-press-office/2016/02/03/remarks-president-islamic-society-baltimore.

———. 2017. "President Obama's Farewell Address: Full Video and Text." *New York Times*, January 10. https://www.nytimes.com/2017/01/10/us/politics/obama-farewell-address-speech.html.

Okin, Susan M., and Joshua Cohen. 1999. *Is Multiculturalism Bad for Women?* Princeton, NJ: Princeton University Press.

Open Society Institute. 2010. "At Home in Europe: Muslims in Europe." https://www.opensocietyfoundations.org/sites/default/files/a-muslims-europe-20110214_0.pdf.

Panagopoulos, Costas. 2006. "The Polls-Trends: Arab and Muslim Americans and Islam in the Aftermath of 9/11." *Public Opinion Quarterly* 70 (4): 608–24.

Park, Jerry Z., and Elaine Howard Ecklund. 2007. "Negotiating Continuity: Family and Religious Socialization for Second-Generation Asian Americans." *Sociological Quarterly* 48 (1): 93–118.

Peek, Lori. 2005. "Becoming Muslim: The Development of a Religious Identity." *Sociology of Religion* 66 (3): 215–42.

———. 2011. *Behind the Backlash: Muslim Americans after 9/11*. Philadelphia: Temple University Press.

Peter, Frank. 2006. "Individualization and Religious Authority in Western European Islam." *Islam and Christian–Muslim Relations* 17 (1): 105–18.

Pettigrew, Thomas F. 1998. "Intergroup Contact Theory." *Annual Review of Psychology* 49 (1): 65-85

Pettigrew, Thomas F., and Linda R. Tropp. 2006. "A Meta-Analytic Test of Intergroup Contact Theory." *Journal of Personality and Social Psychology* 90 (5): 751–83.

Pettigrew, Thomas F., Linda R. Tropp, Ulrich Wagner, and Oliver Christ. 2011. "Recent Advances in Intergroup Contact Theory." *International Journal of Intercultural Relations* 35 (3): 271–80.

Pew Research Center. 2007. "2007 Muslim American Survey."May 22. http://www.people-press.org/2007/05/22/2007-muslim-american-survey.

———. 2010a. "Public Remains Conflicted over Islam." August 24. http://www.pewforum.org/2010/08/24/public-remains-conflicted-over-islam.

———. 2010b. "Widespread Support for Banning Full Veil in Western Europe." July 8. http://www.pewglobal.org/2010/07/08/widespread-support-for-banning-full-islamic-veil-in-western-europe.

———. 2011a. "Muslim Americans: No Signs of Growth in Alienation or Support for Extremism." http://www.pewforum.org/2011/08/30/muslim-americans-no-signs-of-growth-in-alienation-or-support-for-extremism.

———. 2011b. "Section 1: A Demographic Portrait of Muslim Americans." August 30. http://www.people-press.org/2011/08/30/section-1-a-demographic-portrait-of-muslim-americans.

———. 2015. "U.S. Public Becoming Less Religious." http://www.pewforum.org/2015/11/03/u-s-public-becoming-less-religious.

———. 2016a. "On Views of Race and Inequality, Blacks and Whites Are Worlds Apart." http://www.pewsocialtrends.org/2016/06/27/on-views-of-race-and-inequality-blacks-and-whites-are-worlds-apart.

———. 2016b. "Restrictions on Women's Religious Attire." http://www.pewforum.org/2016/04/05/restrictions-on-womens-religious-attire.

Popielarz, Pamela A. 1999. "(In)Voluntary Association: A Multilevel Analysis of Gender Segregation in Voluntary Organizations." *Gender & Society* 13 (2): 234–50.

Prewitt, Kenneth. 2013. *What Is Your Race? The Census and Our Flawed Efforts to Classify Americans.* Princeton, NJ: Princeton University Press. http://public.eblib.com/choice/publicfullrecord.aspx?p=1153313.

Public Policy Polling. 2015. "Trump Getting Stronger in NC; Islamophobia Helps Fuel that Strength." December 8. http://www.publicpolicypolling.com/pdf/2015/PPP_Release_NC_120815.pdf.

Putnam, Robert. 1993. "The Prosperous Community: Social Capital and Public Life." *American Prospect* 4 (13): 35–42.

——. 2000. *Bowling Alone: The Collapse and Revival of American Community.* New York: Simon & Schuster.

——. 2007. "E Pluribus Unum: Diversity and Community in the Twenty-First Century: The 2006 Johan Skytte Prize Lecture." *Scandinavian Political Studies* 30 (2): 137–74.

Rappeport, Alan. 2016. "Feeling GOP Peril, Muslims Try to Get Out Vote." *New York Times,* March 24. https://www.nytimes.com/2016/03/25/us/politics/republicans-muslim-americans-vote.html.

Read, Jen'nan Ghazal. 2007. "Introduction: The Politics of Veiling in Comparative Perspective." *Sociology of Religion* 68 (3): 231–36.

Read, Jen'nan Ghazal, and John P. Bartkowski. 2000. "To Veil or Not to Veil? A Case Study of Identity Negotiation among Muslim Women in Austin, Texas." *Gender & Society* 14 (3): 395–417.

Regnerus, Mark D., Christian Smith, and Brad Smith. 2004. "Social Context in the Development of Adolescent Religiosity." *Applied Developmental Science* 8 (1): 27–38.

Renshon, Stanley. 2011. "The Value of a Hyphenated Identity." Center for Immigration Studies. January 19. http://cis.org/renshon/value-of-a-hyphenated-identity.

Rheault, Magali. 2008. "Headscarves and Secularism: Voices from Turkish Women." Gallup World Poll report. http://www.gallup.com/poll/104257/headscarves-secularism-voices-from-turkish-women.aspx.

Richman, Laura Smart, and Mark R. Leary. 2009. "Reactions to Discrimination, Stigmatization, Ostracism, and Other Forms of Interpersonal Rejection." *Psychological Review* 116 (2): 365–83. http://dx.doi.org/10.1037/a0015250.

Richmond, Kait. 2016. "Muslim Woman: I Don't Feel Safe in the US Wearing a Headscarf." CNN. November 16. http://www.cnn.com/2016/11/16/us/woman-afraid-to-wear-head-scarf-costello-intv-cnntv.

Roberts, Elizabeth. 2016. "NYFW: Hijabs in Every Look at a Landmark Show." *CNN Style.* September 16. http://www.cnn.com/2016/09/15/fashion/nyfw-2016-anniesa-hasibuan-hijabs/index.html.

Roberts, Michael K., and James D. Davidson. 1984. "The Nature and Sources of Religious Involvement." *Review of Religious Research* 25 (4): 334–50.

Roy, Olivier. 1999. *The Failure of Political Islam.* London: I.B. Tauris.

Ruby, Tabassum F. 2006. "Listening to the Voices of Hijab." *Women's Studies International Forum* 29 (1): 54–66.

Ruggiero, K. M., and D. M. Taylor. 1997. "Why Minority Group Members Perceive or Do Not Perceive the Discrimination That Confronts Them: The Role of Self-Esteem and Perceived Control." *Journal of Personality and Social Psychology* 72 (2): 373–89.

Rynard, Pat. 2017 "Outside Iowa Mosque, O'Malley Blasts Muslim Ban As 'Emperor-Like Edict.'" Iowa Starting Line. January 29. http://iowastartingline.com/2017/01/29/outside-iowa-mosque-omalley-blasts-muslim-ban-emperor-like-edict.

Sacirbey, Omar. 2012. "Shiite Muslims Quietly Establish a Foothold in U.S." *Washington Post*, October 2. https://www.washingtonpost.com/national/on-faith/shiite-muslims-quietly-establish-a-foothold-in-us/2012/10/02/f21dc568-0cd6-11e2-ba6c-07bd866eb71a_story.html.

Said, Edward. 1979. *Orientalism*. New York: Vintage.

Sanghani, Radhika. 2015. "Afghan Men Wear Burqas to Campaign for Women's Rights." *Telegraph*, March 6. http://www.telegraph.co.uk/women/womens-life/11453879/Afghan-men-wear-burqas-to-campaign-for-womens-rights.html.

Sarsour, Linda. 2016. "A Muslim Woman Was Set on Fire in New York. Now Just Going Out Requires Courage." Opinion page. *Guardian*, September 13. https://www.theguardian.com/commentisfree/2016/sep/13/new-york-muslim-woman-set-on-fire-eid-al-adha.

Saul, Heather. 2016. "Men in Iran Are Wearing Hijabs in Solidarity with Their Wives." *Independent*, July 28. http://www.independent.co.uk/news/people/men-in-iran-are-wearing-hijabs-in-solidarity-with-their-wives-a7160146.html.

Sayeed, Sarah, Aisha al-Adawiya, and Ihsan Bagby. 2013. *The American Mosque 2011: Women and the American Mosque*. Report No. 3 from the US Mosque Study 2011. New York: Islamic Society of North America.

Schanzer, David, Charles Kurzman, and Ebrahim Moosa. 2010. *Anti-terror Lessons of Muslim-Americans*. Sanford School of Public Policy, Duke University. http://www.sanford.duke.edu/news/Schanzer_Kurzman_Moosa_Anti-Terror_Lessons.pdf.

Scheufele, Dietram A., Bruce W. Hardy, Dominique Brossard, Israel S. Waismel-Manor, and Erik Nisbet. 2006. "Democracy Based on Difference: Examining the Links between Structural Heterogeneity, Heterogeneity of Discussion Networks, and Democratic Citizenship." *Journal of Communication* 56 (4): 728–53.

Scheufele, Dietram A., Matthew C. Nisbet, Dominique Brossard, and Erik Nisbet. 2004. "Social Structure and Citizenship: Examining the Impacts of Social Setting, Network Heterogeneity, and Informational Variables on Political Participation." *Political Communication* 21 (3): 315–38.

Schildkraut, Deborah J. 2002. "The More Things Change . . . American Identity and Mass and Elite Responses to 9/11." *Political Psychology* 23 (3): 511–35.

———. 2009. "The Dynamics of Public Opinion on Ethnic Profiling after 9/11: Results from a Survey Experiment." *American Behavioral Scientist* 53 (1): 61–79.

Schulson, Michael. 2017. "Why Do So Many Americans Believe That Islam Is a Political Ideology, Not a Religion?" Acts of Faith. *Washington Post*, February 3. https://www.washingtonpost.com/news/acts-of-faith/

wp/2017/02/03/why-do-so-many-americans-believe-that-islam-is-a-political-ideology-not-a-religion.

Scott, Joan Wallach. 2007. *The Politics of the Veil*. Princeton, NJ: Princeton University Press.

Secor, Anna J. 2002. "The Veil and Urban Space in Istanbul: Women's Dress, Mobility and Islamic Knowledge." *Gender, Place & Culture* 9 (1): 5–22.

Sen, Amartya. 2007. *Identity and Violence: The Illusion of Destiny*. New York: Norton.

Senzai, Farid. 2012. "Engaging American Muslims: Political Trends and Attitudes." Institute for Social Policy and Understanding, Dearborn, MI. http://www.ispu.org/wp-content/uploads/2016/08/ISPU_Report_Political_Participation.pdf.

Shackford, Scott. 2016. "In America, Muslims Are More Likely to Support Gay Marriage Than Evangelical Christians." *Hit & Run* (blog). Reason.com. June 13. http://reason.com/blog/2016/06/13/in-america-muslims-are-more-likely-to-su.

Shaheed, Aisha Lee Fox. 2008. "How Islamic Is the Veil?" In *The Veil: Women Writers on Its History, Lore, and Politics*, edited by Jennifer Heath, 290–306. Berkeley: University of California Press.

Sha'rāwī, Hudá. 1987. *Harem Years: The Memoirs of an Egyptian Feminist*. London: Virago.

Shechet, Ellie. 2016. "Ilhan Omar, the First Somali-American Lawmaker, Says Cab Driver Threatened to Remove Her Hijab." *Jezebel*, December 7. http://jezebel.com/ilhan-omar-the-first-somali-american-lawmaker-says-ca-1789803961.

Sheffield, Matthew. 2016. "Leading DNC Chair Candidate Keith Ellison Blasted for 'Disqualifying' Remarks about Israel." *Salon*, December 2. http://www.salon.com/2016/12/02/leading-dnc-candidate-keith-ellison-blasted-for-disqualifying-remarks-about-israel.

Sheth, Falguni A. 2006. "Unruly Muslim Women and Threats to Liberal Culture." *Peace Review* 18 (4): 455–63.

Sidahmed, Mazin. 2016. "Muslim Women's Group Inundated with Hate Mail after Endorsing Hillary Clinton." US News. *Guardian*, October 19. https://www.theguardian.com/us-news/2016/oct/19/muslim-womens-group-hate-mail-hillary-clinton-drudge-report.

Simmons, Gwendolyn Zoharah. 2006. "African American Islam as an Expression of Converts' Religious Faiths and Nationalist Dreams and Ambitions." In *Women Embracing Islam: Gender and Conversion in the West*, edited by Karin van Nieuwkerk, 254–80. Austin: University of Texas Press.

——. 2008. "From Muslim Americans to American Muslims." *Journal of Islamic Law and Culture* 10 (3): 254–80.

Siraj, Asifa. 2011. "Meanings of Modesty and the Hijab amongst Muslim Women in Glasgow, Scotland." *Gender, Place & Culture* 18 (6): 716–31.

Sirin, Selcuk R., and Dalal Katsiaficas. 2011. "Religiosity, Discrimination, and Community Engagement: Gendered Pathways of Muslim American Emerging Adults." *Youth & Society* 43 (4): 1528–46.

Smith-Hefner, Nancy J. 2007. "Javanese Women and the Veil in Post-Soeharto Indonesia." *Journal of Asian Studies* 66 (2): 389–420.

Spellberg, Denise. 2013. *Thomas Jefferson's Qur'an: Islam and the Founders*. Repr. ed. New York: Vintage.

Stillman, Yedida Kalfon, and Norman A Stillman. 2003. *Arab Dress: A Short History: From the Dawn of Islam to Modern Times*. Leiden, Neth.: Brill.

Street, Nick. 2015. "First All-Female Mosque Opens in Los Angeles." Al Jazeera America. February 3. http://america.aljazeera.com/articles/2015/2/3/first-all-female-mosque-opens-in-los-angeles.html.

Sue, Derald Wing. 2010. *Microaggressions in Everyday Life: Race, Gender, and Sexual Orientation*. Hoboken, NJ: Wiley.

Tanir, Canan. 2009. "Clothed Bodies That Matter in Search of a Feminist Perspective on the Headscarf Controversy." Istanbul Bilgi Üniversitesi. http://openaccess.bilgi.edu.tr:8080/xmlui/handle/11411/549.

Taylor, Donald M., Stephen C. Wright, Fathali M. Moghaddam, and Richard N. Lalonde. 1990. "The Personal/Group Discrimination Discrepancy: Perceiving My Group, but Not Myself, to Be a Target for Discrimination." *Personality and Social Psychology Bulletin* 16 (2): 254–62.

Taylor, Jessica. 2015. "Trump Calls for 'Total and Complete Shutdown of Muslims Entering' US." National Public Radio. December 7. http://www.npr.org/2015/12/07/458836388/trump-calls-for-total-and-complete-shutdown-of-muslims-entering-u-s.

Tehranian, John. 2009. *Whitewashed: America's Invisible Middle Eastern Minority*. New York: New York University Press.

Thernstrom, Abigail. 1980. "Language: Issues and Legislation." In *Harvard Encyclopedia of American Ethnic Groups*, edited by Stephan Thernstrom, 619–29. Cambridge: Cambridge University Press.

Tilly, Charles. 1997. "A Primer on Citizenship." *Theory and Society* 26 (4): 599–603.

Tobin, Sarah A. 2016. *Everyday Piety: Islam and Economy in Jordan*. Ithaca, NY: Cornell University Press.

Trump, Donald J. 2015. "Donald J. Trump Statement on Preventing Muslim Immigration." December 7. https://www.donaldjtrump.com/press-releases/donald-j.-trump-statement-on-preventing-muslim-immigration.

Turner, Richard Brent. 2003. *Islam in the African Experience*. Bloomington: Indiana University Press.

Turnham, Steve. 2016. "Trump to Father of Fallen Soldier: 'I've Made a Lot of Sacrifices.'" ABC News. August 1. http://abcnews.go.com/Politics/donald-trump-father-fallen-soldier-ive-made-lot/story?id=41015051.

US Census Bureau. 2012. "Computer and Internet Use in the United States: 2010." July. https://www.census.gov/data/tables/2010/demo/computer-internet/computer-use-2010.html.

Vasilaki, Rosa. 2016. "The Politics of Postsecular Feminism." *Theory, Culture & Society* 33 (2): 103–23.

Vatikiotis P. J. 1973. "Tradition and Political Leadership: The Example of Algeria." In *Man, State, and Society in the Contemporary Maghrib*, edited by William I. Zartman, 309–29. New York: Praeger.

Verba, Sidney, Kay Lehman Schlozman, and Henry E Brady. 1995. *Voice and Equality: Civic Voluntarism in American Politics*. Cambridge, MA.: Harvard University Press.

Waggoner, Matt. 2005. "Irony, Embodiment, and the 'Critical Attitude': Engaging Saba Mahmood's Critique of Secular Morality." *Culture and Religion* 6 (2): 237–61.

Wagner, John. 2015. "Visiting a Northern Virginia Mosque, O'Malley Expresses Solidarity with Muslims." *Washington Post*, December 11. https://www. washingtonpost.com/news/post-politics/wp/2015/12/11/visiting-a-northern-virginia-mosque-omalley-expresses-solidarity-with-muslims/?utm_term=. c40b53b09e1c.

Walzer, Michael. 1990. "What Does It Mean to Be an 'American'?" *Social Research* 57 (3): 591–614.

Warner, R. Stephen. 1993. "Work in Progress toward a New Paradigm for the Sociological Study of Religion in the United States." *American Journal of Sociology* 98 (5): 1044–93.

WBUR. 2015. "American Muslims Feel the Heat." *On Point*. National Public Radio. December 9. http://www.wbur.org/onpoint/2015/12/09/san-bernardino-islamophobia-donald-trump.

Weitzer, Ronald, and Steven A. Tuch. 2002. "Perceptions of Racial Profiling: Race, Class, and Personal Experience." *Criminology* 40 (2): 435–56.

Welch, Kevin W. 1981. "An Interpersonal Influence Model of Traditional Religious Commitment." *Sociological Quarterly* 22 (1): 81–92.

Werbner, Pnina. 2005. "Honor, Shame and the Politics of Sexual Embodiment among South Asian Muslims in Britain and Beyond: An Analysis of Debates in the Public Sphere." *International Social Science Review* 6 (1): 25–47.

Westfall, Aubrey, Bozena Welborne, Sarah Tobin, and Özge Çelik Russell. 2016. "The Complexity of Covering: The Religious, Social, and Political Dynamics of Islamic Practice in the United States." *Social Science Quarterly* 97 (3): 771–90.

Wickenden, Dorothy. 2016. "Nailah Lymus Talks to Judith Thurman about Modern Fashion and Islam." *New Yorker*. September 9. http://www.newyorker.com/ podcast/political-scene/nailah-lymus-talks-to-judith-thurman-about-modern-fashion-and-islam.

Wielhouwer, Peter W. 2009. "Religion and American Political Participation." In *The Oxford Handbook of Religion and American Politics*, edited by Corwin E. Smidt, Lyman A. Kellstedt, and James L. Guth, 394–426. Oxford: Oxford University Press.

Williams, Kipling D. 2007. "Ostracism." *Annual Review of Psychology* 58 (1): 425–52.

Williams, Rhys H., and Gira Vashi. 2007. "Hijab and American Muslim Women: Creating the Space for Autonomous Selves." *Sociology of Religion* 68 (3): 269–87. http://dx.doi.org/10.1093/socrel/68.3.269.

Wilson, Chris. 2008. "Are Black Muslims Sunni or Shiite?" *Slate*, June 25. http:// www.slate.com/articles/news_and_politics/explainer/2008/06/are_black_ muslims_sunni_or_shiite.html.

Winchester, Daniel. 2008. "Embodying the Faith: Religious Practice and the Making of a Muslim Moral Habitus." *Social Forces* 86 (4): 1753–80.

Wing, Adrien, and Monica Smith. 2005. "Critical Race Feminism Lifts the Veil? Muslim Women, France, and the Headscarf Ban." *University of California, Davis Law Review* 39 (March): 743–85.

Winter, Bronwyn. 2008. *Hijab & the Republic: Uncovering the French Headscarf Debate*. Syracuse, NY: Syracuse University Press.

Wong, Janelle, and Jane Iwamura. 2007. "The Moral Minority: Race, Religion and Conservative Politics among Asian Americans." In *Religion and Social Justice for Immigrants*, edited by Pierrette Hondagneu-Sotelo, 35–39. New Brunswick, NJ: Rutgers University Press.

Wong, Janelle S., Pei-Te Lien, and M. Margaret Conway. 2005. "Group-Based Resources and Political Participation among Asian Americans." *American Politics Research* 33 (4): 545–76.

Woodhead, Linda. 2013. Foreword to *Modest Fashion: Styling Bodies, Mediating Faith*, edited by Reina Lewis, xvii–xx. London: I.B. Tauris.

Younes, Ali. 2016. "Saba Ahmed: Urging US Muslims to Vote Republican." Al Jazeera. February 24. http://www.aljazeera.com/indepth/features/2016/02/saba-ahmed-urging-muslims-vote-republican-160223122816776.html.

Young, Iris Marion. 2011. *Justice and the Politics of Difference*. Princeton, NJ: Princeton University Press.

Younis, Mohamed. 2011. "Muslim Americans Identify with God and Country." Gallup.com. August 3. http://www.gallup.com/poll/148799/Muslim-Americans-Identify-God-Country.aspx.

Zaal, Mayida, Tahani Salah, and Michelle Fine. 2007. "The Weight of the Hyphen: Freedom, Fusion and Responsibility Embodied by Young Muslim American Women during a Time of Surveillance." *Applied Developmental Science* 11 (3): 164–77.

Zakaria, Fareed. 2016. "Yes, America Is Being Changed—but by Whom?" Opinion page. *Washington Post*, February 11. https://www.washingtonpost.com/opinions/yes-america-is-being-changed--but-by-whom/2016/02/11/834d3dca-d105-11e5-88cd-753e80cd29ad_story.html?utm_term=.392f0801c86b.

Zarya, Valentina. 2016. "How Donald Trump Inspired This Muslim-American Woman to Start a PAC." *Fortune*, October 14. http://fortune.com/2016/10/14/muslim-american-women-pac.

Zogby, John. 2004. "Muslims in the American Public Square: Shifting Political Winds and Fallouts from 9/11, Afghanistan, and Iraq." News Release and Report. http://www.themosqueinmorgantown.com/pdfs/Project MAPSAmericanMuslimPoll.pdf.

❧ Index

Page numbers in *italics* indicate illustrations, tables, and charts.

JUN 0 3 2019